W9-BHS-334

SOURCEBOOK FOR ENVIRONMENTAL EDUCATION

V. EUGENE VIVIAN

Professor of Environmental Studies,
Glassboro State College,
Glassboro, New Jersey; Executive Director,
Conservation and Environmental Studies Center, Inc.,
Browns Mills, New Jersey

SOURCEBOOK FOR ENVIRONMENTAL EDUCATION

with 50 illustrations

Saint Louis
THE C. V. MOSBY COMPANY 1973

Printed in the United States of America

International Standard Book Number 0-8016-5240-5

Library of Congress Catalog Card Number 72-91509

Distributed in Great Britain by Henry Kimpton, London

PREFACE

People have been saying since 1968 that environmental education is needed in schools everywhere. This book is for teachers in preparation or teachers in service and all others who are seeking a curriculum that is irresistible to students and relevant to a significant societal problem, "What can education do for failing environments?" In almost all instances, education and scientific groups envisioned a curriculum from kindergarten through the twelfth grade that would consider the problem of deteriorating environments. At this writing, however, it is doubtful whether even a handful of schools in the United States or elsewhere have developed or adapted a kindergarten to twelfth grade study in environmental education.

On the other hand, the demand for usable curriculum materials in environmental education is increasing daily. This sourcebook is designed to assist school systems in getting started in a comprehensive curriculum by presenting several feasible approaches.

A consideration of the need for environmental education is projected through a set of objectives that, hopefully, will be of practical assistance to teachers and curriculum makers. Ethics or attitudes about environment are analyzed as a most influential aspect of environmental education.

Three approaches are presented in detail. In Chapter 2, a series of unit plans, ranging from primary to secondary grade levels and requiring from 3 to 8 weeks of class time, is presented. The activities and data-collection work sheets are provided in detail sufficient to allow for use in teacher-training programs at either the undergraduate or graduate levels.

How to monitor environmental factors related to air, water, and solid waste pollution is the sole focus of Chapter 3. This approach takes into account that many children prefer to first investigate what is wrong with an environment before embarking on a serious study of ecological relationships. A third, interdisciplinary approach is featured in Chapter 4, with the case study of a community. Sciences, both biological and physical, are intertwined with factors of geography, government, and politics. Since the most degraded environments are those in human communities, most environmental problems will be encountered by studying human communities selected from a broad geographic range.

A fifth chapter on evaluation is intended to delineate some novel means of evaluative procedures.

Materials in Chapters 2 and 3 were contributed by the following persons who are or were environmental education consultants for the Conservation and Environmental Studies Center, Inc., Gayle H. Brent, William M. Coyle, Ernest L. Henderson, Joseph F. Houdart, Barbara J. Riva, and Lois M. Schoeck, and by Fred J. Mason of Biological Sciences Department, Atlantic County Community College (New Jersey), Frank G. Patterson of Department of Life Sciences, Glassboro State College, and the author.

Materials in Chapter 4 were contributed by Marvin C. Creamer and Dr. Charles L. Stansfield, Professors of Geography, Glassboro State College, and by Ernest L. Henderson.

Original editing for Chapters 2, 3, and 4 was done by Norma T. Vivian, Dissemination Consultant, CESC, Inc.

Environmental education has the unique potential not only to rejuvenate children's desire to learn directly, but also to produce a generation of youngsters disposed toward continued involvement with societal progress. It is hoped that this sourcebook will contribute to that end.

V. EUGENE VIVIAN

CONTENTS

SOURCEBOOK FOR ENVIRONMENTAL EDUCATION

1 OBJECTIVES OF ENVIRONMENTAL EDUCATION

WHY ENVIRONMENTAL EDUCATION?

THE NATURAL ENVIRONMENT—EDUCATION'S SOURCE

Environment was mankind's first teacher. Food-gathering man, who sought edible plants and fruits and who hunted flesh on land or in water, studied his environment intensely and constantly. Slowly, through countless individual experiences, a vast array of facts about plant and animal lore, about the ways of water and weather was acquired. This life-sustaining knowledge was transmitted from parents to their children and from wise elders to the young.

The lore and nurture of the land and man's environment were esteemed until man was deluded into believing that he could recklessly impose his will on his surroundings. In earlier times, abuses and destruction could be imposed on the environment with no dire consequences—at worst, only a temporary inconvenience— for man had yet to overpopulate his world and, for all his growing "independence," still held a basic respect for the environment that sustained him. Such a view had to be dominant in an agrarian population.

For technological man this environmental communion has been lost. Succeeding generations of technological men have grown remote from a knowledge of their dependency on environments, immediate or distant—they have lost environmental awareness.

Environmental reality has been lost as the fruits of technology have made our living and working environments more artificial, more controlled, and, in the ultimate, more disquieting. For a child never to have seen a cow being milked is not intrinsically significant, but it is symbolic of the distance to which modern technological man has retreated from basic and life-supporting environments.

Environments of the earth and people have been the source of much of our knowledge and the source of inspiration for abstract wisdom, philosophy, theology, and religions. But modern man has lost this essential contact with his environments.

ENVIRONMENTAL STUDIES—THE "PAVED-OVER" CURRICULUM

An intellectual turning away from the environment came soon after the development of agricultural and trade communities. The *scholarly tradition* signified the separation of those who toiled with their hands and those who dealt with theology, astronomy, education, or the administration of community affairs.

Those who were close to the soil or the trades evolved the *craft tradition,* from which developed the notions of trade secrets, patents, and individualism. Thus, from the beginning, those who were close to the nurture and use of the environment, with both its perils and life-sustaining power, were separated from those who codified knowledge and sought meaning in the events of life. Traditionally, those of the craft tradition were given no education other than apprenticeship, until the rise of the mercantile class during the Renaissance period. But those who did receive formal education did *not* study the environment. Theology, philosophy, mathematics, and metaphysics were the important subjects. Furthermore, an increasing respect for the authority of older teachers and writers soon discouraged students from making firsthand observations and investigations.

Thus the "environmental curriculum" was submerged nearly 2,500 years ago, and verbalism was instituted. This loss is analogous to a productive agricultural field's being paved over with asphalt to become a parking lot. Education today continues to suffer from that verbalism. New curriculum focusing on the environment—with its concern for direct experiences in all the environments of man—is needed to offset the deluge of words that engulfs today's students.

THE ENVIRONMENTAL PARADOX

In all centuries, except the present, there existed numerous unspoiled environments. Many of them had perils for human habitation, such as wild animals, active volcanoes, infertile soils, climates with temperature or moisture extremes, or devastating storms and tidal waves.

As the technological control of various environments was developed and improved, some became relatively suitable for habitation. By the late nineteenth century most cities of the world were safe from plagues and scourges, from famine, and even from international warfare. However, for a variety of reasons the environments of many cities have become decreasingly desirable from the standpoint of adequate housing, nutrition, gainful employment, and personal safety.

Also deteriorating is the self-image for almost all city dwellers, particularly for the masses of people living in ghetto or barrio neighborhoods. The reversal and prevention of decay in large cities throughout the world is an environmental problem of the first magnitude.

The ability of society and individuals in the modern developed countries to control their immediate environments has been greatly increased. In affluent societies individuals may obtain a continuous supply of hot water, air of various temperatures to counteract seasonal extremes, a great variety of electrical laborsaving devices at home, and ready transportation by automobile or other vehicles. In fact, to illustrate the environmental pressure of such affluence, the energy and material resources that a single North American uses are equivalent to those used by *sixty* southeast Asians.

But as the environments of the world yielded to man's ability to control them, they actually became far more perilous than ever. Environmental hazards include pollutants in the atmosphere of the entire earth, even over the polar regions; chemical and pesticide poisons may now be found in the bodies of fish and in the waters of every ocean; only the wildest rivers in a few uninhabited areas are still unpolluted, until they reach areas of human habitation.

Certainly unspoiled environments and those used by much smaller populations held a variety of perils for their human inhabitants. But the technological society, with its much larger populations and its awesome power to change and control, has poured so many poisonous materials into water, air, and earth and is using basic resources so rapidly that it imperils the survival of all human society. Thus the environmental paradox: as technological man's ability to control and modify environments is increased, the quality of those environments is sharply decreased. Even as modern man struggles to develop controls for pollution, many more ways to pollute and assault the environment are developed. The situation is similar to the Malthusian relation between population size and food supply. Environmental pollution controls and safeguards seem to be produced at an arithmetical rate; environmental degradation seems to increase, like population, at a geometrical or exponential rate.

THE DEADLY ENVIRONMENT

More and more poisons are entering the environment. They are present in water, air, foods, and many of the man-made products that we use daily.

The atmosphere surrounding all the larger cities of the world is clearly visible as a brownish haze or a dark, malodorous smog. Houses and clothing are damaged by acidic droplets and continuous accumulation of sooty particles that drop from industrial or household smoke. Far more dangerous to health is the accumulation of poisonous gases in the air, such as carbon monoxide, carbon dioxide, nitrogen oxides, sulfur oxides, phosgene, and unburned compounds resulting from the burning of petroleum fuels, coal of various grades, and trash. Emphysema and other lung disorders are sharply on the increase. The threat of smog disasters such as those experienced in London, England, or Donora, Pennsylvania in this century looms whenever a sustained temperature inversion is possible. (A temperature inversion is the condition resulting when a layer of warm air lies above a layer of cooler air. This upper warm-air blanket tends to prevent heated, and often polluted, air from rising away from the earth's surface to the higher layers, where it can be readily dispersed by prevailing winds. Such warm-air layering is called a temperature inversion because the upper air is normally colder.)

Streams and rivers in the vicinity of and downstream from most large cities are likely to be unfit for bathing or recreation. An abundance of sewage can cause the dissolved oxygen content of the water to be reduced to zero, since it is partially decomposed by microorganisms. Water without dissolved oxygen tends to have unpleasant odors, due to substances produced by anaerobic bacteria (which can live and metabolize without dissolved oxygen) feeding on the decomposable material in sewage. Sewage in water also brings the possibility of waterborne diseases such as cholera, typhoid and paratyphoid fever, and amebic dysentery.

Water pollution is occurring in the Great Lakes, particularly Lake Erie, where the condition of *eutrophication* has been much publicized. Eutrophication refers to a condition in aquatic environments in which the amounts of nutrients are abnormally high, either from natural causes or from accumulations of nutrient-bearing sewage. Eutrophication causes such rapid growth of microorganisms that the dissolved oxygen content falls off to near-zero levels (rate of consumption exceeds rate of exchange with atmosphere). The loss of dissolved oxygen results in the death of many species, essentially by suffocation. Lake Erie, the most shallow of the Great Lakes and also the recipient of effluents from many industrial cities, is particularly vulnerable to the perils of large-scale eutrophication.

Ocean beaches, wherever there is great outflow of sewage and industrial wastes, are extensively polluted and often unfit for bathing. Scarcely a beach in the world, however remote, remains untainted by fuel oil, either from spills that occur when tankers accidentally break up or by the deliberate discharge of oil from passing ships cleaning out their fuel tanks and systems.

How many of today's adults are aware of the environmental impact (and extract) represented by the array of foods and other merchandise on the shelves of a supermarket? The processing of foods in ever-increasing quantities has led to the use of many chemicals for preservation against decay, such as low-cost taste-boosting additives, or for coloration. The long-term effects of consuming chemicals such as benzoate of soda, propionates, and cyclamates are still unknown, but these additives are appearing in the diets of more and more people.

Whereas controversies over fluorides, cyclamates, and monosodium glutamate come to the consumer's attention, the toxicity of many of our fresh and preserved foods is increasing insidiously from environmental poisons such as DDT, mercury, and lead. Mercury, which was presumed to be inert in the environment, has been found in the bodies of many kinds of fish, including tuna, in the poisonous form of methyl mercury. DDT has been found in livers of fish from all oceans of the earth. Lead is entering streams, lakes, and oceans from the exhaust of gasoline-powered engines. All lead compounds are believed to be toxic to humans. The distribution of other pesticides and herbicides in human food has not yet been definitively measured.

These frightening revelations have begun to make the public suspicious of food quality. Although food additives have received much attention, strange chemical names on food labels are still bewildering rather than informative. Perversely, one "whipping boy" is among the oldest of food additives, potassium iodide. The addition of iodide salts to table salt was shown to be effective in supplying iodine essential for proper thyroid function in populations where seafood is scarce in the diet. Now thyroid goiter is again on the increase, since the additive scare has sharply reduced the purchase of iodized salt. The latter case points up the need in this country for better nutritional as well as environmental education.

All these considerations provide abundant evidence that, for many persons, the environment has become increasingly deadly—from the biological, physical, and social viewpoints.

THE RAVAGED ENVIRONMENT

Not only is the environment becoming more deadly for all living species, and man in particular, but it is debilitated and ravaged. Consider our woodland, being used at a rate beyond replacement for lumber, paper, and special products. The demand is so great that only fast-growing tree species are planted in reforestation areas. Unremitting efforts continue to obtain permission to lumber unique redwood stands, even those protected in national parks and forests. The cutting of many timber species from public lands has already been permitted by public "guardian" agencies, often without public knowledge. The demand to harvest resources extends from various timber tree species to minerals of all kinds, including petroleum.

Although efforts to improve and maintain soil quality have been promoted for nearly forty years in the United States, some of our most fertile soils are being used for nonagricultural purposes such as industrial parks, airports, shopping centers, and suburban housing. Soil fertility is being maintained chiefly by the use of chemical fertilizers because they cost less to distribute than natural organic fertilizers. Very few serious attempts are being made to utilize organic wastes of any kind to improve the tilth and composition of soil. This is not to say that chemical fertilizers should be completely replaced by organic additives such as dried sewage sludge, unused slaughterhouse refuse, garbage, tree leaves collected from city streets, and waste cuttings from lumbering. Probably our present agricultural output could not be maintained if the shift were made instantly and completely to organic manures, but the quality of the agricultural produce and the composition of the soil would surely be improved.

Strip-mining operations have left ugly scars on the landscape in Pennsylvania, West Virginia, Kentucky, and other states where it is permitted. Highly acidic and toxic waters from the strip mines flow into many rivers. Although a few mining companies have voluntarily restored some of the mining spoils, and an even smaller number have been forced to cover the stripped area, new requests to carry out still more ambitious plans to mine by stripping, even on public lands, are being made. Little apparent concern or legislation for restoration of environmental quality to these strip mine areas accompany these requests.

Projected for the 1970's is a federally sponsored effort to extract low-sulfur oil from shale rock in Colorado, Utah, and Wyoming as an answer to the need for fuel to power the nation's ever-increasing energy demands. This expensive process is rapidly becoming attractive because of the dependence of the United States on oil imports. Despite tax credits proposed to induce developers to undo environmental damage produced during oil extraction, the outlook is still most discouraging. The proposed 300-foot-high piles of shale waste from this extraction process will probably not be fully vegetated for nearly two centuries because of the aridity of the affected area. This consideration does not seem to inhibit either would-be developers or the federal agencies involved. Only dedicated environmentalists seem to be raising objections and possible legal deterrents.

Planning for community open space, adequate recreation areas, optimum locations for industry and shopping centers, and the specific reservation of highly arable lands is still a rarity in the communities of the world. The quest for increased real-estate tax ratables rather than the quest for short- and long-term environmental quality seems to occupy the attention of most community planners. The use of real-estate holdings as a significant tax base will probably have to be diminished in the next decades.

Although communities have resorted to filling in lowlands and creek beds with their trash, most persons are still concerned with whether or not their wastes are collected and not with where the trash is being dumped. Although mountains of trash create disposal problems, relatively few citizens are concerned with limiting the amount of paper, plastic, or glass discarded. Recycling stations, when they exist, are operated by citizens' groups and seldom by appropriate government agencies.

Except in the cases of toll roads and superhighways, the growth of sight-polluting poles and wires, billboards, and garish roadside stands has gone unchecked, until ugliness characterizes most highways and many city streets. The ravaging of the environment continues.

THE UNVIRONMENT—AN UNINFORMED, UNCOMMITTED SOCIETY

Since the fall of 1969 the news media have done an excellent job of reporting on the state of the deteriorating environment. However, this has not been enough to induce much-needed changes and commitments. The real and present dangers have not been sufficient to stop us from doing business as usual.

- Despite many notable efforts by some industries to reduce air and water pollution, others are continuing to pollute until such time as they are stopped. Many firms plan relocation to areas where production regulations are less stringent.
- Antipollution devices on automobiles and trucks are just beginning to be developed. State requirements for exhaust-emission control on vehicles of all kinds will be instituted slowly during the 1970's. At best, sufficient control will be delayed until all automobiles produced prior to 1973 are no longer in operation.
- Means to solve many pollution problems are already available. Adequate methods of sewage and waste-water disposal are well known, but we continue to build inadequate sewage treatment plants to save tax dollars. Industrial air pollution can also be controlled, in many cases at additional capital or operational cost. Few private citizens have voluntarily changed their automobiles to prevent excess exhaust pollution. Few have changed their home heating systems to reduce harmful effluents. Few have insulated their homes to prevent waste of fuel or energy. The public is apparently not yet committed—many choose to remain uninformed.
- The general public may be tired of hearing about degraded environments. Many are expecting the environmental fad to disappear; they are waiting for the government agencies to alleviate the situation without concerted citizen pressure. The public is not yet sufficiently informed about or committed to ways of improving environmental quality. It may also be that, in an age of instant foods, travel, and gadgets, the public is waiting for "instant" change, now that the problem

has been brought to light. The necessarily slow rate of environmental reclamation is yet to be comprehended by citizens and governments.

- Government agencies have often contributed to environmental degradation by inadequate enforcement of present regulations. Agencies have planned and permitted development of rivers, coastal areas, or mountaintops, without regard to environmental quality. Sometimes these agencies have been stopped by citizens' groups or higher agencies. The holding up of the construction plans for a Florida Everglades jetport is a good example of citizen outcry against environmental destruction. Similar examples can be identified in most states. The 1970-1971 battle over the SST is another instance. Municipal, county, state, and national agencies have all been offenders in permitting changes that adversely affect environmental quality. Most government agencies are not yet committed to the defense of environments against deterioration. In rescue cases like these, enough people simply do not believe the assertions of the scientists, engineers, and economists who represent the government agencies.
- People are also uninformed about many environmental matters. Many persons ignore available information. The labelling of all processed foods has been improved in the past few years because of new legal requirements. The names of many additives are probably unfamiliar to a large segment of the population, but the nutrient content should be understandable to most of the literate public. Yet malnutrition is widespread among persons whose income is more than sufficient to purchase food with adequate nutritional content, indicating that nutritional adequacy has not been a concern of the American public.

Environmental education is just being introduced into scattered areas of public school curricula. But few persons perceive that such education is *education for survival.* An uniformed citizenry can never be concerned or committed to the improvement of environmental quality everywhere. Environmental education is essential—*now.*

OUTDATED ENVIRONMENTAL ETHICS

THE PURPOSE ETHIC

Even though technological man has lost contact with environments that sustain civilization, he has at the same time retained many beliefs developed in food-gathering societies. These hoary beliefs have led to many practices that have produced a progressive deterioration in environmental quality. The rejection of these ideas and the adoption of adequate new environmental ethics will be highly significant steps in reversing the downward trend in environmental quality.

The first of these, the purpose ethic, is that *man has dominion over a world whose parts and inhabitants exist solely for the benefit and welfare of mankind.* This anthropocentric view is repeated every time someone asks, "What good is a mosquito?" (or any other being whose existence may happen to offend us at the moment). It leads to the threatened extinction of wildlife species or the wholesale spraying of shallow wetlands that adjoin many vacationlands. It has sustained the policy of paying bounties on predators such as timber wolves, hawks, owls, bald eagles, or mountain lions and on "vermin" such as skunks, raccoons, or badgers. Even weeds are looked on as a kind of "mistake in Creation" or, at best, a kind of burden that man must bear. For countless generations we have not had reverence for life but have placed a value only on usable living things.

The purpose ethic has made us scornful of all animals whose habits are at variance with our views of right and wrong. Thus blue jays and blacksnakes are "bad" because they steal eggs from birds' nests, despite the multimillion dollar human consumption of hen and duck eggs. The weasel is condemned for the love of killing, but nations glamorize or elect as leaders men whose specialty is the death of members of the human race.

ABANDONING THE FERTILITY GODS

We must cast aside the cult of "fertility," which was an overriding concern of ancient peoples. The lack of fertility in ancient times was considered a catastrophe without parallel. Until the twentieth century, in developed countries, high infant mortality made a large family necessary to ensure the survival of one or two children to childbearing maturity. The fertility rites of those cultures viewed all manifestations of fertility as a signal of favor from the gods—gods now replaced by success with the sciences of agronomy and medicine. We can understand the fertility ethic in historical perspective, but we can no longer give it currency. Runaway population growth, the overwhelming evidence of fertility, will destroy the environment and *all fertility* at the same time.

PROPERTY OWNERSHIP REEXAMINED

In an agrarian society with a majority of the population tilling the soil, land was the only real wealth. Each individual needed land for food production and survival. The agriculturalists and farmers of today are mostly land poor, requiring more and more land for increased crop production to offset the high costs of labor and agricultural machinery.

Land, water, and all other resources are still the only source of wealth and survival; that is why they are called *real estate.* We must consider the question of whether technological society can any longer permit extensive and absolute property ownership in the hands of the few or the privileged. Eventually, regarding all property as essentially public, a land sharing or land trusteeship may be necessary to safeguard the rights of all members of society.

REDUCING ENVIRONMENTAL HOSTILITY

Environments away from human settlements have always been regarded as perilous. To speak of an environment as "cruel," "harsh," or "unfriendly" is another expression of our anthropocentric views of the environment. At the same time, western man in particular has always considered any environment a challenge to be conquered. We thrill to the human conquest of Mount Everest, of undersea depths, of Antarctic winters, or the arrival of men on the moon. The search for new frontiers to master seems to be ingrained in the human psyche. To the quest for these frontiers we *must* add a respect for those environments in their original state. Lack of such respect carried to extremes is seen in the amount of equipment that American astronauts have abandoned on the moon or in the names that people carve or paint on available mountain surfaces to commemorate their short-term visits there.

THE MYTH OF SUPERABUNDANCE

When there were fewer people and much open land, all resources seemed limitless. There always seemed to be more somewhere else. Now we know that all parts of the environment, even air and sunlight, are limited and can be used only with accurate knowledge of those limitations and the rate of replacement for all those renewable resources.

As increasing populations raise the threat of famine or sublevel food supplies, we turn hopefully toward the oceans or the effects of the Green Revolution. Neither of these nor both together can offset the demands that unchecked population growth will make. Instead of abandoning outdated ideas, we seek to remedy the situation while clinging to two views suicidal for future societies—the fertility ethic and the superabundance myth.

The effort to sell more oil without respect to the limitation of supply is another instance of the perpetuation of the idea of superabundance. Oil production and distribution are projected with increasing hazard for ocean waters, for example, the proposed use of increasingly larger tankers whose oil spills could be devastating to the quality of seaside environments. The push for an Alaskan pipeline with only a cursory investigation of safer alternatives couples the superabundance belief with a disregard for the fragile environment of the Arctic tundra.

When we continue to pump fresh water from the earth in excess of the amounts returned to subterranean water reserves by rainfall, our continuing faith in superabundance is demonstrated.

The "cut out and get out" lumbering practices of the past two centuries and the extermination of more than a score of animal species are legacies of our faith in superabundance. We should not forget that the westward migrations of the nineteenth century in the United States originated in part because poor agricultural practices along the eastern seaboard states wore out the land in a few decades of use.

DILUTION IS NOT THE SOLUTION

A converse of the superabundance myth is the expectation that the atmosphere and the waters of the earth can absorb unlimited quantities of pollutants by dilution. Of course, before the advent of technological man and the "population explosion," this method worked quite adequately. Even as streams and lakes show signs of deterioration and biological death or eutrophication, plans are made not to provide a clean and reusable wastewater effluent but rather to transport the unclean water a greater distance to a larger body of water, which will, it is hoped, perform its dilution magic. The present planners of many regional sewage systems do not project a truly reusable water outfall. More public funds based on this outmoded ethic of dilution will be spent.

As a further example, the industrial firm that offends with a high air-polluting emission and that plans to move from an area of high industrial concentration to an area relatively free of air pollution puts its temporary trust in the limited solution called dilution.

THE IDEA OF PROGRESS

From Renaissance times the notion of progress has signified a movement or change toward improvement. That change will occur in all parts of our society and environment is certainly inevitable. The ethical environmentalist can only view "change" as "progress" when an environmental condition has been improved—not worsened.

The cliché "You can't stop progress" is, at best, uncritical or, at worst, irresponsible when referring to a change that may be "something which few people want but most are powerless to prevent." It is necessary for informed citizens to review the plans of government agencies and industries so that changes in the environment may be for the better, that man-made changes be indeed "progress."

UPDATED ENVIRONMENTAL ETHICS—ATTITUDES FOR SURVIVAL

The quest for environmental quality will never become a reality until a new environmental ethic supplants the views and values just described. Any ethic for environmental quality must include three basic beliefs: (1) people should have a reverence for all life; (2) people should respect the right of existence for all environments; and (3) people should accord the highest priority to environmental quality. These simple, but broad, statements can become significant only if stated in terms of desirable or supporting *behaviors.* Some important general behaviors are listed and commented on below with each of the three chief value ideas.

REVERENCE FOR ALL LIFE

1. The control of population growth by each citizen will ensure that present population levels are not raised and that stresses on the environment are not further increased.

To continue or increase the present population growth can only aggravate our problems of food supply and utilization of land, mineral, and fuel resources. Shortages in some or all of the necessities of life can only engender strife, bloodshed, and a reduced quality of life. The reverence for life dictates that the unborn should also be accorded the right to a high-quality environment and life. Runaway population growth is the most potent threat to the quality of life in general and human life in particular.

2. Human warfare as the most devasting of all assaults on human life and all biophysical environments must be actively prevented.

Thomas Malthus, in 1799, in his celebrated *Essay on Population,* pointed to warfare, famine, and disease as three natural checks on human population. In fact, these mechanisms (excepting warfare) are continously effective in the control of other natural populations. However, most human civilizations have considered the Malthusian dictum inconsistent with ethical principles. But is it not obvious that if we do not limit our own numbers, these "natural" mechanisms will eventually do it for us?

Of course, human warfare is not only destructive of human life and social and historical environments but it also accounts for the greatest squandering of mineral, fuel, and biological resources. To change from an economy of warfare to an economy dedicated to human welfare and the improvement of the quality of life and environment is admittedly difficult. It is a challenge that *must* be met.

3. Society, through both private and public agencies, should strive to provide *all* citizens with employment from which to make an apparently meaningful contribution to society's existence.

Employment in a technological society, with its continually increasing automation, will require fewer and fewer hours in the workweek. Furthermore, from many of the jobs the workers acquire a feeling of being a readily dispensable cog in a large machine. These same frustrations are experienced by those receiving government assistance for unemployment or welfare. Environmental quality, so critical to us all, can scarcely be a concern of those who must wrestle with an even more basic question—their own value in the life of society.

4. People must strive to improve environmental quality by the use of available *biological* means to control unwanted populations of insects or other pests, utilizing chemicals only as a last resort.

The technological society has been quick to utilize chemicals before their long-term biological and ecological relationships could be tested or determined. The health of all parts of an ecosystem was probably not an important consideration when scientists first recommended the use of pesticides such as DDT. That DDT in streams would find its way to all the ocean centers of the earth was probably not suspected. Such a complex society of interrelated ecosystems, each with its own set of influential variables, simply cannot tolerate so simplistic a solution to the insect problem as wholesale distribution of a relatively unspecific poison.

5. Although society must convert many "open spaces" into special human-use areas for homes, industries, and shopping centers, any possible plant and animal life must be left intact within those areas.

The familiar practice of levelling an area of all trees and other living things in a building project is a wanton destruction of life. Afterward we often plant trees of a different species, which provide inadequate homes for birds and other animals. Clearing an area by fire is another method designed to save human labor but illustrating total disregard for the inhabitants who might be forced to escape to surrounding environments. Many people go to great lengths to save the life of a fledgling fallen from a nest, but the same sympathetic people seem ignorant of the needless destruction committed by construction projects in hitherto wild areas.

6. People should strive to ensure that examples of unique environments are preserved, not only for the environments themselves but also for the enjoyment and enlightenment of future generations.

The number of environments modified or destroyed for human purposes is bound to continue. However, relatively close to urban centers are many unique environments whose entire populations of animals and plants found nowhere else in the world could be annihilated without proper precautions. Wholesale species extinction could occur on a single construction operation. The Florida Everglades and the New Jersey Pine Barrens, both threatened by jetport plans, are examples of unique environments, as are the famous Sequoia or Big Tree Redwood stands in California. Some such environments have gained the support of citizens' groups to protect them from extinction, but many more are in jeopardy. Citizens and government agencies will need to work together to ensure their preservation.

The belief that unique environments should be preserved is exemplified by groups such as the Sierra Club, in promoting the designation and protection of an area as "Forever Wild." The Forever Wild category is in reality a unique environment, since there are few environments indeed not already modified by man.

Ecologists cannot describe and interpret the relationships that have developed within an ecosystem if disturbance has already changed those relationships. When some conservationists seek a Forever Wild land use for an area, they are really proposing that persons like themselves be allowed to enter an area but that the general public be kept out. Is this proprietary inconsistency valid? Even the ecologist who studies the Forever Wild area would be disturbing it to some extent.

Another important reason for preserving unique environments is the likelihood that many of our forests of today will lose their present species make-up. As the demand for lumber increases, newer, fast-growing trees may be planted in place of the original forest species. This wholesale modification of forest environments can lead to the extinction of many plant and animal types. Original ecosystems must be preserved not only as a matter of ecological interest but also to provide base-line data for the development of optimum quality in areas whose dominant populations have been changed.

THE RIGHT OF EXISTENCE FOR ALL ENVIRONMENTS

The second value for an environmental ethic is a restatement of man's place in nature.

1. People must actively support the idea that human beings are only *one* of many plant and animal species that may be part of various environments.

This attitude is designed to counteract the view that mankind has dominion over all the earth and that all living beings have a purpose only in man's scheme of things.

Man, as the only steward for the life of the other species, must recognize the inherent right of each species to exist for its own purpose (whatever that may be). The human race cannot decide whether or not a species has the right to exist. The human view of the value of a particular species may vary from generation to generation or age to age. The elimination of a species is, however, an irreversible act.

2. We all must realize and actively support the principle that environments vary in their capacity to support human communities.

People also have been so misled by the increased ability to control environments that they have begun to ignore the terrifying "old" dangers. Increasingly, houses are built on unprotected beaches and bays, in the backwashes at baselevels of streams with a history of flooding, in the paths of potential avalanches, mud slides, and volcanic overflows, and along geological fault zones. When a catastrophe in such an environment finally occurs, a needless waste of human and material resources is the result. The persons who live in threatening environments seem to do so from ignorance or from disrespect for the character of an environment.

3. The quality of environments will be improved if people strive to maintain existing ecosystems and compensate adequately for disturbed ones.

The draining of a swamp or wetlands area illustrates a widespread practice of *destroying* an existing ecosystem. Lowering the water level forces out of existence many plants and animals inhabiting the area. Probably the wetland in question is a vital link in the food supply (food chain) of animals living in distant areas. For example, many ocean fish are spawned in shallow bogs and coastal wetlands; therefore the destruction of these wetlands may reduce the number of fish in the ocean, disturb the ecology of the wetland *and* the ocean, and reduce an important human food supply.

The conversion of any grassland or woodland area to cropland is a common example of *disturbing* an ecosystem. Partial compensation for this disturbed ecosystem is possible. For example, maintaining some of the original tree species in the form of hedgerows is essential in preventing extensive wind erosion as well as maintaining bird and animal populations to control crop-destroying insect and rodent populations. Croplands, because they often consist of a population of one or only a few species of food or other plants, are the most vulnerable of new ecosystems. Any single overwhelming disease or animal enemy can wipe out the entire population; this threat often becomes a reality when an area of high species diversity is repopulated with only a few species.

4. Fragile environments must be protected from irreparable damage.

Fragile environments are those in which living things are severely limited by one or more environmental factors, such as low amounts of moisture or low average annual temperatures (short growing seasons).

The tundra in Alaska is an example of a fragile environment. The heated oil pipeline proposed to be built across Alaska and possibly through parts of Canada to the United States is believed by many ecologists to be a threat to the fragile tundra environment. It is anticipated that the heat from the pipeline will melt much of the nonrock material that remains permanently frozen inches below the earth's surface. This melting, in turn, can destroy much of the moss and ground cover on which many animals, such as caribou, depend for their existence. Opponents of the proposed pipeline believe that the economic rationale advanced is simply not valid. Their view is that the pipeline is not necessarily the only feasible means to provide needed crude oil to the United States. These opponents believe that alternate oil sources and means of transportation have neither been fully explored nor made public. This controversy illustrates the need for more knowledge about the effect of and the demonstrable need for a proposed and possibly irreversible environmental change.

ACCORDING THE HIGHEST PRIORITY TO ENVIRONMENTAL QUALITY

1. People must relinquish the "rights" that accompany absolute ownership of property.

The privilege of absolute ownership cannot be granted by a complex society dedicated to desirable environmental quality. For too long, individuals have treated their property and conducted activities thereon as if it were all quite unrelated to anyone else's rights. "What I do with and on my own property is my own business!" Not so any more. The population explosion has made that attitude intolerable. We are all exposed daily to various kinds of pollution—visual, noise, air, chemical—

emanating from someone else's house, yard, auto, or whatever.

Actually, absolute property ownership enjoys only hypothetical status in our society. Already many apartments in condominiums and other large complexes are sold essentially as leases. There are strict rules by which to live, and proper maintenance, etc., is automatic—for which the inhabitants are financially assessed as a condition of "ownership." Similar leases are sold for separate dwellings, for example, in retirement villages. The ultimate solution may be the limiting of all property ownership to "trusteeships" granted by society to individuals or groups. This type of arrangement obviously already exists.

Furthermore, municipal zoning laws provide many curbs and restrictions on present owners. It is likely that the jurisdiction for zoning will pass from municipalities to states to prevent inequities in neighboring areas. This loss of home rule is already threatened with the imposition of federal quality standards for water and air. This erosion of the privileges accorded to property owners illustrates how *relative* all present property ownership is, in point of fact.

2. It must be realized that the excellence or poverty of environmental quality in one area has a definite effect on quality in many more distant environments.

In human societies, even distant environments are increasingly interdependent and interrelated. The existence of this ethic is implicit in all the riparian rights, which have been developed over the past few millennia. Riparian, or river, rights were originally involked to guarantee the quantity, and later quality, of water for people who lived or owned property downstream. In all agricultural situations requiring extensive irrigation or diversion of river or lake waters, the quantity of water allotted and guaranteed to each user was and is a matter of essential importance. Changes in water levels with accompanying changes in land areas in tidal zones gave rise to the practice of granting underwater land rights to owners of land on a riverbank or shoreline. This privilege is being withdrawn with the development of state and federal regulations and claims to jurisdiction over tidewater lands. For example, in New Jersey the Wetlands Act of 1970 gave the state regulatory powers and responsibility for all land up to 5 feet above the average high-tide level.

The collection and expenditure of taxes by states and the federal government, as it assumes increasing responsibility for environmental quality, indicate that the interdependence of environments is a recognized condition. Our new ethic must make such responsibilities by government agencies a matter of expectation, rather than a matter of emergency or special consideration, as it most often is now. In particular, the interrelated-distant-environment ethic means that the traditional political rural and urban coalitions will lose their *raison d'être*. Legislators and politicians may no longer indulge in the luxury of pitting the interests of one environment against others. Old animosities will have to dissolve with the realization and conviction that each environment is essential to the well-being of the others.

3. All citizens in general and designated agencies in particular must assume responsibility for the trusteeship of public property.

This ethic not only indicates that public land is in trusteeship already but that all citizens share in that responsibility. This thrust is essential in bringing about a shift in the common perception that each citizen is not individually responsible for public property and that current practices of vandalism are "too bad, but not my problem." The littering and other defacing of state and national parks is a case in point. Public opinion must be turned around so that individuals would report cases of littering and vandalism to the proper authorities.

4. All citizens must assume responsibility for the

trusteeship of abandoned buildings or property, whether publicly or privately held.

Abandoned or uninhabited buildings and property have been more and more subject to vandalism, and, of course, they present health and safety hazards as well. Public opinion needs to be directed in such a way that responsibility for any property is accepted by all citizens.

The use and discarding of all other kinds of property also needs to be reexamined. This new ethic encompassing true individual responsibility for property could produce desirable results for environmental quality.

5. People must not infringe on the rights of some or all citizens by dumping private property on or in public property.

In this view, all gaseous emissions, waste water, or storm effluents and any biological, chemical, or mineral solid wastes are private property. The disposal of any private property is the responsibility of the owner. As a matter of fact, this ethic is consistent with the federal no-dumping ban enacted in 1899, and its implications are far reaching. To accept a no-dumping belief would place responsibility for exhaust emissions from motor vehicles, factories, industrial parks, and homes squarely on the shoulders of the property owner(s) or lessee(s). Destructive rainfall or snowfall runoff and drainage would also be the owner's responsibility.

All these new responsibilities for helping to maintain desirable environmental quality will impose many difficulties on all property owners, especially individuals. For this reason a greater share and a greater overall expenditure of tax funds will need to be used for environmental protection. Merely to provide tax reductions for those individuals, groups, or corporations who act responsibly toward the environment is, in fact, a denial of this much-needed ethic. By this means, various pollution emissions or other acts of environmental degradation by property owners are considered acceptable as long as the owner or polluter pays more taxes. This kind of license for environmental deterioration may ultimately bring about the very environmental decay that the tax-incentive policy is designed to prevent. All citizens should expect to pay their just share of taxes and should acknowledge that an increasing proportion of those taxes will be allocated for environmental-protection methods and facilities not available to the individual property owner.

In effect, the acceptance of this ethic would remove the need of standards for air and water quality. Instead of regulating the acceptable degree of air and water pollution, the no-dumping ethic would be aimed at nonpollution as a standard.

6. People should consume resources according to their *needs* rather than their *wants.*

The acceptance and practice of this ethic will reduce the assault on the environment that is now being made by Western technological man. Our present goal for continued economic well-being is the expansion of all markets. The result of this has been an increasing per capita consumption of an ever-increasing variety of goods and products.

Present escalating rates of consumption of oil, coal, minerals, lumber, and wood products, coupled with a growing population, constitute the most formidable threat yet known to man. A new ethic for consumption must replace our present acceptance of the profligate use of resources.

7. Materials and fuels should be used in such a way that they are recycled on a global scale.

The recycling of all resources cannot be initiated too soon. Plans for recycling on an earth-wide basis must be developed and put into practice. Plans for global recycling will not be made until the idea of recycling becomes a widely held ethic.

8. People must be ready to spend more of their personal income as well as more of the gross national product toward the improvement and maintenance of environmental quality.

Costs for pollution control, environmental cleanup, and recycling will require expenditures hitherto not considered the responsibility of each citizen. Each citizen must be willing to pay for an environment that is fit and pleasant to live in, even if it means increases in prices and taxes. Up to the present time we have never thought of having to pay much for environmental quality.

• • •

People must dedicate themselves to, and take an active part in, the protection of our natural environment. All citizens have a stake and a role in its maintenance and improvement. The inertia of events and systems that now lead to environmental degradation is hard to stop or to reverse. Governmental agencies alone cannot be expected to see to it that the environment is protected. Only an interested, informed, and vigilant public can maintain pressure to ensure that the wisest environmental decisions are made by agencies or individuals with the power to effect environmental change.

The changing of priorities and spending, both of individuals and their governments, is first a matter of ethics. It is the task of environmental education to nurture a new ethic for the environment. This formidable task represents the real challenge in the quest for environmental quality. Ultimately it is the only road to survival.

THE "WHAT" OF ENVIRONMENTAL EDUCATION

GOALS

The improvement of environmental quality is the ultimate and significant goal of environmental education. More specifically, this goal is to create a concern for all environments—a concern that leads to a commitment to preserve or develop optimum environments and to improve less desirable ones.

The study of man and all his environments falls in the broad realm of environmental education. The promulgation of the wise use of natural resources was the goal of *conservation education*. The environmental education purview includes an equal concern for the environmental problems of overcrowding in cities, unemployment, adequate nutrition for all citizens, and the many forms of discrimination that degrade the environments of many people. It is not enough to be concerned about pollution in our waters or in the air, not enough to be alert to the dangers of radioactive wastes from new atomic-powered generating plants, not enough to perceive the dangers of urban sprawl, not enough to know the fundamental principles of ecology. Each of these concerns forms an essential segment of environmental education —a curriculum must include all of them.

Because it has such a diversity and such a growing content, environmental education should have an important place in every grade in the K-12 span, as well as in higher and general public education. But the *content* of the curriculum as it pertains to environmental education is not nearly so important as the *concern* for whatever environment is being considered.

For at least thirty years continuous but ineffective attempts have been made to put conservation education, with its emphasis on land- and other resource management practices, an integral part of the curriculum in all schools. These attempts failed for a number of reasons:

1. The impetus for conservation education did not originate in the schools. Professional conservationists, foreseeing the impending environmental crisis, sought to assist schools in getting started, but teachers were not prepared either with a conviction engendered by adequate environmental ethics or by a knowledge of practices needed to maintain quality environments.

2. Teachers called in a variety of experts on conservation to give talks or demonstrations, but

the teachers never acquired this ability for themselves. They continued to expect that conservation education goals could be met by the experts alone.

3. The preparation of teachers was inadequate both in content and urgency to create a will to make environmental quality an important segment of the changing curriculum.

4. The content of conservation education seemed remote from schools in the larger communities and great cities. Conservation education seemed more suitable for rural or small suburban schools.

Environmental education will be unsuccessful as well unless the rank-and-file teachers perceive the societal need for a curricular concern for environmental quality in every grade.

THE LEARNING ENVIRONMENT

For teachers, in particular, environmental education has a very special meaning for all situations where learning itself is nurtured. Environmental education requires a commitment by educators to develop and utilize situations where learning can flourish.

Learning environments are found not only in the classroom. Away from the classroom, individually or in small or large groups, children and adults may study the diverse environments around them. The firsthand experience, the opportunity to use all senses in observing or investigating, the opportunity to raise questions and get answers directly—all these are available to any school where the environments of man are accepted for serious study.

The desire to provide direct experiences as attractive means for learning is the legacy of Dr. Lloyd B. Sharp, who inspired many teachers, school administrators, and other leaders of youth at Columbia, New York, and Southern Illinois universities. Dr. Sharp's method—use of learning environments away from the classroom—was called "camping education" and "school camping" at first because it was generally practiced with groups of youngsters from the classroom who lived and learned for several days at a resident center. As the implications of these firsthand experiences became more clear, Dr. Sharp renamed his method "outdoor education." He was joined early by men such as Dr. Julian Smith of Michigan State University and Dr. Hugh B. Masters of the University of Georgia. At present there are many adherents of the outdoor education methodology.

Environmental education is not the same as either outdoor education or conservation education. Environmental education contains all of both but has the restrictions of neither. Its frame of reference is larger than a combination of both. Instead of being concerned chiefly with the management of resources such as soil, water, forests, wildlife, and air, environmental education is also concerned with all aspects of the social environments of man, with man-made environments and their effects both on man and on all of the "natural environment." The focus is on man and his relationship to, and use and control of, all environments.

An environmental education program will provide many learning situations outdoors but will use any environments where firsthand experiences may be obtained. The practice of having students gather reliable, reportable data about the quality of any environment, as well as using firsthand sources of information about environments, is indicative of the more inclusive scope of environmental education. Students who are well informed about ecological relationships in general and local environmental conditions in particular and who are disposed to take social action through available means and agencies represent the epitome of environmental education.

To concern students with social problems of the magnitude of the environmental crisis is a position hitherto avoided by American education. This undeniable relevance provides environmental education with its highest potential for all education.

CRITERIA FOR A K-12 ENVIRONMENTAL EDUCATION CURRICULUM

A K-12 curriculum in environmental studies should be distinguished by these characteristics:

1. An all-out effort to develop a new set of environmental ethics
2. At least one unit of study of environments or ecology in every grade, including the secondary years
3. The teaching of skills in monitoring various aspects of the environment and in reporting that information to responsible agencies
4. The use of firsthand sources of information in every grade
5. An opportunity for youngsters to raise questions and develop hypotheses and to work out research means for answering their questions directly and for testing their hypotheses
6. The use of both multidisciplinary and interdisciplinary approaches
7. The organization of all instruction around generalizations or concepts
8. An evaluation of instruction in terms of student behaviors, which include desirable ecoaction
9. The study of "healthy" as well as "sick" environments, that is, the study of balanced, functioning ecosystems as well as disturbed, polluted ecosystems
10. Consideration of alternatives and ecoaction to implement change.

Concerns for elementary grades

In the primary grades, K-3, units on air, water, land, plants, and animals, as well as studies on home, school, and community environments, will provide basic ecological knowledge. In intermediate grades, 4, 5, and 6, units of soils, forests, and special environments can continue development of ecological knowledge, while studies of urban environments, nutrition, ecoaction, and monitoring environmental quality can also be introduced.

Most of these units may be organized as interdisciplinary studies. Significant distinctions can be made between interdisciplinary and multidisciplinary organization. If the study of environmental concepts or attitudes is approached via several subject disciplines, that approach is multidisciplinary. The multidisciplinary effort is, perforce, done in bits and pieces, and the separate components are often poorly articulated. Even when a teacher in a self-contained classroom utilizes a multidisciplinary approach, he or she may need to take great care to draw the entire complex into a unified whole. Interdisciplinary teaching of environmental studies is even more difficult. It may be done by one teacher or a team of teachers. The hallmark of an interdisciplinary effort is indistinct or undiscernible boundaries between the various disciplines involved. The significant syntheses are made by pupils and teachers together.

Perhaps nowhere in the elementary school is the interdisciplinary approach practiced more obviously than in the early primary grades. At this level teachers seem less confined by subject boundaries and are more inclined to explore topics from several angles. Primary grade teachers may seldom be aware that they use the interdisciplinary approach because this has always been their traditional style of teaching.

The study of water at a middle-grade level might appropriately consist of considerations of chemical composition, physical characteristics, geographical distribution, economics of wastewater disposal, the water-energy cycle, historical significance of water, environmental ethics in grade-level literature, artistic and musical expressions involving water, political jurisdiction in water regulation, or the mathematics of water pressure.

Concerns for secondary grades

For the secondary grades, units of study may be presented in one or more subject curricula, particularly the social studies and the sciences, or they may be offered in a teaching organization with potential for interdisciplinary contributions. For example, if all or most of the students are in a biology course, that course could have at least one unit on environmental studies or, preferably, the entire curriculum organized around man, other organisms, and their environments. Other units could include considerations of ecological succession, carrying capacity, recycling, monitoring of air and water constituents, land use, urban problems and urban planning, recreation and environmental quality, and the function of government agencies at all levels in maintaining environmental standards.

CONCEPTUAL SCHEMES

The development of curricula in all fields has been increasingly characterized by organization around conceptual schemes, a series of broad interlocking generalizations that encompass and relate many lesser concepts or generalizations. The selection of conceptual schemes forms the intellectual framework for all curricular planning. Environmental ethics or attitudes should be placed in a similar framework. Some of the most useful conceptual schemes for environmental studies follow.

Interdependence ideas

1. All parts of any environment, living or nonliving, are interdependent: their stability and existence are interconnected.

2. Environmental stresses placed on part of any community tends to produce additional stresses on other or all segments of that community.

Interaction ideas

3. Change is the most constant characteristic of the living or nonliving parts of any environment.

4. The continuous interaction between heredity and environment determines the characteristics of all life forms.

5. The relationships that develop among individuals, groups, and their environments determine the characteristics of those groups.

6. The history of any group of persons is a record of the interaction of individuals in that group, of that group with other groups, and the interaction of all of them with their environments.

7. The characteristics and behavior of an individual are a result of the interaction of his heredity and all his environments—the biophysical, the social, and the cultural.

Perception ideas

8. Governments are stabilized by tradition and law; governments are changed by modification of the people's perception of the governmental function.

9. The way an individual uses his environment is influenced by his perception of that environment.

10. The economy of a society is influenced by its perception of the relation of that society to its natural and human skills and resources.

Take, for instance, the central idea: All parts of any environment, living or nonliving, are interdependent; their stability and existence are interconnected. Disturbing the environment produces a situation much like the series of predicaments encountered by the old woman in the nursery tale when she wanted her pig to go over the stile. In her case, feeding the cat led to threatening the mouse to gnawing the rope to hanging the butcher to killing the ox to drinking the water to quenching the fire to burning the stick to hitting the dog to biting the pig to going over the stile.

This central idea is called a *conceptual scheme* because it relates or connects many other important concepts in ecology. The interdependence idea pulls together concepts such as the following:

1. When a series of larger animals feeds (and depends) on smaller animals or plants, that whole series is known as a food chain. For example, mice, which feed on seeds or grain, may be eaten by snakes, which, in turn, are caught by hawks or owls. This food chain is disturbed by people who

deliberately try to exterminate snakes, hawks, and owls. The resulting change may produce a plague of mice. This leads to a second concept.

2. When one or more members of a food chain are eliminated, disastrous consequences may result for one or more other members of the chain.

3. The more complex the food chains and other interrelationships in an environment, the more difficult it is to disrupt the web of interrelationships. Conversely, more simplified environments such as a farmer's field of corn are far more susceptible to disruption, by insect pests, for example, than a more complex community such as mixed vegetation, forests, or grasslands.

4. Any section of land on which people or animals are dependent for food has a definite limit or carrying capacity of population that it can support.

Each of these four broad concepts is, in itself, an illustration of the conceptual scheme of "interdependence."

ENVIRONMENTAL EDUCATION MODULES FOR THE ELEMENTARY GRADES

Following are examples of topics that might be taught in the elementary grades using interdisciplinary and multidisciplinary approaches. For each topic activities from a number of different subject areas are suggested.

Interdisciplinary organization

Primary grades

Animals

In the primary grades an interdisciplinary organization may be structured around a major activity such as a visit to a farm, a trip to the zoo, or a children's pet show. Each of these major events may serve as the focal point for many significant lesson and subsidiary activities. If a children's pet show is used, these activities and others will produce a desirable interdisciplinary blend.

Children might do the following:

Give the name of the pet and reasons for choosing the name.
Discuss age, weight, and sex of the pet.
Classify the pet (mammal, bird, etc.).
Group pets according to similar characteristics.
Compute the amount and kind of food consumed by the animal.
Compare cost of purchasing various pets.
Imitate sounds made by the pet.
Discuss the role of family members in helping to care for the pet.
Feel the animal and describe outer covering (fur, feathers).
Determine the amount of space required for keeping the pet.
Write poems about different pets.
Imitate the movements of pets.
Draw pictures or sketches of their favorite pet.
Compose and sing songs about animals.
Try to guess animal riddles from descriptions given by classmates.

Intermediate grades

Microclimates

An example of the effective correlation of mathematics and sciences is the study of a microclimate. A microclimate is a small area in which at least one life-support factor is at variance with those in the areas surrounding it. Life-support factors include temperature, light intensity, soil moisture, relative humidity, and soil fertility. Many classrooms have a thermometer just outside the window. The purpose of the thermometer is generally to indicate the outside air temperature. However, what it really indicates is the temperature of the air in the vicinity of the thermometer, since the temperature of the air varies from place to place within a given area.

An excellent activity is to have the class measure and record the temperature in several locations around the school with several thermometers. Questions such as these listed would direct the children's learning experiences. The temperatures at the various locations may be recorded in a table and/or graph.

What differences are found between high and low places?
How does the temperature vary between sunny and shaded areas?

- Is the temperature of concrete the same as the temperature of brick?
- Which side of the building is warmest?
- How does the difference in temperature of several places affect the way man lives?
- Do different plants or animals live in places where the temperature is different?
- Do areas of different temperatures have variations in other microclimatic factors such as light intensity, moisture, humidity, or soil characteristics?

Urban studies

A study of the urban environment may fit logically into the social studies curriculum, since most people live in cities. However, material from other disciplines may be woven in to make the study meaningful:

Architecture and design of building	(Art)
Racial and ethnic relationships	(Social Studies)
Unemployment statistics and effects	(Mathematics-Economics)
Air and water pollution	(Science)
Cultural institutions, that is, libraries, museums, etc.	(Art, Music, Social Studies)
Collection and interpretation of data	(Mathematics)

Water cycle

A series of lessons commonly taught in the elementary grades is organized around the idea of the *water cycle.* Concepts of evaporation, condensation, and precipitation are naturally included. The usual purpose of these lessons is to show how water leaves the surface of the earth through evaporation, condenses, and returns to earth as precipitation. The following are some environmental questions that could be included in the lesson series:

- What happens to rainwater when it reaches the earth?
- What effect does runoff have on soil?
- Why is it important that some water sink into the ground?
- What happens to water when a parking lot is built over open land?
- Where does most of the precipitation that falls in the city go?

Rusting and oxidation

In the intermediate elementary grades, consider a typical science lesson on the characteristics of rust. The following facts may be emphasized:

- Rust is a chemical compound.
- Rust is formed from iron and oxygen atoms.
- Rust is sometimes called iron oxide.

However, we might expand the lesson to include the effects of rust on man:

- Rust is responsible for millions of dollars worth of property damage.
- Man has spent great amounts of time, money, and effort developing new materials that will not rust.
- Rust is capable of destroying some metals that litter our landscape.
- Items such as aluminum cans, which will not rust if discarded on the landscape, will remain for many years.

Carbon-oxygen cycle

In a study of the carbon-oxygen cycle, most upper elementary students are able to explain the following:

- Carbon dioxide is a compound of carbon and oxygen.
- Plants use carbon dioxide in manufacturing food.
- Plants give off oxygen into the air, while producing food.
- Animals need oxygen to live.
- Animals inhale air containing oxygen and exhale air containing carbon dioxide.

However, carbon dioxide is important to man in other ways. Children could examine such ideas as these:

- Carbon dioxide prevents some of the sun's rays from reaching the earth—a good thing except where the carbon dioxide is in such abundance as to adversely affect the existence and activities of living beings.
- High carbon dioxide levels pose yet another important threat: an increase of carbon dioxide in the air may prevent the reflected heat waves of the earth from escaping into the atmosphere. This situation, called the "greenhouse effect," may increase the temperature of the earth to the point of threatening man's existence —by melting present polar ice caps and flooding many coastal areas.
- Carbon dioxide is used to provide the carbonation bubbles of soft drinks.
- Carbon dioxide is mixed with oxygen in small amounts to

increase the breathing rate of hospital patients or astronauts who use "pure" oxygen.

Carbon dioxide is used in fire extinguishers for electrical fires.

Carbon dioxide, produced by the bacterial decay of plant and animal material, is responsible for most of the acidity in soil, since it dissolves in soil water. The production of carbon dioxide from decaying plant or animal remains signals the recycling that generally occurs in environments not disturbed by man.

Multidisciplinary organization

Intermediate grades

Trees

SCIENCE

- Look for next year's buds on the trees in September, before the leaves fall, and observe growth through the winter and spring, until the buds open.
- Collect fallen leaves and classify according to color, shapes, and sizes.
- Examine the bark of different trees for variations in texture.
- Plant a small tree near the school.

MATHEMATICS

- Walk around the school building or block and count various types of trees or the number of one particular kind.
- Set up a tree calendar to record significant dates in the annual life of the tree.
- By counting or addition and subtraction, determine the length of time from the first leaf color change until no more is observed, or the number of days for a swelling bud to grow into a stem or leaves.
- Gather acorns for counting games.
- Count the annual rings of a tree stump.
- Measure the length of tree shadows at different times of the day or year and develop conclusions.

LANGUAGE ARTS

- Read poems and stories about trees.
- Look for likenesses and differences in tree sizes, shapes, bark, leaves, twig color.
- Let children suggest their own descriptive or comparative words.
- Have children develop a clue chart to distinguish some of the common trees in the neighborhood area.
- Develop experience charts or description of activities with trees.

ART

- Sketch shapes of trees with crayon or charcoal.
- Prepare a bulletin board of tree pictures.
- Make leaf dolls: paste leaves on paper, stems up, and sketch heads and limbs, using the stem for the torso and the leaf blade for the skirt.

MUSIC

- Choose songs about trees. Perhaps the children will compose their own songs.
- Make rhythm instruments from fallen tree branches or sections of hollow tree trunks.

SOCIAL STUDIES

- Discuss how trees are used by people.
- Have children identify trees as a source of specific items in the classroom and school.

Weather

LANGUAGE ARTS

- Listen to recordings of wind, rain, thunder.
- Read stories with weather or seasonal themes.
- Discuss signs of various seasons. Have children select and use appropriate word or sentence descriptions for these weather or climate signs.

These may lead easily into numerous weather-related art or craft activities.

MATHEMATICS

- Read thermometers.
- Keep a chart of daily temperatures at the beginning and end of the class day. Count or compute temperature differences.
- Maintain monthly weather calendar, recording such conveniently gathered data as temperature, wind speed, amount of rainfall or snowfall.

This information will provide abundant opportunities to develop questions that may utilize mathematical processes such as counting, selecting sets, addition, and subtraction.

SOCIAL STUDIES

- Discuss how weather affects our lives (clothing, activities, feelings).

SCIENCE

- Collect and measure rainfall in suitable containers.
- Measure how deep the snow is in the various parts of the school yard. Have children try to account for the variations.
- Use the wind clue chart to estimate wind speeds.

Although there are numerous recipes and directions for making simple weather instruments in the classroom from inexpensive materials, such instruments are of little value unless they initiate a series of measurements of some weather factor. The measurements usually yield greater learning dividends when they are recorded and interpreted.

MUSIC AND ART

All these activities can be articulated with all the familiar weather rhythms and many of the well-known seasonal activities.

2 DEVELOPING AND USING INSTRUCTIONAL MATERIALS

No body of knowledge in education, regardless of its simplicity or complexity, can be taught with maximum effectiveness in a haphazard, loosely organized manner. To have the greatest impact on the learner, the material must have purposes clear to both the teacher and the prospective learner. The methods and materials for study should then be planned carefully to realize these purposes.

This is especially true in environmental education in which the knowledge learned is truly a means to an end. In the final analysis the learner will, it is hoped, use his knowledge as a foundation to shape those attitudes that will lead to a commitment to strive for the improvement of environmental quality.

The Environmental Education Instruction Plan (EEIP) is a structured unit approach to environmental education, organized to be an effective tool for teachers. The EEIP is designed so that the teacher and the class begin with definite, clearly defined objectives. Through the presentation of a series of sequentially arranged lessons the class may achieve those objectives.

Following is a brief description of each component of the EEIP.

OBJECTIVES

The objectives of each Environmental Education Instruction Plan are written in behavioral terms and include both the cognitive and affective domains. The cognitive domain includes pertinent knowledge in the form of facts and generalizations. In addition, the cognitive domain is concerned with the intellectual skills involved in locating information, classifying information, synthesizing facts into generalities, and inferring the consequences, or prediction value of broad general statements. The cognitive objectives are stated in terms of actions in which the students will be motivated to engage during the conduct of the unit. These actions will ostensibly demonstrate the students' mastery of selected items of knowledge. The writing of such objectives in behavioral terms should facilitate the preparation of effective evaluation procedures for the teacher.

The objectives written for the affective domain are those which reflect attitudes, feelings, and social skills to be developed by the learner. By their very nature, affective objectives are difficult to measure. But a promising means to detect a particular attitude in a student is the selection of actions in which students might engage if they had that attitude. A discussion of procedures for measuring achievement in cognitive objectives will be presented in Chapter 5.

GENERALIZATIONS

Along with the skills, abilities, and attitudes to be developed from the EEIP, the broad concepts to be learned are a vital part of the package. These ideas are referred to as generalizations. Generalizations provide cogent summaries and relationships for numerous factual items of knowledge. Generalizations are significant objects of instruction in that they form the basis on which the attitudes toward environmental quality are to be formed.

STRATEGY

The strategy is that part of the plan providing the rationale and the general explanation of the methods and approaches to be used in exploring the topic. Because environmental education is not found in the existing curricula of many school systems, some curricular adjustment may be necessary if the general goals of environmental education are to be realized.

EEIPs such as those included in this book are designed to be brief enough to be utilized without serious dislocation of the existing curriculum or self-contained classroom. They may also be used conveniently in departmentalized classes in a variety of disciplinary concerns.

If neither of these procedures is feasible, some teachers may introduce environmental components into a less flexible curriculum by selecting appropriate lessons from the EEIPs.

LESSON OUTLINES

The specific lessons are arranged to provide a useful or meaningful continuity, many lessons being derived from previous ones. Activities accompany each lesson and often require either a direct encounter with a specific environment or the gathering or interpretation of data pertinent to a particular environment. These activities are directly related to the generalizations of the unit and are designed to reinforce the learning. Many of the activities can be conducted effectively in the classroom, whereas others require the students to leave the classroom to work in a variety of environments.

MATERIALS

A suggested list of materials for use in teaching the unit is provided but is by no means complete. Teachers are encouraged to provide additional materials that may be available and useful in their particular situations.

EVALUATION

Each Environmental Education Instruction Plan includes suggestions for evaluating achievement of the objectives. These suggestions are intended to assist the teacher in detecting those student behaviors needed for evaluation. These suggestions are also made to enable the teacher to determine quickly the effectiveness of the plan and the areas requiring additional instruction.

BIBLIOGRAPHY

The bibliography includes listings of those books, films, and teaching aids used in preparing the EEIPs. These may be employed by teachers when implementing or extending the plans.

INTERDISCIPLINARY ASPECTS

Although the general area of emphasis of an Environmental Education Instruction Plan may seem to fit quite logically into a particular discipline such as science, social studies, and mathematics, closer examination will reveal that many subject areas can be involved. This interdisciplinary aspect allows the use of several approaches to the study of environments.

For example, an EEIP dealing with water pollution may be science oriented. However, in the course of teaching the unit, the teacher may have students determine stream flow and volume, capacity of a watershed, or average water consumption by various groups. These determinations will require the use of one or more mathematical processes. The mathematical expressions provide a special kind of description—a special language.

The impact of water pollution on the health of human beings could be included in such a unit. Such activities as writing letters to public officials to describe an environmental condition or interviewing private citizens would utilize the language arts. The responsibility of the individual citizen and the government would be a social studies concern within the same study. Although these activities are not labeled science, math, language arts, social studies, they may be interwoven with the EEIP in an effort to give many aspects of a significant social problem more meaning and purpose to students and teachers.

ENVIRONMENTAL EDUCATION INSTRUCTION PLANS

Here are some Environmental Education Instruction Plans that have been field tested. The lessons and activities have been utilized in both classroom and extraclassroom situations. Lessons have been rewritten, revised, rearranged, or eliminated in accordance with teacher evaluations. So that the appropriate step-by-step learnings may occur, each EEIP should be adopted (or adapted) in its entirety, rather than be used solely as a source for a few outdoor activities.

I am vitally interested in the continuous revision of this curriculum material and would appreciate feedback on any EEIPs that you may actually use in your teaching. The information below would be of great value.

1. Are you a: teacher
   principal
   superintendent
   curriculum coordinator
   other (list)
2. Grade level(s) for which EEIP was used? (Please answer for each EEIP.)
3. Title(s) of EEIPs used.
4. How were EEIPs used?
   ________ Used entire plans
   ________ Selected individual lessons from plans
   ________ Other: ________________________________
5. What were the most valuable features of the EEIPs?
6. What problems did you have in using them?
7. For what areas of study would you like to see new EEIP material developed?
8. Have you been able to develop similar curriculum plans for environmental study from your textbooks and school curriculum guides?
9. What suggestions do you have for improving the EEIPs that you have reviewed above?

EEIP 1—MAIN STREET, U.S.A.

Interdisciplinary—emphasizing social and ecological relationships
Primary grades

Overview

Man by his social nature has chosen to live in groups. Throughout time these groups have been designed to help individuals meet their basic needs of food, clothing, shelter, and protection. To ensure survival and enhance life, man has begun to realize that he must act in an interdependent manner with other men and his environment.

As evidenced by the history of the United States of America, change—whether good or bad—has been constant. However, the basic living group of the family has remained fairly stable, and today 87% of all Americans live in family groups. Obviously these small cultural groups have banded together for reasons relating to anthropology, geography, and economics and have created communities. In turn, communities influence an individual's way of doing things, and the people residing therein are never completely independent of their habitat.

The major purpose of our educational system is to ensure the continuation of our society, and this would include the preparation of children for roles in this society. To carry out an effective role, children must be aware of existing human groupings and environmental relationships. A study of the basic family group and the local community provides the fundamental step in gaining an understanding of the American culture.

Objectives

Cognitive. Lessons primarily pertinent only to specific objectives are noted in parentheses.

1. To observe and describe changes in one or more aspects of the total environment.
2. To ask questions about the environmental impact of projected changes such as building and construction (Lessons I, IV).
3. To make comparisons between one's environment and the environments of others (Lessons I, VI, IX).
4. To transfer environmental context into other areas, that is, stories, pictures, vocabulary (Lesson XI).
5. To present or demonstrate original ideas concerning one's role in the environment.
6. To identify the needs of the individual in the community (Lessons II, V, VII, VIII, XII, XIV, XV).
7. To identify the interrelationships of people and their environment (Lessons I, V, VII, VIII, XII-XV).
8. To point out some changes in the environment (Lesson IV).
9. To classify and organize materials and/or objects (Lessons VII, IX, XI).
10. To ask questions about the environment.
11. To ask exploratory questions—"How come?" "Why?" "What for?" etc.—concerning the environment (Lessons I, III-V, VII-IX, XI, XII).
12. To design investigations or observations to answer questions about environments (Lesson VII).
13. To involve other children and adults in answering questions (Lessons VI, XII).
14. To avoid making predictions not based on evidence.
15. To make predictions based on evidence (if opportunity is provided).
16. To draw inferences from material presented (Lesson IX).
17. To draw conclusions from observations.
18. To manipulate class materials independently.
19. To use environmental vocabulary correctly in context, in lessons other than this study unit.

Affective—attitudes. Objectives in the affective domain have been stated as generalizations of desired conducts. For each, any one of a number of index behaviors may indicate progress toward the desired affective objectives. Frequently, of course, these behaviors overlap. Several index behaviors are listed with each attitudinal generalization, so that the teacher may utilize any for which the class activities would provide behavioral evidence. The teacher may also devise additional or alternative index behaviors for any or all of the attitudinal generalizations.

1. People should not permit environmental changes if convinced that the proposed change will deteriorate the quality of that environment.

   Related index behaviors

   a. Not knowingly damage or harm trees or other plants.
   b. Attempt to place litter and refuse in the proper receptacles.
   c. Demonstrate proper health habits to prevent the spread of disease.
   d. Consciously plan to prevent hazards by placing objects in the proper places and following general safety rules.
   e. Demonstrate a respect for the value of food by handling it properly and not wasting it.
   f. Not knowingly harm domestic or wild animals and their habitats.

2. People should strive to improve environmental quality.

   Related index behaviors

   a. Attempt to care for existing trees and plants or, if possible, replace them where they may be of use.
   b. Pick up litter or refuse and deposit it in a proper container.
   c. Attempt to correct unsanitary conditions.
   d. Attempt, to the best of their ability to remove hazardous conditions, for example, bicycles blocking a sidewalk, broken glass on the playground.
   e. Show awareness of air and water pollution problems by bringing these matters to the attention of a responsible adult.
   f. Improve conditions for wild animals by providing for them in winter or attempting to protect their natural habitat.
   g. Participate as individuals.*
   h. Interact with group.*
   i. Listen to and try ideas of others.*

3. All property ownership is really a trusteeship granted by a society to individuals.

   Related index behaviors

   a. Not make changes that will deteriorate the environment of any privately held property or that will deteriorate more distant environments.
   b. Will not knowingly contribute to the deterioration of the inside or the outside of a building.
   c. Care for and be responsible for their own belongings and the property of others.
   d. Consider trusteeship of public property a responsibility of all citizens in general and designated public agencies in particular.
   e. Show concern and respect for public lands and property by using them as they were intended to be used.
   f. Report the unwarranted use or vandalism of public property or land to the proper authority.
   g. Consider trusteeship of abandoned buildings or property, although privately held, as requiring the supportive trusteeship of all citizens.

---

*These behaviors contribute to the improvement of a social environment.

Generalizations

1. Communities help to meet the needs of the individuals who live there by supplying them with some essential services such as schools, medical care, police protection, safe drinking water, and sanitary sewage disposal. When any of these needs are not met, environmental deterioration probably occurs.
2. Every individual has a responsibility to know his community and take an active part in its affairs.
3. Workers are paid to produce goods or to perform services. They in turn use this money to obtain goods and services. Occasionally a limited salary does not permit a worker to obtain some desired goods or services.
4. Cultural background and life styles influence a person's behavior and attitudes toward all aspects of the environment.
5. Many environments help to make up a community. According to their condition and the purpose they serve, these environments may add to or detract from the total community.
6. Man has the ability to alter his environment. If it is necessary to change the environment, it should be done with care for the consequences of the environmental change on people and the environment, for the immediate and more distant future.
7. Awareness of and concern for the environment should lead to a commitment to optimum environments and to the improvement of unhealthy environments by persons at all age levels.

Strategy

This EEIP, comprised of several interrelated lessons, has been designed to introduce the primary grade child to the concept of the community and to help develop understandings about the environment. As the child is discovering the relationships that exist between the population and the physical community, it is hoped that he will be able to view and understand the continuity and balance that is present and that helps shape the identifying characteristics of his surroundings.

The material and information concerning the community that is presented to the child by the teacher should be suitable and authentic. Above all, it should be relevant to the child and his world. The ideas set forth here can be used by the teacher as a basic outline and should be modified or implemented to meet the needs of the individual class; if Main Street does exist, it must certainly do so in endless varieties.

Lesson outlines

Lesson I. In the classroom—A lead-up activity

Post a large map of the United States and maps of other countries if your class has foreign-born children. Have the children make cutouts of themselves and mark them with their names and places of birth. Fasten the cutouts to the appropriate places on the map.

Have the children locate their present community. Mark plainly.

A discussion should follow, noting the places of birth. Elicit reasons why some families have moved to this community. Some of the reasons may include jobs, family, new or different houses, proximity to a large metropolitan area, or better living conditions. List reasons on chart paper.

If the majority of the children were born in this community, determine reasons why their ancestors came to this community. List these reasons on second chart.

Text continued on p. 32.

A LOOK AT OUR COMMUNITY

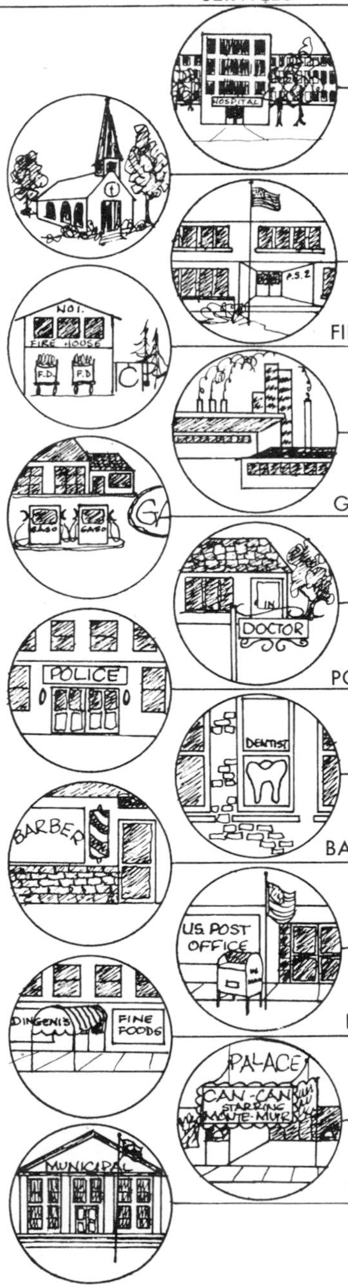

SERVICES	NO. OF TIMES SEEN	WHAT IS DONE IN THIS BUILDING?
HOSPITAL		
CHURCH		
SCHOOL		
FIREHOUSE		
FACTORY		
GAS STATION		
DOCTOR		
POLICE STATION		
DENTIST		
BARBERSHOP		
POST OFFICE		
RESTAURANT		
THEATER		
TOWN HALL		

Fig. 2-1

A LOOK AT OUR COMMUNITY

AREAS	NO. OF TIMES SEEN	WHAT IS DONE IN EACH AREA?
PLAYGROUND		
PARKING LOT		
SHOPPING CENTER		
PARK		
BASEBALL FIELD		
VACANT LOT		
INDUSTRIAL AREA		
NATURAL AREA		
RESIDENTIAL AREA		

You may add other stores to your list.

Continued.

A LOOK AT OUR COMMUNITY

STORES	NO. OF TIMES SEEN	WHAT IS SOLD IN THIS STORE?
FOOD STORE		
CLOTHING STORE		
DEPARTMENT STORE		
DELICATESSEN		
DRUGSTORE		
PET SHOP		
SHOE STORE		
HARDWARE STORE		
JEWELRY STORE		
FURNITURE STORE		
SPORTING GOODS STORE		
TOY AND HOBBY SHOP		

You may add other buildings to your list.

Fig. 2-1, cont'd

A LOOK AT OUR COMMUNITY

PEOPLE	NO. OF TIMES SEEN						WHAT DOES EACH PERSON DO?
SCHOOL CROSSING GUARD							
POSTMAN							
POLICEMAN							
REPAIRMAN							
WAITRESS							
STORE CLERK							
TRUCK DRIVER							
CONTRACTOR							
BUS DRIVER							
TAXI DRIVER							
DELIVERYMAN							
FIREMAN							
BARBER							

You may add other people to your list.

Lesson II. In the classroom—Identifying human needs

Prepare a large bulletin board with pictures showing needs of individuals as well as needs of a group (that is, food, clothing, shelter, hospitals, schools, recreational areas, policemen, firemen, garbage collectors, stores, banks, churches, people engaged in work, etc.). These pictures should be relevant to your class and community.

Elicit a discussion in which the children can identify the needs as their own or as those of their family or community. Note if any of the needs identified are similar to the reasons given in Lesson I as to why people have moved to this community.

Have the children contribute drawings or pictures to the bulletin board and encourage them to explain their contributions.

Urge the children to note some of these needs and how they are met while they are on their way to and from school. Discuss.

Divide the class into study groups and, using the corresponding work sheets, assign each group one of the following subjects: services, stores, people, or areas. While on walking trips near the school grounds or into nearby neighborhoods, the children will then be able to survey the community.

After returning to the classroom, complete work sheets such as those suggested on pp. 28 to 31, compiling your information and drawing conclusions concerning your community and environment based on what the children have observed.

Lesson III. In the classroom—Locating within the community

NOTE: Local planning board, government, merchants, Chamber of Commerce may be a source for map(s) of community.

Obtain and post an enlarged map showing your local community. Have the children locate and mark the school and their homes with colored straight pins and trace the route they take to school with their fingers. Decide on boundaries for the community and neighborhoods.

Locate and mark the following on the map: shopping area, industrial area, residential area, recreational areas, theater, churches, hospital, and others. Ask the following questions:

1. Do several children live in one area? Why?
2. Where are the public buildings located? Why?
3. What are the means of transportation used? Why?
4. What is the locational relationship between the residential area and the shopping area? Explain.
5. Are there reasons for the existing boundaries of the communities? Natural barriers? Man-made barriers?
6. Have children label environments and identify characteristics of each.

Lesson IV. In the community

A. Take a trip into the community. Look for changes in the community and for buildings, objects, or landmarks that have been in the community for a long time. Working in their study groups the children can survey the community with the aid of the Suggested Work Sheet on opposite page.

In the classroom have each group compile the information that was collected. Initiate a discussion and consider the following questions:

1. Where are the old buildings, objects, or landmarks located? Why are they found here?
2. What is the approximate age of these structures?
3. What is the apparent condition of the buildings?
4. For what purpose are these structures being used?
5. Are any of these structures historic,

"haunted," or different from buildings that are familiar to the children?

6. What is the condition of the environment surrounding the building? How did this condition come about? Can it be improved?

Ask similar questions concerning the changes that were noted. Compare and contrast these buildings and the areas in which they are found. Draw conclusions about the future of these buildings and the surrounding areas.

Make a list of the old buildings and landmarks of the community. Collect and exhibit pictures of these very old places. Write stories to go with these pictures.

B. If possible, view the community from a tall building. Locate various buildings and areas. Draw simple maps showing buildings, roads, and other features in relation to each other.

In the classroom the children may prepare a large floor map of the area seen. It is easier if the streets form a simple grid and the cutouts representing the buildings and objects are of relative size. Include a key and directions.

C. Identify your community (for example, a farming community, an industrial community, a resort community). With the information gathered on the trip, have the children decide what kind of community they live in. Discuss other types of communities or environments. What might they look like? Why?

Lesson V. In the classroom—Food for the community

Prepare a bulletin board showing the kinds of food eaten by the children. Have the children bring in pictures, labels, cartons, and wrappers for the bulletin board. Discuss the following questions:

1. Where does your family purchase food?
2. How is your family able to purchase food?
3. How do families get their money?
4. Where do stores get their food?
5. Where is some food processed or prepared?
6. Where is the food grown?
7. How does the food get to the stores?
8. What are the various kinds of food stores?
9. Where are the food stores? Locate on maps.
10. Who works in the stores? Why?
11. Where do they live?
12. How do they get to work?
13. What do the stores do with the money they get from sales?
14. Do the food stores remain the same or do they change?
15. Does the time of the year have something to do with what the food store sells?
16. Food stores must maintain certain health standards. What are some of them?
17. Who sets the standards?
18. How are these standards maintained?

SUGGESTED WORK SHEET

FINDING CHANGES IN BUILDINGS

CHANGES	OLD BUILDINGS OBJECTS, LANDMARKS	LOCATION	CONDITION	
			GOOD	POOR
Example: New post office			X	

Have the children prepare a mural showing the various steps of food from farm to store to table.

Build a store in your classroom. Allow the children to decide what is to be sold and stock it with food containers that are representative of the community. Price the items accordingly. The store should provide an opportunity for the children to be involved in the buying and selling of goods and the handling of money. The children can assume the roles of store clerks and customers and, by playacting, conduct business. By using play money or similar facsimiles, the children can be actively involved in the exchange of money and goods.

Lesson VI. In the classroom—Foods of the community

NOTE: In this lesson the teacher has a choice of either a buffet luncheon planned, prepared, and served by the children, so that they can be introduced to new foods, or the preparation of a recipe book, so that the children can gain an understanding of other people's choices of food.

A. Plan a buffet luncheon. Discuss the kinds of food the children have at home. Identify some of the more popular foods and determine their origins. In your community perhaps there will be foods particular to various ethnic groups such as Italian or Mexican or foods that have historical backgrounds such as maple sugar candy or cranberry sauce.

Decide on a simple menu that illustrates these popular foods and assign class groups the task of planning for the luncheon. Each group's responsibilities should include choosing the recipe from home, preparing, setting out, and serving the food, and general cleanup. The children will have to take into account the need to plan a balanced diet and the cost of the food. The children can compare their various roles to those of persons in their families.

The planning of the luncheon can be initiated at this time, but the actual activity can be held at a later time as a culminating event and an evaluation.

B. Perhaps your class can write and illustrate their own recipe booklet, including recipes and cooking ideas from a child's point of view. Encourage the children to write stories or legends to go with their recipes.

1. The recipe book can be illustrated by the children.
2. These recipe books could be typed and reproduced for distribution to each member of the class, the appropriate parent organization, other classes, and teachers.

Lesson VII. In or away from the classroom—Trips into the community

Plan field trips to various local places such as an orchard, a truck farm, or a poultry farm. If such places are not readily available, plan a trip to a food-processing plant, a food-supply warehouse, or the food-storage area of a large food store.

Class discussions before the trip should familiarize the children with the purpose of the trip and what to expect to find when they arrive.

Following are some of the points that should be discussed before the trip:

1. The name and location of the place to be visited.
2. The purpose and kind of work done.
3. Services to the community in terms of supplying needs.
4. The persons who work there.
   a. Who?
   b. How many?
   c. How do they get there?
   d. What are some of the jobs?
5. The inside and outside environment.
   a. Is the inside of the building neat?
   b. Would you like to work there?

c. What would you do to improve conditions?
d. Is the immediate area and the surrounding neighborhood pleasant?
e. How would you keep it pleasant or what could you do to improve the area?

Many of the questions will not be answered until the trip has been completed. The work sheet suggested will help the children to collect their data.

After returning to the classroom, prepare a mural, telling the story of the trip, or write and illustrate a story of the trip.

SUGGESTED WORK SHEET

HOW BUILDINGS LOOK

1. Look at the outside of the building. Put a check next to the words that best tell about it.

________ neat	________ not clean	________ many windows
________ clean	________ needs fixing	________ few windows
________ old	________ large	________ pleasant
________ new	________ small	________ unsightly

2. Look at the area near the building. Put a check next to the words that best tell about it.

________ farm area	________ other buildings	________ many animals
________ grassy	________ neat	________ many cars
________ bare ground	________ littered	________ signs
________ citylike	________ many roads	________ many sidewalks

3. Look at the inside of the building. Put a check next to the words that best tell about it.

________ many rooms	________ clean	________ cold
________ few rooms	________ pleasant	________ hot
________ quiet	________ littered	________ many people
________ noisy	________ smelly	________ few people

4. Do many people work here? ________ yes ________ no
5. What are some of the jobs these people do?
6. Do they wear special clothes? ________ yes ________ no
   Draw a picture of their special clothes.
7. Do they use special tools? ________ yes ________ no
   Draw a picture of their special tools.

Lesson VIII. In and away from the classroom—Clothing for the community

A. Families need clothing. Have the children determine that we get our clothing by purchasing it in a store or having someone make it for us. Prepare a bulletin board showing various types of clothing needed by people who live in your community. Deduce that the type of clothing worn depends on the weather. Discuss the relationship between essential clothing and popular types.

List the various articles of clothing. Have the children survey the different clothing stores to determine the type of store, goods sold, and number of stores. Mark on map. Do the stores meet the people's needs? Also consider the cost of clothing.

B. Take a trip to a large retail store, mill, garment house, or warehouse. Consider these points in planning the trip:

1. What are the basic sources of material for all clothing?
2. How and in what quantity is clothing made commercially?
3. How do items of clothing get to our community?
4. Where do you shop for clothes?
5. Where are the stores?
6. Who works in them?
7. How do the people get to work?
8. Do clothing stores always sell the same type of clothes? Why not?
9. What do the stores do with the money they get from sales?
10. What environmental factors affect the type of clothing featured in stores?
11. What environmental factors affect the type of clothes you wear?
12. What animals will eventually disappear from the earth if their skins are made into fur coats?

C. At this point a discussion about money can be initiated. The following points should be emphasized:

1. People work to earn money.
2. Money we have earned is exchanged for goods or services that we need.
3. Money is a way of saving for future use.
4. Money circulates.

Have the children draw pictures of things people do to earn money. Some examples are jobs requiring skilled or unskilled labor, services, producing goods or products, and special abilities.

Have the children draw pictures of what can be obtained or done with money. For example, include such items as food, clothing, pay for household expenses, education, entertainment, recreation, insurance, and things the children may want.

Lesson IX. In the classroom—Community dwellings

With the children discuss how homes fulfill many of the needs of the people who inhabit them. Be sure to include such points as sheltering from the weather and providing a place to cook, eat, and sleep, a place to keep one's belongings, and a place to entertain. Encourage the children to contribute their ideas of a home.

Initiate a discussion that contrasts homes from an earlier environment and homes from a modern-day environment.

1. In the "olden days" what did people do without in their homes?
2. What rooms are usually found in a modern home?
3. How do you tell the difference between a modern home and an old one?

Take a walk in the area near the school and observe the different kinds of homes. For instance, note single-unit dwellings, multiunit dwellings, apartment complexes, mobile homes, or retirement villages. See sample work sheet on p. 37.

In class determine why there are so many kinds of houses and in what kind of environment we

COMMUNITY DWELLINGS

What kind of houses do people live in?

Fig. 2-2

find these houses. Why do some houses cost more than others, and why does some land cost more than other land?

Have the children prepare a bulletin board of pictures of dwellings common to your community. Determine why some families live in certain homes and in certain environments, noting such facts as large families, low-cost housing, proximity to schools, work, transportation, and recreational areas.

Have the children compare their own homes to the home and environment they would prefer.

Lesson X. In and away from the classroom—Studying a house

For study choose a house near your school that is typical of your community. Draw a picture of the house and answer the following questions:

1. What is the size of the house?
2. How many floors are there?
3. Is there a cellar and an attic? How do you know?
4. How many windows, rooms, and outside doors are there?
5. What color is the house? What color is the trim?
6. What materials were used in the construction of this house? Where were these materials obtained in the community?
7. Is there a lawn, play yard, or other similar areas?
8. Are there trees, flowers, or grass? Why or why not?
9. Does this house have a telephone and electricity? How can you tell?
10. What is the approximate age and condition of this house?
11. Estimate the size of the family or the number of people who live here?
12. How is the house adapted to meet weather conditions?
13. Are any children living here? How do you know?
14. Is there a pet? How can you tell?
15. Does this family have a car? How can you tell?
16. Is this house near to stores?
17. How does this house contribute to or detract from its environment?

Have each child draw and color a picture of a house he would like to live in and write a story telling about the house.

Lesson XI. In the classroom—Building a new house

NOTE: If a new housing development is located in your community, obtain a floor plan or blueprints from them. Ask if you can bring your class to the site to observe houses in various stages of construction. Perhaps the developer or sales agent would answer questions for the children.

Obtain a simple floor plan or a blueprint of a house. (The real estate section of your newspaper is an excellent source.) Study the floor plan and locate all areas—sleeping, cooking, living, and others. Have the children determine the steps in building a house. Observe the construction of a house that is typical of your community. Answer the following questions:

1. Who will live here?
2. What are the needs of this family?
3. How will the construction of this house affect the environment?
4. Is the house right for the land? For the weather?
5. What building materials are being used? Where have they been obtained?
6. What are the skills of workmen who are building this house? Where do they live? What tools do they need?
7. What are they working on here? What are their jobs?

BUILDING A NEW HOUSE

What is a house made of?

 Wood		 Metal		 Bricks		 Stone		 Glass	

Fig. 2-3

8. How long does it take them to build a house?
9. How does a family obtain enough money to buy a house?

Using the suggested work sheet on p. 39, have the children list or draw the objects used in the construction of a house under the correct materials-source column and include the skilled worker who uses this material.

Lesson XII. In the classroom—Local government

Families have rules that must be obeyed, such as children must put their belongings away or help with certain household chores. Encourage the children to tell about some of the rules of their families.

Communities also have rules and laws so that the people will be safe and the community, orderly. Discuss some of the rules and the reasons why they should be enforced. Include such laws as obeying traffic lights, driving on the right side of the road, and stopping for the loading and unloading of school buses. Also consider such responsibilities as the proper use of public and private property and buildings and the following of health rules.

Discuss government and the role of the government in maintaining a safe and orderly community. Have the children invite an elected local government official to visit your class. Ask him to tell about his job and the responsibility of the government to the people and the people to the government.

Prior to his coming have each group develop its own questions that they can direct to the official. Consider questions such as the following:

1. What are some of the services provided by the local government?
2. How do you get to be a government official?
3. Where does the government get its money?
4. How does the government try to protect the environment?

Lesson XIII. In and away from the classroom—Responsibilities of local government

A. Governments provide many services for the community. Have the children review the services provided by the community government. (The visit of the local official should have helped them determine services.)

Have the class invite a police officer or a fireman to your classroom to explain his job. Perhaps he could bring some equipment to demonstrate.

Following is a list of some governmental services. Visit the locations or headquarters of as many as possible. Mark these places on the map:

1. Police protection
2. Fire protection
3. Refuse collection
4. Libraries
5. Health services
6. Recreation facilities
7. Schools
8. Water and sewage removal
9. Streets and highways
10. Community government
11. Utilities
12. Transportation

During these visits stress the following points:

1. In a community, individuals need one another.
2. Communities attempt to keep people safe and healthy.
3. Community environments are everybody's concern.
4. Communities need workers.
5. Communities must pay their workers.

Also consider the following questions:

1. Are the services that are provided sufficient? If not, what could be done about improving them?
2. Are some services not provided that should be? How do we go about obtaining these services?

B. Taxes are collected to pay for the services provided by the government and also to pay the salaries of government employees. Some of this tax money is collected from the people who live in the community.

Knowing some of the services provided by the community, have the children discuss with their parents or guardians some of the taxes they pay.

Compile a list of taxes and discuss the use of the money for such items as maintaining schools, roads, and the fire and police departments.

Lesson XIV. In the classroom—Communications

Introduce the word *communications.* Compare the word to *communities* and help the children discover the relationship between the two words. List several ways in which people in your community communicate. If possible, visit a newspaper or magazine publisher, a telephone office, or a radio or television station.

Messages transmitted by the various means of communication affect the persons that read and hear them, and they, in turn, affect the environment. These messages inform the public of such things as advertised sales, community events, road closings for repairs, and warnings of storms.

Have the children bring in copies of a local newspaper. Locate articles or advertisements directed at the general public. Discuss how they will affect the individuals who read them and how they might affect the environment.

Example: An article telling about the last game of the season for the local high school football team will bring out many spectators for an afternoon of entertainment.

The great number of persons converging at one place may cause problems in traffic safety, and many policemen may have to be on hand to keep traffic moving safely. Trash from food and souvenirs may litter the ground, and extra trash collectors will be needed to aid in the cleanup. These and other environmental problems must be taken care of, so that the persons attending the game will have a safe and enjoyable time.

Lesson XV. In the classroom—Transportation

A. Discuss the various means of transportation used today. Have each child draw a picture of one method of transportation. As a group, look through the pictures and decide whether the method of transportation is used basically for passengers or for freight. Compile a list of this information. Decide which of these means of transportation are used in your community.

B. Have the children study some bus or train timetables. Note that there must be good communications before there is reliable transportation. If possible, visit a bus or train station or an airport. Have the children discover the importance of these transportation modes in affecting their environments.

C. Return to the classroom store and read the labels, wrappers, and cartons used in Lesson V to determine where they were produced and if they had to be transported into the community. Discuss whether fresh produce, clothing, and other manufactured goods must be brought into the community.

D. Assign each group one of the following means of transportation: truck, train, ship, and airplane. By writing letters to transportation companies to obtain information and using the school library, each group can prepare a short report about its means of transportation studied.

The following items should be included:

1. Pictures or drawings of the type of transportation.
2. What is brought into the community by this means of transportation.
3. What facilities are needed by this means of transportation (tracks, station, runways).
4. How this means of transportation affects the environment.
5. What would happen to the community if this means of transportation were suddenly not available.

Lesson XVI. In the classroom—Community murals

As a culminating activity have each group prepare a large mural about some aspect of the community and write a story to accompany each mural.

The following are some suggestions for topics for the murals:

1. Our community.
2. How we affect our environment.
3. Different environments within our community.

Lesson XVII. In an appropriate location—Buffet luncheon

In Lesson VI a buffet luncheon was planned. At this time, if it is possible, the actual luncheon can be prepared and served. Parents can be asked to help the children with the preparations.

Materials

1. Large outline map of the United States
2. Large map of local area or community
3. Individual community maps for each child
4. Craft paper for floor map
5. Cardboard cartons and boxes for model city
6. Work sheets

Evaluation

Evaluation may be made in terms of the behavioral objectives stated at the beginning of this EEIP. The first five cognitive objectives relate to four characteristics desirable in young children—sensitivity (1), curiosity (2, 3), creativity and imagination (4, 5). The remaining cognitive objectives relate directly to the development of the skills of observing (6-9), questioning (10, 11), seeking answers (12, 13), and hypothesizing (14-17), and to general skills useful throughout these processes (18, 19). The lesson numbers included in the list of objectives refer to specific lessons that bear direct relevance to a particular behavior.

In addition, many of the objectives can be observed in an optional evaluative activity that may be undertaken by the teacher and class—the planning and building of a model city (community). Begin with an imaginary, undeveloped, natural area located near other communities. Portray the area on individual maps, so that the children can visualize the situation. Plan a class story telling how the land will be used.

Transfer the plan to a model. The city (community) can be constructed from boxes and other household articles and assembled on a sand table. Inhabit the community with several families and individuals and have the children provide for the needs of these persons.

While the children are planning and working, observe their actions and comments closely. The teacher may determine if the children's attitudes and acknowledgments of people's wants and needs show favorable progress in terms of the affective objectives. The children will also display much knowledge and skill in planning the physical community.

BIBLIOGRAPHY

A place to live, The Yearbook of Agriculture, Washington, D. C., 1963. U. S. Department of Agriculture.

Brehm, Shirley A.: A teacher's handbook for study outside the classroom, Columbus, Ohio, 1969, Charles E. Merrill Publishing Co.

Burton, Virginia Lee: The little house, Boston, Houghton Mifflin Co.

Darling, F. Fraser, and Milton, John P., editors: Future environments of North America, Garden City, L. I., 1966, The Natural History Press.

Kane, Elmer R.: How money and credit help us, Chicago, 1966, Benefic Press.

King, Frederick M., Bracken, Dorothy, and Sloan, Margaret A.: Families and social needs, River Forest, Ill., 1968, Laidlaw Brothers.

King, Frederick M., Bracken, Dorothy, and Sloan, Margaret A.: Communities and social needs, River Forest, Ill., 1968, Laidlaw Brothers.

Mand, Charles L.: Outdoor education, New York, 1967, J. Lowell Pratt & Co., Inc.

Outdoors, U.S.A., the yearbook of agriculture, Washington, D. C., 1967, U. S. Department of Agriculture.

Wilcox, Louise K., and Burks, Gordon E.: What is money? Austin, Texas, 1959, The Steck Co.

EEIP 2—TUNING UP THE FIVE SENSES

Interdisciplinary—emphasizing observation and communication skills
Middle grades through Junior High

Overview

Imagine before us the painting "Christina's World" by Andrew Wyeth. In it the artist has chosen to depict a woman crawling through a grassy field toward a distant farmhouse and outbuildings. If we were to seat a fifth-grade teacher and one of her pupils in front of this picture, we would observe a curious dissimilarity in their reactions. To the teacher the subject of the work is the woman in the foreground, whereas the youngster views the entire painting as relevant. This divergence of viewpoint is the result of a cultural screening action, which has been developing since birth in the mental process of the adult but which has not yet occurred in the mind of the child.

Since the world outside our minds is composed of an infinite number of objects and their interactions (events), we must develop some criteria for choosing those items that are of most importance. The screening process, however, should not evolve haphazardly, as it has in most of us, but should rather be the result of direct multisensory interplay with the environment in teacher-guided learning situations. Educational researchers maintain that the more variety of sensory experiences provided in such learning situations, the greater the understanding of a particular idea or generalization will be.

Objectives

Cognitive

1. To categorize information received according to the sense used for reception (Lessons I-III, IV, VII-X).
2. To write a description of an object using words that convey sensory images (Lessons II, III, VII-IX).
3. To draw rough sketches of small environmental areas (Lessons XIV-XVI).
4. To list several characteristics of various objects (Lessons VI-X, XII, XIII).
5. To "test" objects by the use of their senses (Lessons I-IV, VIII).
6. To utilize library-research methods to learn more about individual objects (Lessons XI, XIII, XV, XVII).
7. To identify selected species of flora and fauna by use of "keys" (Lessons XI, XIII-XV).
8. To use effectively such tools as the hand lens, binoculars, or microscopes to increase sensory effectiveness (Lesson XIII).

Affective

1. To identify subjectively with "pet" objects and convey feelings and beliefs about these through varied means of creative expression (Lessons VII-X).
2. To demonstrate formation of an environmental ethic, by showing selectivity in removing objects from their natural environment (Lessons VII, XII-XVI).
3. To demonstrate an increase in ability to pursue further study of the environment (Lessons XIII-XVII).

Generalizations

1. Descriptions of any environment are more complete when as many human sensory impressions as possible are utilized (Lessons I-V, VII-X).
2. Accurate descriptions of the environment are provided in terms of a variety of measurements, but the qualitative components gained from sense impressions can add interest and fascination to any environmental description (Lessons XIII-XVII).
3. Whenever data are collected from an environment, care must be taken to ensure that the data collection does not impair the quality

of the environment being studied (Lessons VII, XIII-XVI).

Strategy

The following series of lessons is designed to provide a stimulating learning climate focusing on the process of learning rather than on content. Included are several outdoor experiences that require the student to function in the realm of problem solving and imagination. Also present are a number of opportunities for the utilization of words that can communicate what the student saw, heard, felt, smelled, or tasted when he was examining his environment. This is especially valuable to the intermediate-level student, who is adding word building blocks to the foundation of his adult vocabulary.

The suggested flow of the lessons is from a macroscopical observation of the student's world toward a more microscopical focus on smaller environmental areas. The structure of the series is not rigid, and any lesson can serve as an initiatory device for a myriad of new learnings. It is hoped that teachers using this environmental instruction plan will provide time for students to follow up with further research any tangential discoveries that they may make in the out-of-doors.

Lesson outlines

Lesson I. In the classroom—Preliminary discussion: sense

Use an initiatory device such as the actual popping of corn or observation of a small flame to discuss the following:

1. What are "senses"?
2. How do we learn about objects?

Invite students to attempt either a written or oral description of an imagined experience with fire.

Lesson II. In an outdoor environment—Sensory impression hunt

The class may take an outdoor hike in which individual students, working in previously established groups, are to gather sights, sounds, smells, tastes, and tactile impressions and record these on work sheets according to the appropriate sense. Emphasize caution in touching and tasting. A work sheet such as the example on the opposite page will facilitate this activity.

Lesson III. In the classroom—Stories about "Our Hunt"

Discuss sensory experiences gathered in the previous lesson. Have each student group attempt to put together a group story based on their sensory impression hunt, using words that convey some of their sensory experiences. The activity could be entitled "Using Sensory Words." Urge the students to use words that tell what they saw, heard, felt, touched, or tasted (words like *fluffy* fur, *sticky* leaves, *pillow* clouds).

Lesson IV. In the classroom—Sensory impression games

Prepare a cardboard box so that it has an access area such that the contents are not readily visible. Following are some suggestions for use of this device to develop sensory awareness:

1. Touch box: Place one or several items of various shapes and textures in the box. Have students reach in, touch the item, and describe orally what they felt within the container.
2. Odor box: Saturate small pieces of sponge with various scents. Have students describe the scent to their classmates.

Motivation can be provided within the group-process format by having each group try to guess

SUGGESTED WORK SHEET

USING MY SENSES

Instructions: Find seven ways to use each of your senses to learn more about the outdoors. List them under appropriate columns. (*Examples:* hear birds' songs; see animal tracks.)

	SEE	HEAR	TOUCH	SMELL	TASTE
1					
2					
3					
4					
5					
6					
7					

what their representative is describing and awarding points on a 5- to 0-point scale, subtracting a point for each question or guess required before positive identification. The team having the most points after an equal number of "describers" from each team have participated would be the winner.

Similar games can be played with a tape recorder and earphones for sounds and various tasting materials for taste. Even "sight" games are possible if the describer is required to write down an imagined object or scene and then describe the situation as if he were actually seeing it.

Lesson V. In a variety of learning environments—Framing part of the world

Have students bend wire coat hangers into a diamond shape. These should then be used as viewfinders, with the hangers at arm's length so as to narrow the students' area of visual focus. Have them (1) look straight ahead, (2) look up, and (3) look down, and then make a rough draft sketch of what they see.

Have 8½- by 11-inch paper turned to form an approximate diamond shape for this sketching. See Suggested Work Sheet on p. 46. The "looking down" activity will provide experience that will prepare students for the later quadrat or microquadrat studies.

Lesson VI. In the classroom—Preliminary discussion: object characteristics

Present students with a collection of material objects. Hold an informal discussion focused on the following:

1. What is an object?
2. What are some characteristics of objects?
3. What words do we use to name or describe these characteristics?

SUGGESTED WORK SHEET

FRAMING MY WORLD

Instructions: Bend a wire coat hanger into a diamond shape ( ). While holding the hanger at arm's length, *look* (1) straight in front of you, (2) at the sky overhead, and (3) at the ground beneath you. In the spaces below or on three separate sheets of paper, sketch what you see framed by your coat hanger.

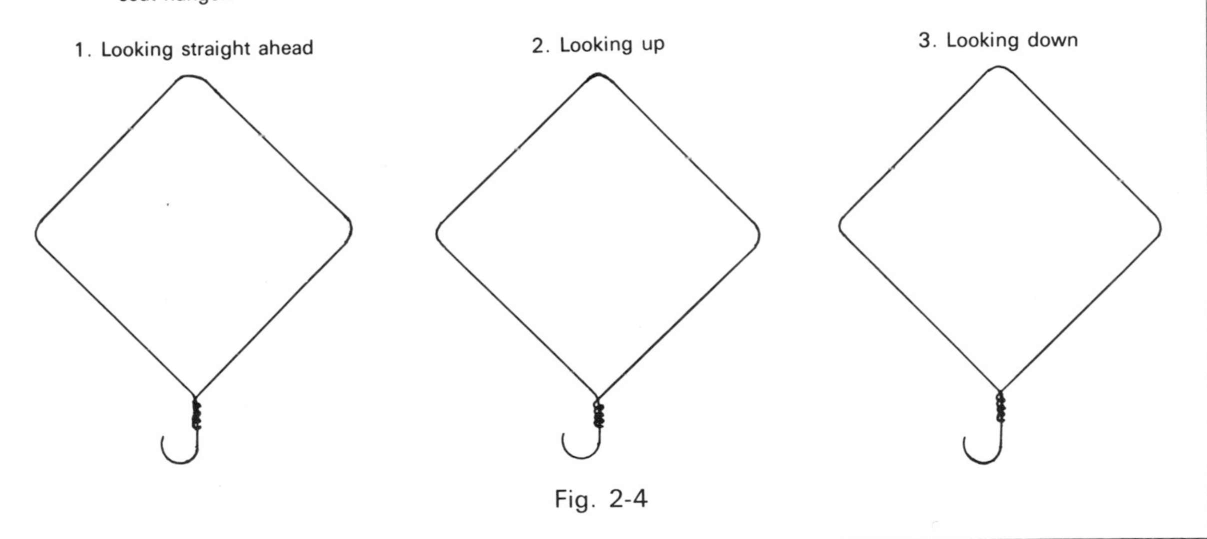

Fig. 2-4

Have students point out various classroom objects that exhibit characteristics similar to those in the collection.

Lesson VII. In a variety of learning environments —Object characteristic hunt

Objects (pebbles, sticks, leaves, dog, cat, fish, and others) have certain traits distinctively theirs, such as color, shape, and feel. These are called the characteristics of the object.

Divide students into teams of two. Have each team choose one characteristic (for example, all red, all round, all with points). While on an outdoor hike, they are to collect objects possessing this characteristic. Caution them not to tell anyone what characteristic their collection possesses. Have each group display its collection and encourage other students to try guessing what the common characteristic is for each collection. Discuss what objects cannot or should not be brought back (for physical or conservational reasons). Have students sketch such objects.

Lesson VIII. In a variety of learning environments —Choosing an object for study

Instruct children to choose an outdoor object that interests them and about which they would like to learn. Tell them to draw a rough picture

SUGGESTED WORK SHEET

MY "PET" OBJECT

Instructions: Find an outdoor object that interests you and that you would like to learn more about. Use each of your senses to test this object. List information obtained in this way. Find out as much as you can about your "pet" object.

SEE

Draw a picture of your object.

HEAR

TOUCH

SMELL

TASTE: Only under supervision of your teacher.

of the object first and then to test the object with each of their senses. Each child should list such information. See Suggested Work Sheet above.

Lesson IX. In the classroom—Describing your object

This may be the time to stimulate students to read by suggesting that, instead of writing their own descriptions of an object, they find an already written description in the several books, articles, and other material that you will conveniently provide within the classroom.

To set the tenor of this lesson, the teacher should read some descriptions of outdoor objects or scenes. Include both poetry and prose. Pictorial materials (color slides, paintings, sketches, etc.) might also be provided around the room to stimulate mental "pictures."

Ask students to describe their pet object in their own poetry or prose, paying particular attention to the use of sensory words. Be sure they understand the meaning of *sensory* words—words conveying sense data or impression of what was heard, felt, touched, tasted, or seen for example, sticky liquid, bumpy rock, prickly leaf.

Lesson X. In student-selected learning environments—My object's diary

Suggest to students that they play a "Let's Pretend" game. Tell them to pretend that they are their pet outdoor object. Have them write a short diary telling what happens to them during a one-hour time period. This may require further outdoor observation, or they may be able to generalize and predict what might happen on the basis of what they have already learned about the outdoors.

Specifically instruct students not to include name of object in the main portion of their diary but rather to place the name of the object at the end of their papers.

When students have completed their diaries, have them tape-record them, leaving out the name of the object. The teacher can then play back the tapes and ask for guesses as to what the object is.

Lesson XI. In the classroom—How much can we learn about birds?

Introduce students to the idea of an identification "key" by discussing some of the common birds seen on their previous field experiences. Develop some type of bird clue chart, such as suggested later, which will require students to discriminate among various colors, silhouettes, sizes, habitats, songs, and flight patterns.

Have students list known characteristics of common birds under appropriate headings on their charts. Leave blank any unknown items for further field or library research. Show how someone would use a field study guide or key to find the name of a bird when most of the characteristics are observed and recorded mentally or in a notebook. In actual field use the accompanying Clue Chart for Birds will serve as a recording system for observed data that can be compared with appropriate bird guides or keys to obtain the common or scientific names for birds seen by the students.

Lesson XII. In the classroom and in an environment suitable for viewing birds—Extending the senses with observational tools

In an indoor session introduce children to the advantages gained by the use of such sense-expanding devices as the hand lens, binoculars, and compound microscopes, and the nomenclature.

If several pairs of binoculars are available from school equipment or from those which the students can bring to class, take students on an outdoor observational trip, using the bird clue chart format in Lesson XI to give them experience in the use of binoculars. They may also collect interesting items for later microscopy work. Provide sufficient bird keys for identification work.

Lesson XIII. In the classroom—Microscopy

Have students (working in teams of four or less) examine and sketch items and organisms gathered on the previous lesson's outdoor hike. Depending on the items collected, it may be possible to introduce the concept of food web, or ecosystem, or other pertinent ecological generalizations. If such be the case, encourage them to draw a partial food web, including some of the organisms that they have collected. Extend the use of keys to the microscopic organisms and plant specimens gathered.

Lesson XIV. In a variety of learning environments—Studying a microquadrat

Have students mark off a small outdoor area for intensive study by using the coat hanger from Lesson V to establish boundaries. Encourage identification by use of appropriate field guides:

1. Soil or rock types
2. Plant specimens
3. Animal organisms
4. Climatic factors

SUGGESTED WORK SHEET

CLUE CHART FOR BIRDS

SIZE	COLOR	SILHOUETTE	HABITAT	FLIGHT PATTERN	SONG

BIRD CHARACTERISTICS

Size Write down estimated size of bird. Compare with known objects to make estimate.

Color Note color and area of body where color is located.

Silhouette Draw outline profile of bird, paying special attention to shape of body, head, bill, tail, wing, and leg.

Habitat Where did you see the bird? Have you seen the same type of bird in other locations? List three locations.

Flight pattern Note the movements made by the bird's wings. Describe these movements. What was the speed of flight? Did any noise accompany takeoff?

Song Use words or syllables to approximate the sounds of the bird's song.

Compare these clues with those given in various bird field guides (for example, Peterson) to identify the bird.

SUGGESTED WORK SHEET

LOG AND STUMP STUDY

Instructions: Find a dead log or tree stump to study and answer the following questions about your study object, basing your decisions on personal observation and library research.

1. Are there leaves on or near your log?
2. Is bark still present?
3. What kind of tree was your object?
4. Is the wood hard or soft?
5. Is any moisture in the wood?
6. Why did the tree die?
7. Can you guess how long ago it died?
8. Is your study log or stump serving as an animal den?
9. Are any plants growing on the dead tree?
10. Are any birds living in the tree?
11. Are any insects living in or on the decaying wood?
12. List animals observed:
13. List the plants found:
    (On a separate piece of paper sketch unidentified plants.)
14. List types of birds seen:
15. List insects seen:
16. On a separate piece of paper make a pictorial sketch of the food web of your decaying log or stump. Show feeding relationships among the various inhabitants (animals, birds, insects, and others) by means of arrows from ''eater'' to its food. (Example: Birds eat insects. Draw a line from the bird to insect eaten.)

Lesson XV. In a woodland environment—Study of a decaying log or tree stump

The task of each student group is to discover and study a log or tree stump in an advanced stage of decay. They should identify the organisms present and describe conditions of the log or tree stump and surrounding area in a "scientific" report for oral presentation to the class. See accompanying Suggested Work Sheet.

Lesson XVI. In selected environments—Quadrat study

Have students establish quadrats of 9 yards or meters on a side, 81 square yards or meters in area, for continued study over relatively long periods of time, noting changes that occur within the area and analyzing the causes of such change. Detailed instructions for this long-term study may be given to the students as suggested in the Appendix to this EEIP.

Lesson XVII. In student-selected learning environments—Individual research projects

Encourage students to choose some outdoor situation (for example, birds in a nest, the behavior of squirrels, a ten-foot-square area of the playground, a group of plants) for further study and reporting. Continue the study for whatever period of time seems appropriate: then require a carefully detailed written report on the events that occurred to the chosen object or within the selected area. Request illustrations if deemed necessary for clarification.

The following is a suggested form for the report:

1. Problem—the reason for conducting the study—most readily stated as a question.
2. Hypothesis—the student's predicted answer to the question.
3. Procedure—how the student carried out his investigation.
4. Conclusions—the results of the observations and investigations in summary form. The student should confirm, modify, or reject the statement of the hypothesis.

NOTE: By now many of your students have become involved in personally interesting studies. Encourage this, especially by rewarding them with your approval for unique collections of knowledgeable reports.

Materials

1. A candle or popcorn and associated equipment
2. Cardboard box
3. Tape recorder and earphones
4. Miscellaneous scents such as ammonia, syrup, animal musk (for example, deer lure), and Carbona (carbon tetrachloride) and pieces of sponge
5. Miscellaneous materials for tasting such as sugar, salt, lemon, Tabasco, and cola
6. Wire coat hangers for each student
7. Microscopes } as required for groups
8. Binoculars } as required for groups
9. Hand lenses } as required for groups
10. Work sheets where necessary (see Appendix for samples)
11. Materials needed for quadrat study (see Appendix)
12. Poetry and prose selections about the outdoors (for example, Robert Frost, Henry David Thoreau, Carl Sandburg)

IDENTIFICATION AIDS

Doubleday Nature Guides, Doubleday & Co., Inc., New York, N. Y.

Golden Nature Guides Series, Golden Press, Publishers, New York, N. Y.

Peterson Film Guide Series, Houghton Mifflin Co., Boston, Mass.

Putnam Nature Field Books, G. P. Putnam's Sons, New York, N. Y.

FILMS

Life in a Pond, 11 minutes, color, Syracuse University Film Library.

Principles of the Microscope, 30 minutes, color or black and white, Encyclopaedia Brittanica Films, Inc.

The World at Your Feet (observing soil), 22 minutes, color, Audubon Society.

World in a Marsh, 21 minutes 7 seconds, color, National Film Board of Canada.

FILMSTRIPS

Introduction to the Microscope, 42 frames, color, Society of Visual Education.

Story of Lenses, 42 frames, color, McGraw-Hill Text-Films.

Evaluation

The chart on p. 52 indicates in which lessons you may observe or collect evidence for each of the objectives and generalizations.

Although the objectives for this instructional plan provide some specific behaviors that can be interpreted as evidence of success in meeting objectives, another somewhat unusual method may be used in conjunction with such behavioral evaluation.

If at all possible, try to arrange the occurrence of some highly charged situation in the classroom prior to Lesson I. Afterward ask the students to describe what occurred. File their descriptions for

OBJECTIVES	APPROPRIATE LESSONS	OBJECTIVES	APPROPRIATE LESSONS
Cognitive		Affective	
1	I, II, III, IV, VIII	1	VII, VIII, IX, X
2	II, III, VII, VIII, IX	2	VII, XIII, XIV, XV, XVI
3	V, XIV, XV, XVI	3	XII, XIII, XIV, XV, XVI, XVII
4	VI, VII, VIII, IX, X, XII, XIII		
5	I, II, III, IV, VI, VII, VIII, XI, XII, XIII, XV, XVI	Generalizations	
6	XI, XIII, XV, XVI, XVII	1	I, II, III, IV, V, VII, VIII, IX, X
7	XI, XII, XIII, XIV, XV, XVI	2	XIII, XIV, XV, XVI, XVII
8	XII, XIII, XVI	3	VII, XIII, XIV, XV, XVI

future reference. A situation that I once used was to have a fellow teacher from another district visit the classroom. He was made up as an old sailor, dressed in outlandish garb, smoking a clay pipe, and carrying a stuffed great horned owl under his arm. This visit occurred just when I had been called to the principal's office for "important business." Such a situation may be difficult to duplicate. But if two such experiences (differing totally in character) are provided, one prior to and one following the lesson series, and a written description is called for in each case, the teacher will have examples of the students' descriptive skills. It is hoped that the teacher will be able to recognize some improvements after the use of this Environmental Education Instruction Plan.

BIBLIOGRAPHY

Bale, Robert O.: Conservation for camp and classroom, Minneapolis, Minn., 1962, Burgess Publishing Co.

Hug, John W., and Wilson, P. J.: Curriculum enrichment outdoors, Evanston, Ill., 1965, Harper & Row, Publishers.

Navarra, John Gabriel, Zafforoni, Joseph, and Garone, John Edward: Life and the molecule, Evanston, Ill., 1966, Harper & Row, Publishers.

Science curriculum improvement study, material objects—a teacher's guide, Chicago, Ill., 1966, Rand McNally & Co.

APPENDIX QUADRAT STUDY GUIDE

Purpose

To study a natural area in an organized way; to learn what kinds of plants and animals can live together in a small community environment.

To have students work together in a team. Assignment should be designated for each member.

Materials needed for one team

The following materials are needed for a team of no more than twelve children:

- 1 ball of string
- 12 wooden stakes (4 stakes 2 feet long; 8 stakes 1 foot long)
- 4 yard sticks
- 1 Silva compass
- 4 hand lenses
- Soil-testing kit(s)
- Soil Borer(s) or auger(s)
- 2 soil thermometers
- Weather station, to include barometer and hygrometer
- 1 small field library including keys for trees, shrubs, mosses, ferns, insects, animals, and others
- 1 small hammer
- 1 pair of binoculars
- 1 herbarium press
- Data sheets including:
  - Grid form
  - Profile diagram
  - Soil profile charts
  - Weather analysis summary sheet

Procedure for laying out the quadrat

A quadrat is a sampling area, usually square—most commonly 1 square meter—used for analyzing vegetation or animal populations. Large quadrats are usually 10 square meters.

Select a natural area:

Field
Woodlot
Edge of the woods
Vacant city lot
Near a stream
Burned-over area
Near a lake shore
School playground not covered by asphalt

Lay out a large square area within the location you have chosen. Use the four large stakes to make the corners. Run the string along the ground from corner to corner. Make sure the corners are square. Use the compass to line up the quadrat like Fig. 2-5. Each side should be 9 yards or meters long.

After you have set up the outside lines, you should lay out what is called a grid in your quadrat. With the short stakes and the rest of the string, divide the quadrat into nine equal squares. If time and equipment are available, set up the weather station.

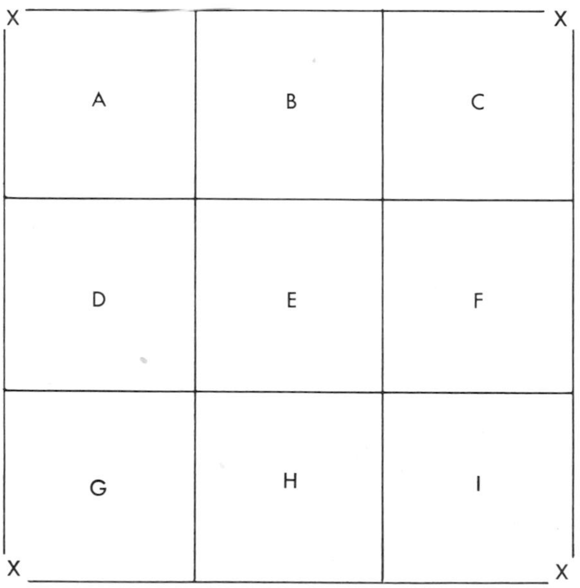

X			X
	A	B	C
	D	E	F
	G	H	I
X			X

Fig. 2-5

Activities in and around the quadrat

Mapping the quadrat. With the help of the teacher and a field library, try to identify many of the plants in your quadrat. You should try especially hard to identify all trees and shrubs. As you do this, locate each plant by number on a paper grid form—a map of your quadrat. Once a plant is given a number, that number should be used for that kind of plant only every time that plant is found and recorded.

Study of a microquadrat. Within your 81 square yard quadrat lay out an area that measures 6 inches long by 6 inches wide by 1 inch deep.

What is the surface area?

What is the volume?

Use a hand lens to find out the following information:

How many different kinds of living organisms are present?
How many can you name?
How many are plants?
How many are animals?
What kinds of decaying things are present?
How big do you think the soil particles are?

Establishing a profile diagram. A profile diagram is a record of the kinds of trees and shrubs

Text continued on p. 56.

Questions:

What is the area of the quadrat?

What is the area of an individual section?

Multiply the second answer by 9.

Your answer should be the same as the answer to the first question.

SUGGESTED WORK SHEET

QUADRAT PROFILE DIAGRAM AND RECORD

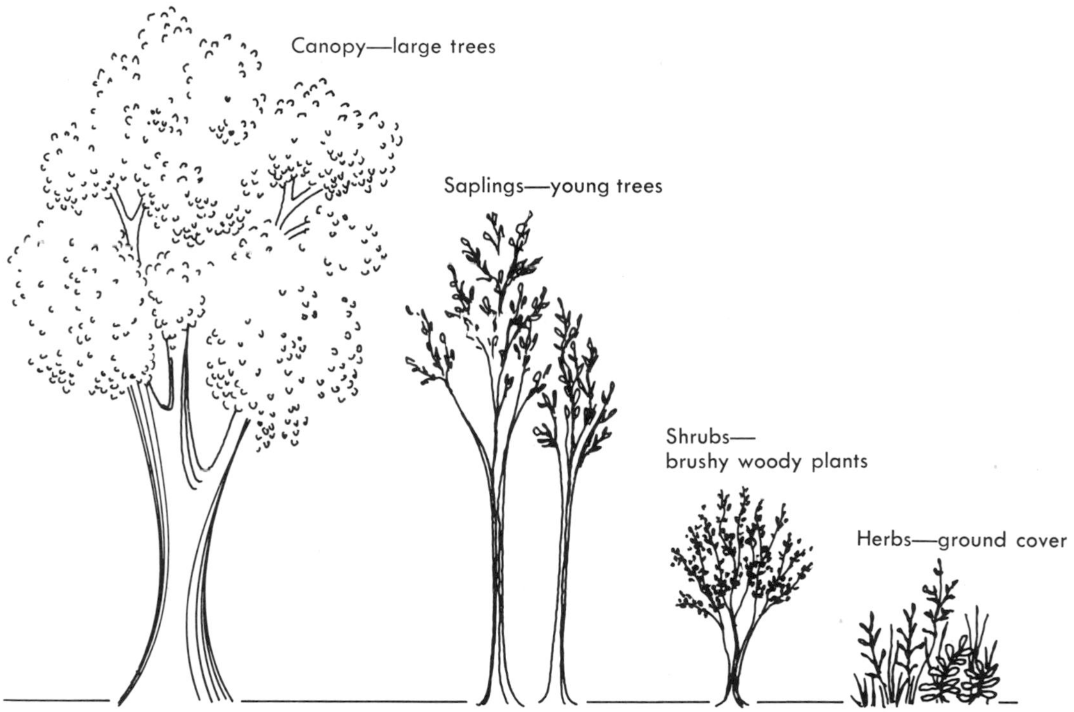

Canopy—large trees

Saplings—young trees

Shrubs—
brushy woody plants

Herbs—ground cover

SPECIES	NUMBER (1)	OBSERVATIONS

VEGETATION AT STATION
Canopy (large trees)

1. ______
2. ______
3. ______
4. ______
5. ______

QUADRAT PROFILE DIAGRAM AND RECORD—cont'd

SPECIES	NUMBER (1)	OBSERVATIONS

Saplings (young trees)

1. ____________________
2. ____________________
3. ____________________
4. ____________________
5. ____________________

Shrubs (bushy woody plants)

1. ____________________
2. ____________________
3. ____________________
4. ____________________
5. ____________________

Herbs (ground cover)

1. ____________________
2. ____________________
3. ____________________
4. ____________________
5. ____________________
6. ____________________
7. ____________________
8. ____________________
9. ____________________
10. ____________________

ANIMALS AT STATION	HOW DID YOU IDENTIFY THE ANIMAL?

1. ____________________
2. ____________________

Continued.

QUADRAT PROFILE DIAGRAM AND RECORD—cont'd

ANIMALS AT STATION	HOW DID YOU IDENTIFY THE ANIMAL?
3. ______	
4. ______	
5. ______	
6. ______	
7. ______	
8. ______	
9. ______	

A. The air temperature was ______ °F. ______ ° C.

B. The temperature of the soil at 2 inches depth was ______ °F. ______ ° C.

C. The relative humidity was ______ %.

D. The barometric pressure was ______ inches.

E. The light intensity was ______ footcandles.

F. The greatest number of plants was found in the ______ layer.

G. The greatest number of species was found in the ______ layer.

in each layer of your quadrat. The profile should be done after the grid is completed.

Trees, shrubs, and other plants should be located in three layers:

Canopy—roof or top of the forest

Understory—shrubs and saplings below the canopy to 10 feet above the ground

Herbs (nonwoody plants) and other ground cover

On the accompanying Quadrat Profile Diagram and Record Sheet record each plant (only once by name) in the left column; then every time you record one of the same name, just place a stroke (/) in the number column.

When all trees and shrubs are recorded, total the strokes for each plant in each layer.

After you total each column, complete statements A through G following the diagram and records.

Weather analysis. If you have placed a weather station near your quadrat area, some team member should be assigned to take weather-instrument readings three times each day. Use the Weather Analysis Summary Sheet to record your finding.

SUGGESTED WORK SHEET

WEATHER ANALYSIS SUMMARY SHEET

By ____________ Date ____________ Time ____________ Location ____________

Wet bulb ____________ Dry bulb ____________

Relative humidity ____________ Present temperature ____________

High since last reading ____________ Low since last reading ____________

Barometric reading ____________ Barometric tendency ____________

Wind velocity ____________ Wind direction ____________

Sky cover ____________ Cloud type ____________

Precipitation: Type ____________ Amount ____________

Clothing recommendation—next part of day (circle one): Fair Foul

Miscellaneous observations: ____________

____

____

Prediction: ____________

For your quadrat study it is well to know the relative humidity and temperature of the air above your quadrat, as well as the daily amount of precipitation.

Soil analysis. The depth, soil acidity or pH, and temperature of the different layers of the soil in your quadrat can be easily determined. With the soil borer or auger, go down about 1 foot and remove a sample of soil. You will readily see color and texture changes from top to bottom of the sample. These colors help you to locate the different layers. Measure the depth of each layer and record it on the Soil Profile Chart. By following the directions at the bottom left-hand side of the chart, draw a sketch of the sample. Do this once in each section of the grid. When finished, you should have nine samples recorded. On the reverse side of the chart answer the questions found at the bottom right-hand corner of the chart.

Ask your teacher to show you how to use the soil-testing kit to find the soil acidity or pH of the soil. What can pH tell us about the soil?

With the help of your teacher learn how to use the soil thermometer. Is the temperature underground the same as the temperature of the air just above the ground? How do you explain the answer to the last question?

EEIP 3—FORESTS, A DICHOTOMY BETWEEN DOLLARS AND DREAMS

Interdisciplinary—Emphasizing science and social studies

Upper elementary grades or junior high school

Overview

Before an individual can "care" for something, he must have some knowledge about the object(s)

SUGGESTED WORK SHEET

SOIL PROFILE CHART

Section A	Section B	Section C	Section D	Section E	Section F	Section G	Section H	Section I

Sketch the profile:

1. Record the depth in inches.
2. Record the temperature of each layer.
3. Record the pH of each layer.
4. On the reverse side write a description of the things you find in the top or humus layers.

Answer why or why not to the following questions on the reverse side:

1. Are all layers the same thickness in each sample?
2. Are all temperatures the same at each layer of each sample?
3. Are all top-layer temperatures the same?
4. Are all bottom-layer temperatures the same?

of his concern. If an instructor wishes to promote an attitude favorable toward conserving forest resources, he must first have his students develop their own values about woodlands. This series of lessons is so directed.

Objectives

Cognitive

1. To identify at least five important commercial trees (Lessons II, X).
2. To measure distance by pacing or other means (Lessons V, VI, VIII).
3. To construct a Biltmore stick (Lessons IV, VII).
4. To determine the number of *board feet* and *sawlogs* in a tree (Lesson VIII).
5. To estimate the commercial value of a tree (Lesson VIII).
6. To demonstrate evidence of familiarity with the ideas in generalizations 1, 2, and 3 in their discussions and by other means of expression (Lessons III, VIII, XI-XIII).

Affective

1. To express feelings or beliefs about the value of forests by one or more means of communication and expression (Lessons I, XI, XIII, XIV).
2. To demonstrate an interest in forest conservation by making independent studies of or visits to such agencies as the State Bureau of Forests, State Fish and Game Commission, State Forest Fire Service, U. S. Park Service, U. S. Department of Agriculture and Bureau of Forests, U. S. Corps of Army Engineers, and U. S. Bureau of Reclamation (Lessons XII, XV).
3. To demonstrate responsibility by working productively within a group (Lessons II-IV, VII, VIII, XII, XIII, XV).
4. To utilize group processes for problem solving (Lessons III, VI, VIII, XV).

Generalizations

1. Forests are not only valuable sources of unique raw materials such as lumber, wood pulp for paper, resins, and chemicals but also are indispensable in preventing soil from sliding down steep slopes, increasing the intake of rainwater into the soil, maintaining populations of plants and animals, and providing aesthetic enjoyment and recreation (Lessons I, VIII, XI, XIII).
2. Forests may be cut down and replanted to produce a "crop" of new lumber over a period of fifteen to fifty years or longer, depending on the "lumber" species desired (Lesson VIII).
3. When forests are cut for lumber, the method used should provide for reseeding by leaving scattered seed trees standing, removing and utilizing "slash" (branches and twigs), and disturbing the soil as little as possible (Lesson VIII).
4. National parks, national forests, and national monuments or similar areas serving states, counties, or municipalities should be used by the public in such a way that the area will remain in optimum condition for all to enjoy. This means that the public should not only refrain from littering, lumbering, or defacing trees, land, and buildings but also should help to encourage other citizens to demonstrate respect for woodland environments. Forest lands in private ownership must also be maintained in similar condition, not only by the owners but also by the general public (Lessons XIII-XV).
5. Examples of each unique ecological type of forest land must be protected and preserved in a "Forever Wild" state, which means that no visitors would be permitted to enter or use those areas (Lessons VII, XIII-XV).
6. All forests have a worth not only in the dollar value of marketable trees but also in

an immeasurable and irreplaceable value for many forms of life including man (Lessons I, III, XI-XIII).

Strategy

The following unit of lessons has been organized in such a manner that students, through their everyday classroom subjects, can develop a set of values concerning forest lands. This unit, or series, is "open-ended" and should not be considered completed with the last lesson. Also there is no strict sequential order to the specific lessons found in this study unit. The time span is at the instructor's discretion.

Lesson outlines

Lesson I. In the classroom—Trees: What do they mean to people?

Use Joyce Kilmer's poem "Trees" or other poems or lines about trees.

Develop a discussion to determine the following:

1. What are students' feelings and concepts about trees?
2. How important is a simple tree in their lives?
3. How important are forests (groups of trees)?

Assign students to choose a poem, novel, story and/or essay that describes or emphasizes some desirable or important characteristics of trees.

Lesson II. In a park or woodland environment—Observing trees

Organize class into small groups for the purpose of this lesson and future lessons. Each group should designate a recorder, who will present the report.

Have students observe five different types of trees by taking note of their size, shape, color, odor (if any), bark, texture, and leaves.

The size, shape, color, odor (if any), and texture of the leaf of each tree should also be observed and noted. Have students make a rough drawing of each leaf design.

When students return to the classroom, have them use simple pictorial references to identify the kinds of trees they observed.

Lesson III. In the classroom—Trees and dollars

The class groups should be assigned to research projects. Some examples of group research projects on various types of trees and their economic value and use are the following:

1. To compute the value of an acre of softwood when lumbered (use bibliography or direct information from lumberyard or lumber company such as Weyerhaeuser or Georgia-Pacific).
2. To determine the value of an acre of hardwood when lumbered or harvested periodically for (a) Christmas trees (should this practice be continued?) and (b) firewood.
3. To estimate the value of an acre of land used for recreation, such as a picnic area (obtain direct information from the owners of a commercial picnic area, the tax assessor's office in a community where such a picnic area is located, the superintendent of a state park, or the state, county, or local planning board or similar agency).

Lesson IV. In the classroom—Biltmore sticks

The amount of usable lumber in a forest area or woodlot may be estimated by a simple hand-held device called a Biltmore stick. The name refers to the Biltmore forest tract near Asheville, North Carolina, where the method originated.

School children may obtain paper strips (Biltmore stick covers), which may be pasted on a yardstick or similar piece of wood to make individual Biltmore sticks. Directions for use are printed on the strip, along with other interesting information.

Have class compose letter requesting Biltmore stick covers and information about the history of the U. S. Forest Service and then choose a representative to write the letter on behalf of the entire class to the following address:

The U. S. Forest Service
U. S. Department of Agriculture
Washington, D. C. 20202

Lesson V. In the school yard, gymnasium, or hallway—Learning to pace

NOTE: A pace is two steps and everyone's pace is different.

Develop the concept of *pace* as a means of measuring distance. Have students determine their own pace by pacing off a marked 100-foot distance. Have students walk the length several times.

By using ratios have each student determine the length of his own pace in feet and the number of his own paces required to cover a distance of 50, 66, and 100 feet.

Lesson VI. In the classroom—Using pacing techniques to measure short distances

Conduct a drill and review exercise in which students compute the number of their own individual paces required to measure various distances. Students may move outdoors to test their computations.

Lesson VII. In the classroom—"Something Called Heritage"

If possible, have a student committee consult a local lumberyard or sawmill to find out the cost per board foot of lumber for the species of trees available for measurement in their area.

Have each student or group of students construct a Biltmore stick by following directions found on the Biltmore stick cover.

Discuss "Something Called Heritage" on the Biltmore stick cover with the class.

Lesson VIII. In a park or woodland environment—Forests with usable lumber are worth many dollars

Review methods of determining distance by pace. Have each pupil compute the number of paces he must walk to measure off 66 feet.

Demonstrate the technique of using a Biltmore stick. (Follow directions listed on the Biltmore stick cover.)

Using references listed in the bibliography and on Biltmore sticks, have students locate and identify several types of trees and compute the commercial value of each.

Have small groups of students pace off a wooded square, 50 feet by 50 feet, and compute the commercial value of the timber therein.

Discuss generalizations 2 and 3.

Lesson IX. In the classroom—Teaching others to estimate forests and lumber value

Orally review the previous outdoor activity. Have students develop lessons to teach other students not in their class how to use the Biltmore stick. If another class seems receptive, let the students in your class teach the others how to use a Biltmore stick and explain its purpose.

Groups of students may move outdoors to demonstrate the Biltmore stick to members of another class.

Lesson X. In feasible learning environments—How to know some forest trees

Have available for each student a "Master Tree Finder" by May Watts (or another tree key of equal simplicity). If a woodlot, park, or other forested area is available near the school, take the class out of doors to *key out* trees. Determine how a dichotomous tree key is used.

Have students key out several tree species from samples brought into the classroom. Be sure to encourage students to use texts to corroborate the indications of the tree keys. Students should be encouraged to determine which trees are best suited for lumbering, wood pulp, reforesting, and other purposes.

Lesson XI. In the classroom—Forests are more than lumber trees: discussion of noncommercial uses of forests

1. Have pupils list noncommercial uses of a forest such as recreation, camping, providing open space, water recharge and storage, research, hunting, fishing, boating, hiking, photography, observing plants and animals, sketching, "back to nature," inspiration, or "just to dream."
2. Have each student prepare arguments to advance his or her ideas of the values inherent in one or more of the listed uses.

Lesson XII. In the classroom, in a public park, or both—What forest resources are available to the public?

Following are some of the means by which the teacher and class could make a survey of their own municipal, county, and state parks:

1. Writing a single letter to appropriate county and state agencies to request information for the class about all public lands, including fish and game areas.
   a. What size and number of forested areas are available to the public?
   b. What facilities are available to persons in these areas?
2. Studying county and state road maps.
3. Making a similar request to the Superintendent of Public Documents, Washington, D. C. 20202, for information about facilities and activities available in national parks and forests.

The class should note that hunting is usually prohibited in lands designated as parks but not in those designated as forests. Other lands identified by various names are maintained primarily for fishing and hunting.

With the information that has been obtained, the class should list all the uses that individuals may make of their forested public lands.

The class should take special notice of parks and forests that have information centers or educational centers. The desirability of visiting the information center or superintendent's office before travelling through or otherwise using unfamiliar public lands should be discussed. Visitors can usually learn much about what to see and much about the special features of a park by spending some time at an information or education center.

Lesson XIII. In the classroom—Forests are for . . .

Encourage students to write, debate, or prepare an oral presentation on such topics as the following:

Forests are for hunting		A landscape without trees?
Forests are for people		How much is a tree worth?
Forests are for animals		Do cities need trees?
Forests are for insects	**or**	Do forests need care?
Forests are for naturalists		Do people need trees?
Forests are for lumber		Do animals need trees?
Forests are for paper		

Discuss generalization 6.

Have the class compose a booklet "Forests are for . . ." to be distributed to other classes in the school.

Lesson XIV. In the classroom—What problems do we face in maintaining optimum quality in forested lands?

In preparation for this lesson or series of discussions, the class teacher should encourage the students to collect newspaper or magazine articles or to make notes on television or radio reports concerning any use or abuse of forests. Plans for new parks and forests should also be noted.

The teacher should direct the discussion to the ideas in generalization 4.

Some of the more serious problems that threaten the quality of forest environments and that should be considered are the following:

1. Pressures to permit lumbering in national forests and parks
2. The general problem of multiple use of forested lands for recreation, hunting, camping, and the commercial interests of lumbering, mining, or recreational services by concessionaires
3. Overcrowding and overuse
4. The loss of tax revenues for municipalities if new wooded lands are acquired to reserve more open space for public use (should such municipalities receive a guarantee of in-land tax payments by government?)
5. Personal safety
6. Threats to forested lands by new strip-mining ventures to meet rising fuel demands
7. The threat to forested lands posed by new highways and new housing areas
8. The need for more public forests to meet the needs of an increasing population
9. Rising maintenance costs from littering and vandalism

These problems should point up the dilemma—the dichotomy between dollars and dreams—the dreams of having forests for the purposes that the students have discovered. The students may wish to discuss how serious the dichotomy is and whether or not the situation is improving or deteriorating.

Lesson XV. In the classroom or appropriate learning environments—What can students do to protect woodland environments?

The students may wish to visit one or more public forested areas as a class, in small groups, or in family groups. Their purpose would be to assess the successes and failures of the area in terms of its designated functions. A rating scale such as the following might be employed:

	EXCELLENT	ADEQUATE	POOR
1. Is the park equipped with motor roads?			
2. Is the park equipped with hiking trails?			
3. Is the park equipped with bicycle paths?			
4. Is the park equipped with swimming, boating, sports, picnic tables?			
5. Is the park equipped with information center?			
6. Is the park equipped with educational center?			
7. Is the park equipped to handle an increasing number of visitors?			
8. How is the general cleanliness? (To be asked if the superintendent or other responsible park official is available.)			
9. Does the park presently serve enough visitors to justify its maintenance costs?			
10. What are the chief problems now encountered by the park? What recommendations would you make for the improvement of this park?			

The members of the class may wish to undertake some of these measures to help forest environmental quality:

1. Visit the municipal governing body or the park commission to find out what the projected plans for park development and/or expansion are and what students may do to assist. The students may also submit their suggestions and assessments developed in their survey.
2. Students should visit county and state park officials to exchange similar information.
3. Students may volunteer to clean up an area that has been littered or vandalized.
4. Students should write to their congressional representatives to encourage support of an objection to national forest legislation or usage.

Materials

1. Clipboards
2. Paper and pencils
3. 100-foot tape measure
4. Furring strips, ¼ inch × 1½ inches × 36 inches
5. Biltmore stick covers from the U. S. Department of Agriculture
6. Tree keys (''Master Tree Finder'' by May Watts)

FILMS

Extra Forest Dollars, 19 minutes, color, U. S. Forest Service.
Living Forest, 41 minutes, color, Syracuse University.
Challenge of Forestry, 22 minutes, color, New York State Conservation Department.
The Changing Forest, 11 minutes, color, BFA Educational Media.

FILMSTRIPS

Resources for Tomorrow—Forests, 64 frames, color, Ward's.
The Story of West Coast Lumber, 75 frames, color, Society for Visual Education.
Using Our Forests Wisely, 53 frames, color, McGraw-Hill.

TRANSPARENCIES

Creative Visuals, Big Spring, Texas—Conservation:
The Importance of Our Forests
Potential Enemies of the Forest
Distribution of U. S. Forest Types
Woodlot Improvement Cutting
Four Types of Harvesting Forest Resources

Evaluation

The lessons in this guide have been designed to provide for a number of student behaviors and activities that will indicate progress toward the stated objectives.

The following chart indicates in which lessons

OBJECTIVES	APPROPRIATE LESSONS	OBJECTIVES	APPROPRIATE LESSONS
Cognitive		Affective	
1	II, X	1	I, XI, XIII, XIV
2	V, VI, VIII	2	XII, XV
3	IV, VII	3	II-IV, VII, VIII, XII, XIII, XV
4	VIII	4	II, III, VIII
5	VIII		
6	III, VIII, XI, XII, XIII	Generalizations	
		1	I, VIII, XI
		2	VIII
		3	VIII
		4	XIII-XV
		5	XIII-XV
		6	I, III, XI-XIII

evidence for each of the objectives and generalizations may be observed or collected.

1. Students should be given opportunity to indicate their impressions of their own progress to the teacher.
2. The teacher should get student suggestions or criticisms of the learning climate developed during these studies.

BIBLIOGRAPHY

Forest Products, Forest Products Statistics. In Yearbook for 1966, U. S. Department of Agriculture.

Hug, J., and Wilson P.: Curriculum enrichment outdoors, Evanston, Ill., 1965, Harper & Row, Publishers.

Trees. In Yearbook for 1949, U. S. Department of Agriculture.

Vivian, V. Eugene, and Vivian, Norma T.: The world out-of-doors, Browns Mills, N. J., 1967, CESC press.

Watts, May T.: Master tree finder, Berkeley, Calif., 1963, Nature study Guild.

EEIP 4—THE URBAN WORLD

Interdisciplinary—Emphasizing social studies and science

Middle grades through junior high school

Overview

Concern for the environment has been long in coming and has only recently begun to make its impact felt on the citizens of America. The problem of deterioration of our natural resources has aroused young and old alike to reevaluate man's use of his environments.

Nowhere is there a greater need for environmental concern than in our nation's cities. The problems of urban blight, traffic congestion, air pollution, and the like have made the environments of many cities undesirable places to live.

The purpose of this series of environmental education components is to provide urban teachers with materials that can be used to create an awareness and concern for urban environmental problems on the part of students.

"The Urban World" is open-ended. New components may be developed to supplement those currently included, such as People of the City, Economics of the City, and Solid Waste Disposal in a City.

Objectives

1. To recognize different types of land use within one's community (Lesson I).
2. To prepare a graph showing the land use of an area near the school (Lesson I).
3. To discuss signs of physical change within a given area (Lesson I).
4. To recognize nonconforming land uses (Lesson I).
5. To recognize different types of streets such as through, dead-end, connecting, and one-way streets, as well as other special streets such as expressways, parkways, and play streets (Lessons II, IV).
6. To discuss ways in which streets are maintained (Lesson VIII).
7. To demonstrate how streets serve people (Lessons II, IV).
8. To monitor traffic flow within a city (Lessons V-VII).
9. To demonstrate a knowledge of how persons contribute to or influence a street system (Lessons IV, VIII).
10. To discuss ways in which various types of streets and buildings serve as watersheds and affect the rest of the environment in a community (Lessons IX-XI).
11. To discuss and give examples of the generalizations sought (Lessons XIII, XIV, XVI).
12. To identify sources of noise within the community (Lessons XII, XV, XVI).
13. To distinguish between necessary and unnecessary noise (Lessons XIII, XV, XVI).
14. To monitor noise levels in different areas of the community (Lessons XV, XVI).

Generalizations

1. Buildings within a city block may be classified according to use (Lesson I).
2. The manner in which buildings are arranged within a block creates an environmental design (Lesson I).
3. Certain land uses within a given area may not conform to the general design of the area (Lesson I).
4. The land uses within a city block affect the people who live in or near the block (Lesson I).
5. All streets serve the main purpose of providing convenient space for people to travel from one place to another (Lessons II, III).
6. Good street planning begins with a general plan to create a beautiful and useful city, but in many cities old trails, streams, riverbanks, or high ground formed the first unplanned pathways or streets (Lesson III).
7. Turnpikes and other toll roads are supported by fees charged to all travelers who use them. This method of obtaining road-building funds removes some of the financial burden from people who live in cities connected by toll roads (Lesson IV).
8. Street usage for traffic is influenced by geographical location, relation to other streets, proximity to public buildings, shopping centers, hotels, or industrial plants, and time of day, week, or year (Lessons V-VII).
9. Most streets are paid for largely by taxes collected from persons who live in the cities and towns that provide the streets (Lessons II, VIII).
10. Climate and traffic gradually cause the street surface to wear out or become uneven as the paving grows older (Lesson VIII).
11. Some water seeps into the ground to become a part of the groundwater. Other water lies on the surface of the earth, trees, or buildings and evaporates. Some water runs off from the higher areas to the lower and finds its way into streams and rivers (Lessons IX-XI).
12. In the city, where there are many buildings and hard-surface areas, the bulk of the rainwater cannot seep into the ground. Instead, it runs off the roofs, sidewalks, paved areas, parking lots, and streets into storm sewers and rivers (Lessons IX-XI).
13. Streets should be constructed so that they permit water to drain readily into the gutters along the street. If streets are flat, water will tend to remain on the surface. A slight rise in the middle of the street will make for good drainage (Lessons X, XI).
14. Water moving along gutters tends to pick up soil, debris, and oil and carry it into storm sewers and into streams and rivers (Lessons IX, X).
15. The loudness of a sound decreases as the square of the distance from the source (Lesson XIII).
16. The loudness, or intensity, of a sound depends on the quantity of energy in the sound waves (Lesson XIII).
17. The pitch of a sound depends on the frequency of the vibrations producing that sound. The intensity of sound is dependent on the amount of energy expended in producing the sound (Lessons XIII, XIV).
18. Regular sources of vibration produce musical sounds; irregular ones produce noise (Lessons XV, XVI).
19. Noise is dangerous or harmful to one's health when it is loud, meaningless, irregular, or unpleasant (Lessons XV, XVI).

Strategy

These environmental education components are intended to initiate a series of active studies focusing on the environment most familiar to a majority of students. The span of time over which these activities are conducted, the intensity of involvement by the children, as well as the continuations that may be developed, will vary with each class and its teacher.

Lesson outlines

Lesson I. Indoors and outdoors—A city block: an environmental design

Obtain a community land-use map or section of such a map that locates the school and surrounding area from a community agency such as the chamber of commerce, planning board, zoning board, or road department.

This lesson can be expanded to include a neighborhood area of several blocks. Children can do individual or group observations as an extra assignment.

Conduct an introductory discussion of the overall layout of the community. Consider the following questions about the community:

1. Where do most of the people live?
2. Is there a shopping district? In what part of the community is this area located?
3. In what part is most of the industry found?
4. Where are the recreational areas located?
5. What types of buildings might be found on a city block?

Distribute work sheets on land use. Review the work sheet before children go out of doors.

Have the class walk around the block or other area to be considered. Collect data to be recorded on a survey sheet such as the one suggested.

Discuss the work sheet and data gathered:

1. What is the most common land use of the area?
2. What other land uses were observed?
3. What buildings or houses looked out of place?
4. Did the "out-of-place" buildings improve or downgrade the block or area studied?

LAND USE SURVEY SHEET

Instructions: Use tally marks to record data.

I. Number of buildings per block used for the following:
- A. Commercial
  - Retail
  - Wholesale
  - Warehouse
  - Service
  - Other
- B. Residential
  - Apartment
  - Row house
  - Single family
- C. Industrial
  - (list types of industry)
- D. Public
  - (list types of public buildings)

II. Number of other features
- E. Open space
  - Playground
  - Vacant lot
  - Parking lot
  - Other
- F. Natural features
  - Trees
  - Gardens
  - Other
- G. Environmental health
  - Trash collection
  - Garbage collection
  - Litter
  - Animals, pets
  - Pests

RATING FORM

Instructions: On this work sheet you are asked to rate the area you have studied. Answer the following questions by circling your choice. Please give reasons for your answers.

A. How would you rate the area:

1. As a place to live?

Good	Fair	Poor

2. As a place to attend school?

Good	Fair	Poor

3. As a place to play?

Good	Fair	Poor

4. As a place to work?

Good	Fair	Poor

B. What would you add to this area to improve it?

C. What would you take out of this area to improve it?

5. What signs of recent changes are there within the block? What signs of future changes?
6. Was the block well planned? Why or why not? How would you change the design of the block?

Have the class rate their block (using a form such as the accompanying sample). Have students prepare graphs showing land use in the block and draw a map of the block showing various land uses.

Lesson II. In the classroom—The streets of the city: kinds of streets

Obtain enough street maps of the city for each student's use. These can serve several purposes during the course of this study.

Conduct an introductory discussion on "what makes up a city" (buildings, people, schools, streets, etc.). Develop the discussion around "streets and their importance to a city."

Consider the following questions:

What purposes do streets serve? (In the planning of a city, what determines the street pattern; for example, traffic, residential areas, businesses, factories, public buildings? What are some of the different kinds of streets in the city; for example, expressways, boulevards, avenues, one-way and dead-end streets?)

Why do we have so many different kinds of streets? (Different streets have different uses. Large volumes of traffic require special streets. Residential areas may have less traffic and thus many one-way and dead-end streets.)

What materials are used to build streets? (Most city streets are paved with brick, concrete, or bituminous materials, made from asphalt mixed with stone and sand.)

Who pays for the building of streets? (Taxes paid by the people of the cities help pay for streets. Some state funds are given to cities for building streets. The federal government may assist in building streets into a city.)

Is the street pattern, or plan, a useful and/or attractive one? How can you decide about the usefulness and attractiveness of streets?

Lesson III. In an outdoor environment—How do the streets in your city vary?

NOTE: If the city is of such a size as to make the following activity difficult, a portion of the city may be used. If student transportation or bussing is not available, plan for students to study a variety of streets within walking distance of home or school.

Conduct a field trip around the city. Provide opportunities for the class to travel on the types of streets discussed indoors. Make frequent stops along the way to discuss the characteristics of each kind of street. Consider the following factors in investigating the streets:

1. Area in which street is located (industrial, commercial, residential)
2. Population density of the street
3. Parking accommodations (meters, lots, and other arrangements)
4. General cleanliness and maintenance

Lesson IV. In the classroom—Evaluating present street usage

Discuss the field trip. Have students prepare an outline showing each kind of street and the characteristics noted. Where possible, students should be encouraged to make photographs or sketches of street types.

Using the map of the city, set up a color key and in crayon note the main streets, expressways, one-way streets, and other routes.

Set up a hypothetical situation in which you eliminate one of the main streets such as in the case of building a shopping mall or plaza. How would the lives of city residents change? What problems would be created? How would traffic patterns change?

Using the map of the city, find a street that follows several directions through the city. Imagine that the street could be rerouted to follow a straight course. What changes would have to take place to achieve this? What would happen to the buildings and properties that stood in the way of the proposed street? How do you think the property owners would feel? Do you think the change would be desirable, considering all these factors?

If there are turnpikes, toll roads, or freeways leading into or through the city find out (1) how the road building was financed, (2) how road maintenance and improvement is financed, (3) whether the road has good traffic flow or frequent traffic tie-ups, and (4) what the accident or fatality rates are.

Lesson V. In the classroom—Traffic of the city

NOTE: To avoid harassing a public official by flooding his desk with identical requests from each student, contact the official's office in advance of this study and outline the kind of information the students will need to conduct their study.

Discuss the main types of vehicles used in your city for transportation. How is the flow of traffic controlled? What methods for monitoring traffic are used in your city?

Have a representative of the class write a letter to the city traffic engineer expressing interest of the class in learning about city traffic. Request that the traffic engineer prepare a data sheet on local traffic for use by the students. How many streets are used for one-way traffic? What are peak traffic times on streets?

Lesson VI. In an outdoor environment—Monitoring traffic on city streets

Select several locations at which to monitor traffic flow. Choose locations with varying amounts of traffic volume. The suggested work sheet would be convenient for recording information.

Gather information on several different days to provide a basis for future monitoring.

TRAFFIC MONITORING WORK SHEET

Date and day of week	Time	Location (name of street or streets at intersection)	Weather conditions	Type of street (one-way, expressway, etc.)	Direction of traffic flow (north, south, east, west)	Traffic count				Other
	to					Cars	Trucks	Buses	Pedestrians	

Distribute additional work sheets to students for independent monitoring of traffic within their neighborhoods. Individual assignments should be made to assure monitoring of desired areas. This activity lends itself well to group work. Children living in the same neighborhood may wish to work together.

Have students return work sheets at the end of a week. Individual students should discuss results with the class.

Lesson VII. In the classroom — Analyzing traffic flow data

Interpret data collected in Lesson VI. What conclusions can be drawn concerning the differences found? What does the information tell about life in your city?

In interpreting the data collected, consider the following questions:

1. What is the average number of vehicles passing a certain point at noon each day?
2. What kinds of streets carry the most traffic?
3. How do weather or climatic conditions affect the amount of traffic on a street?
4. What time of day is the traffic heaviest?

Lesson VIII. Indoor and outdoor—Maintenance of city streets

Discuss the fact that if streets are to serve people, they must be kept in good condition.

What are some factors that cause damage to streets?

1. Salt and other chemicals. (These are used by man to help melt snow from the streets. They also cause damage to the streets, which must then be repaired.)
2. Extremes of heat and cold.
3. Heavy automobile, bus, and truck traffic.

Which of these factors can man control?

Arrange for the class to visit the maintenance yards of the street department. On the way, look for signs of streets that are in need of repair and make a record. Have students devise the method of recording. If possible, visit a site where street maintenance is in progress. Discuss the methods being used to maintain roadways.

Have the students use the information they have collected to write a report on "How Our City Streets Are Maintained."

While at the street department, use the following questions as guides for gathering information.

Snow and ice removal

1. What procedures are used in your city by the street department when heavy snow is forecast?
2. Does snow removal provide extra jobs for some persons in the city?
3. What special kinds of equipment are used for removing snow from city streets?
4. What is a snow emergency route?

5. How much does it cost each year for snow removal in your city?
6. Where does the money come from to pay for snow and ice removal?
7. Which streets are cleaned first?
8. Why would some streets be cleaned before others?
9. If there are labor problems, how are they resolved?

Street repair

1. What kinds of streets need to be repaired most often?
2. What are some of the methods of repairing streets?
3. Is there a special time of year for repairing streets?
4. Where do the materials come from that are used to repair the streets?
5. How does the street department know what streets need repair?
6. What would happen if the city streets were never repaired?
7. If there are labor problems, how are they resolved?

Street cleaning

1. What kind of equipment is used to clean streets?
2. How often are the city streets cleaned?
3. What streets need cleaning most often?
4. What time of day are the streets cleaned?
5. Why would you want to keep streets cleaned?
6. If there are labor problems, how are they resolved?

Lesson IX. In the classroom—Street drainage

Consider the following questions in class discussion:

1. What other functions do streets perform besides serving as traffic and pedestrian lanes (for example, drainage area for rainwater)?
2. What do we usually see at the curbs of streets that help carry water away? Does every street have one or more "catch basins"?
3. Discuss the term "watershed." (A watershed is a regional drainage pattern or an area contributing to the drainage pattern. Thus a building or parking lot can be a mini-watershed.)
4. What happens to rainwater after it falls to earth?
5. When it rains in the city, where does the water go? Into what body of water do the city's storm sewers flow?

Lesson X. In outdoor environments—Streets as stream beds

Activity 1 (during rainstorm if possible)

Have class conduct a study of the school building as the beginning of a watershed. Examine the roof of the building from the ground. How many surfaces does the roof have for shedding water? Walk around the building and locate the rain gutters. Does each surface have a rain gutter? Find the downspouts. Trace the route of water from the various surfaces of the roof to the rain gutters, to the downspouts, to the streets, and down the storm sewers. Repeat this activity at each side of the building. Observe the school yard for signs of low spots where water might collect after a rain.

(Children should be encouraged to conduct similar watershed studies of buildings in their neighborhood. This can be done in groups or individually.)

How does the construction of streets affect the drainage of water from them?

Activity 2

Determine if the street near the school is level from one side to the other. Place a cord across the street; allow each end to rest on the curb; pull string taut. Using a ruler or yardstick, measure the distance from the string to the surface of the street near the middle. Repeat measurement near the curb on either side. If measurements are the same in the middle of the street as near the edges, the street surface is on a single plane. To determine whether the street is level, use a small carpenter's bubble level.

1. How can the shape or level at the street best be described? Can you make a cross-sectional sketch?
2. Does this shape assist the runoff of rainwater from the street?
3. What waste of water resources is represented by "storm water runoff"?
4. How could the waste of water by street runoff be reduced?

Activity 3

What effect does the movement of water along streets have on the litter and soil found in the gutter?

Why should we keep our streets and gutters clean?

Have class monitor streets for litter. Distribute plastic bags for collecting litter along gutters on specific streets. Collect soil in separate bag. Prepare a chart showing the amount of soil and litter collected on various streets.

Lesson XI. In the classroom and at home—Houses as watersheds

Assign each member of the class the task of investigating his home as a watershed, using the technique developed in class. Have students measure their street to demonstrate whether it has good or poor drainage. Students should monitor litter and soil found on their streets.

Have students give individual reports to the class.

Lesson XII. In the classroom—Sound sources

Conduct a general discussion on using the five senses. Emphasize the reduced use of the sense of hearing in today's noise-laden environment. Consider the following:

How is sound produced? (Strike the prongs of a tuning fork with a rubber hammer and listen to the tone. Rub your fingernail across the cloth cover of a book. What substance was vibrating to produce the sound in each of the examples?)

Students should make lists of sounds and sources, using a work sheet such as the accompanying example.

Lesson XIII. In the classroom—The loudness of sound

Using a spring-wound clock, have the children who can hear the ticking of the clock raise their hands. Those students near the back of the room will not be able to hear as clearly as those near the source of the ticking.

Have students give evidence to demonstrate that the closer the source, the louder the sound.

Strike a tuning fork softly. A soft sound is pro-

SOUNDMAKERS

SOURCE OF SOUND	SOURCE OF ENERGY	VIBRATING PART(S)
1. Drum	Muscular contraction	Drumhead
2.		
3.		
4.		

duced. Strike the tuning fork vigorously, and a loud sound results.

Strike a xylophone with very little force. Increase the force, a little at a time. What differences can you notice? The students may record results as suggested in the accompanying work sheet.

Lesson XIV. In the classroom—The pitch of sound

Obtain three rubber bands of the same length but of different widths or thicknesses. Stretch these over an empty cigar box with the lid removed. Pluck each rubber band in turn and listen to the sounds. Which band vibrates faster? Slower? Which has the higher pitch, or tone? Lower pitch, or tone?

Have the class make a list of sources of high-pitched and low-pitched tones as suggested in the accompanying work sheet.

Have the students describe their findings in a general statement or rule of behavior.

Lesson XV. Indoors and outdoors—Sounds, noises, and people

If possible, bring an electric blender (93 db.) and a vacuum cleaner (81 db.) to class. Demonstrate the noise produced by both of these in combination. Discuss the effect of the noise on the students.

Produce a sudden loud sound in class such as bursting a hidden balloon or dropping a pile of silverware. How were the students affected by the sudden noise?

Additional facts about noises and people

1. The autonomic nervous system begins to react at 70 decibels. Increases in the sound level show dilation of the pupils, drying of the mouth and tongue, loss of skin color, excitation of the heart, and contraction of muscles.
2. Sufferers from diseases such as heart trouble, asthma, ulcers, and gastrointestinal spasms may all be adversely affected by sudden or prolonged noise.

THE LOUDNESS OF SOUND

SOURCE OF SOUND	DISTANCE AT WHICH SOUND CAN NO LONGER BE HEARD	DISTANCE AT WHICH SOUND CAN NO LONGER BE HEARD WHEN THE ENERGY INPUT TO THE SOUND SOURCE IS DOUBLED

HIGH- AND LOW-PITCHED SOUNDS

SOURCE OF SOUND	HIGH PITCH	LOW PITCH
1.		
2.		

3. Noise is a definite stress factor and can cause emotional damage to the individual.
4. Noise can affect the brain during sleeping hours. Noise-interrupted sleep can have damaging effects on aged or sick people.

Take the class on a field trip to various parts of the city. Use a tape recorder to record the sounds found in each area.

Consider the following questions:

1. In what areas did you find the most noise?
2. Were people living in this area?
3. What single source produced the greatest amount of noise?
4. What other sources of noise did you discover?
5. Were any of the noises necessary? Why?
6. What steps could be taken to reduce the noise level in your city?

Students may also wish to estimate loudness of sounds heard at various locations by using the accompanying chart and suggested work sheet.

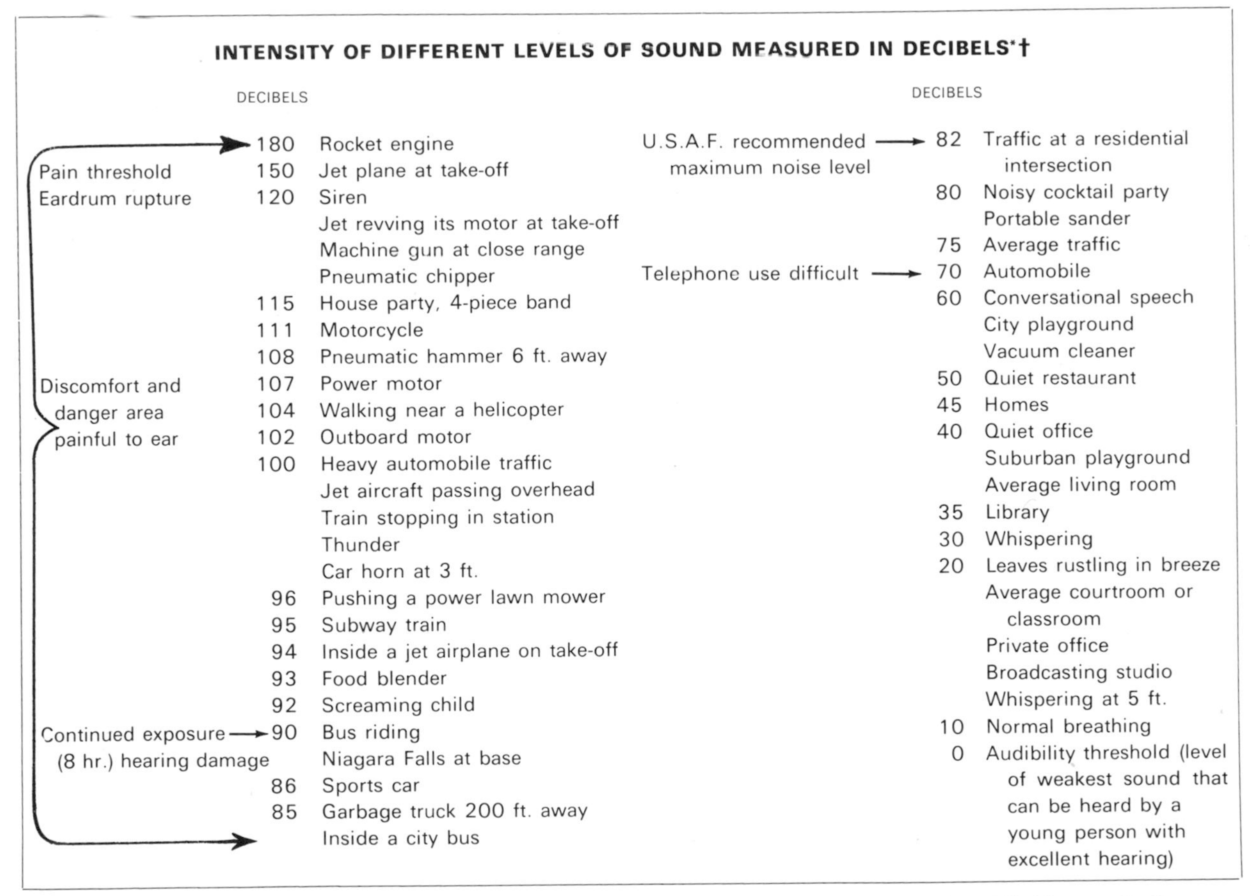

INTENSITY OF DIFFERENT LEVELS OF SOUND MEASURED IN DECIBELS*†

	DECIBELS	
	180	Rocket engine
Pain threshold	150	Jet plane at take-off
Eardrum rupture	120	Siren
		Jet revving its motor at take-off
		Machine gun at close range
		Pneumatic chipper
	115	House party, 4-piece band
	111	Motorcycle
	108	Pneumatic hammer 6 ft. away
Discomfort and danger area painful to ear	107	Power motor
	104	Walking near a helicopter
	102	Outboard motor
	100	Heavy automobile traffic
		Jet aircraft passing overhead
		Train stopping in station
		Thunder
		Car horn at 3 ft.
	96	Pushing a power lawn mower
	95	Subway train
	94	Inside a jet airplane on take-off
	93	Food blender
	92	Screaming child
Continued exposure (8 hr.) hearing damage →	90	Bus riding
		Niagara Falls at base
	86	Sports car
	85	Garbage truck 200 ft. away
		Inside a city bus

	DECIBELS	
U.S.A.F. recommended maximum noise level →	82	Traffic at a residential intersection
	80	Noisy cocktail party
		Portable sander
	75	Average traffic
Telephone use difficult →	70	Automobile
	60	Conversational speech
		City playground
		Vacuum cleaner
	50	Quiet restaurant
	45	Homes
	40	Quiet office
		Suburban playground
		Average living room
	35	Library
	30	Whispering
	20	Leaves rustling in breeze
		Average courtroom or classroom
		Private office
		Broadcasting studio
		Whispering at 5 ft.
	10	Normal breathing
	0	Audibility threshold (level of weakest sound that can be heard by a young person with excellent hearing)

*Reprinted from the book "Our Poisoned Planet," copyright 1970 U. S. News & World Report, Inc., Washington, D. C.

†The decibel is a logarithmic, not a linear unit; 10 decibels equal 10 times the power of 1 decibel; 20 decibels equal 10 times the power of 10 decibels or 100 times the power of 1 decibel.

SUGGESTED WORK SHEET

SOURCE	LOCATION	ESTIMATED LOUDNESS IN DECIBELS (USE CHART)	NECESSARY (YES OR NO)	HOW DID THIS NOISE MAKE YOU FEEL?

Lesson XVI. In the classroom—Evaluating noise

NOTE: The field trip may be repeated at several different times of the day. This will enable the student to determine how noise levels vary at different times and places.

Discuss the information and data collected on the Noise Trip.

Play back recordings. Gather student reaction to noise levels in the city.

What steps have been taken by your city to control noise?

Evaluate the statement "Because of increased intensity of noise levels, persons of younger ages are less able to hear sounds on the lower intensity (loudness) levels."

If possible, have an architect or builder visit the class to discuss how the noise problem affects construction and vice versa.

OBJECTIVES	APPROPRIATE LESSONS	OBJECTIVES	APPROPRIATE LESSONS
		Generalizations	
1	I	1	I
2	I	2	I
3	I	3	I
4	I	4	I
5	II, IV	5	II, III
6	VIII	6	III
7	II, IV	7	IV
8	V-VII	8	V-VII
9	IV, VIII	9	VIII
10	IX-XI	10	VIII
11	XIII, XIV, XVI	11	IX-XI
12	XIII-XV	12	IX-XI
13	XIII-XV	13	X, XI
14	XV, XVI	14	IX-XI
		15	XIII
		16	XIII
		17	XIII, XIV
		18	XV, XVI
		19	XV, XVI

FILMS
Noise Boom, 26 minutes, color, NBC Films.

FILMSTRIPS
Centron Educational Films, Lawrence, Kan.
Noise: The Latest Pollution, 98 frames, color.
Awareness in the City, 65 frames, color.

TRANSPARENCIES
The Lansford Publishing Co., San Jose, Calif.
Noises That Disturb People
Levels of Sound

Evaluation

Evaluation should be carried out in terms of the behavioral objectives stated. The chart on p. 75 indicates in which lessons evidence for each of the objectives and generalizations may be observed or collected.

EEIP 5—ADVENTURES IN THE HYDROSPHERE

Interdisciplinary—Emphasizing science and mathematics
Secondary grades

Overview

To study the dynamics of any body of water, whether stream, pond, bay, ocean, river, or lake, it is most desirable to initiate the effort as a carefully planned scientific adventure, an adventure in learning.

In this Environmental Education Instruction Plan the method of carrying out such a study will be described, as well as side trips into other areas of water analysis.

Water areas have been extensively studied for their biological contents in many high schools. This EEIP, however, concentrates on the physical components of the body of water and leaves the biotic studies for an additional effort.

This plan might be used in conjunction with a ninth or tenth grade unit intended to examine the hydrosphere and the EEIP made a part of that unit rather than a separate learning device.

Objectives

Cognitive

1. To determine temperature, specific gravity, color, and other physical variables of water both at the surface and at various depths (Lessons III-V).
2. To chart generalized current patterns in the water system under study and determine the velocity of the current (Lessons II, VII, VIII).
3. To describe possible causes of the environmental effects observed (Lessons VIII, IX).
4. To obtain and study samples of bottom material from various bodies of water (Lesson VIII).
5. To solve basic problems relating to physical study of streams and ponds, utilizing mathematical language and methods (Lessons IV, V, VII).
6. To list five basic physical characteristics of water (Lessons III-V).
7. To demonstrate knowledge of the generalizations in class discussions and class or individual activities (Lessons III-X).

Affective

1. To demonstrate increased concern for accuracy in obtaining scientific data (Lessons I, II, IV, V, VII, VIII).
2. To evidence a concern for environmental quality by participating in efforts to improve deteriorated environments and to protect unimpaired ones (Lessons IX, X).
3. To use care in handling equipment and taking readings (Lessons III-V, VII, VIII).
4. To demonstrate responsibility by working productively within a group (Lessons I-III, V-VIII).
5. To utilize group processes for problem solving (Lessons I-III, V-VIII).

Generalizations

1. The temperature of water in ponds and streams is influenced by air temperature, sunlight, depth, and temperature of water flowing into the body of water being studied (Lesson IV).
2. The specific gravity of water is increased by salts dissolved from the soil and upper layers of the earth's crust, by decreases in temperature (except at the range from 4° to 0° C.), and by dissolved or suspended pollutants (Lesson V).
3. The pressure developed in a liquid depends on its depth and its density (specific gravity) (Lesson III).
4. The rate of stream flow is generally most rapid in the center of the stream, since the shorelines and bottom present resistance to the flow (Lesson VII).
5. Water pollution may be detected by the appearance of color and odor developed in samples that have been standing for twenty-four hours, by low dissolved oxygen values, by high specific gravities, and by high temperatures not attributable to climatic or topographical influences (Lessons VIII, IX).
6. Water quality information collected by student investigation should be reported to citizen groups and appropriate governmental agencies (Lesson X).

Strategy

Systematize, quantify, interpret—these are the keys to the treasure of our physical study of a water system. Use them carefully and you unlock the mysteries. Use them carelessly and you may jam the lock of learning.

Carefully, by first defining the system under study, by locating precisely several landmarks from which to map data-gathering points, by displaying data gathered on overlays on the map, and finally by drawing conclusions about this data, we may arrive at a much clearer understanding of what is actually taking place in "our pond," or the body of water we are studying.

One additional note: Mathematics makes molehills out of mountains. This EEIP offers an opportunity for developing practical mathematics skills in a working situation. The teacher is urged to take full advantage of this opportunity.

Lesson outlines

Lesson I. In the classroom—Methods and equipment

All research trips by oceanographers are called "cruises." Each cruise is composed of a number of data-gathering "stations." Our cruise through the aquatic environment will also involve a number of stations.

Divide thc class into research teams of approximately six students. Appoint or elect a captain and a recorder for each team. Issue a specific notebook and a supply of work sheets to each group. The recorder will be responsible for keeping accurate records of all data obtained by the team. The team captain will organize all data gathering. If possible, records should be kept in metric system units, but English system units may be utilized if desirable.

Teachers should use imagination and creativity to provide variations on any lesson. Student teams should label all samples immediately and record all locations accurately.

Each team should prepare its own equipment, having first consulted the equipment illustrated in Figs. 2-6 to 2-11. Each team is then responsible for the care and maintenance of that equipment. Teachers should issue other needed supplies.

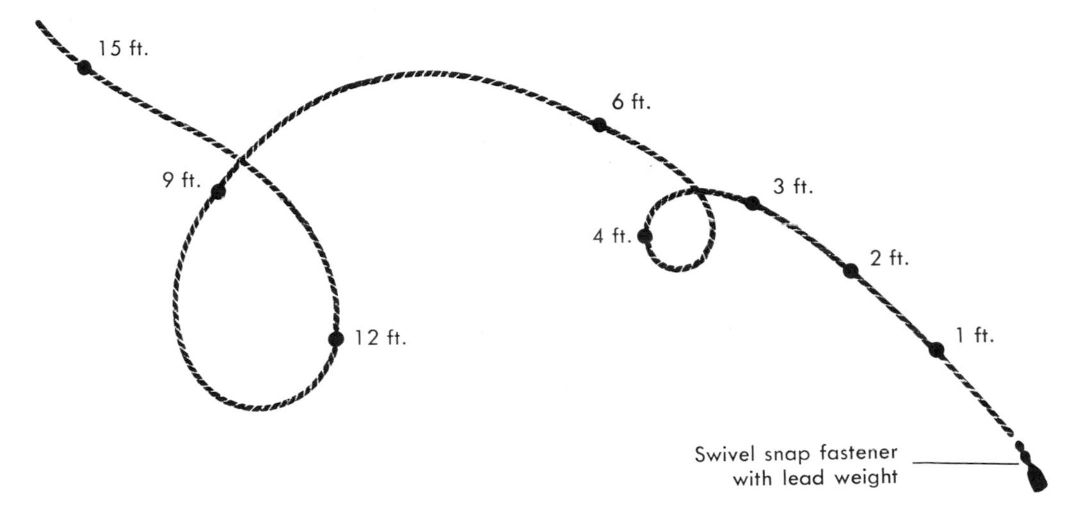

Fig. 2-6. Sounding line.

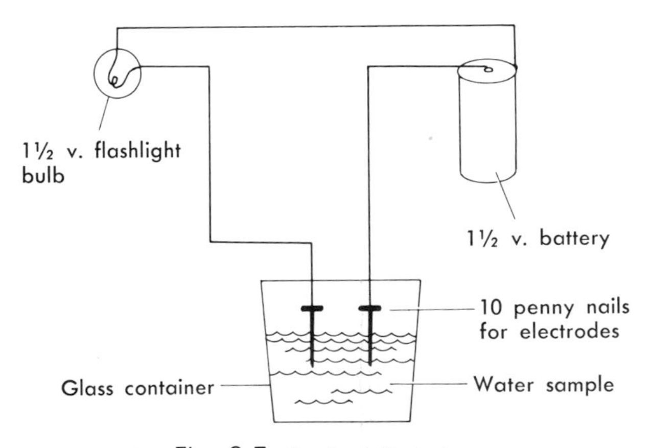

Fig. 2-7. Conductivity tester.

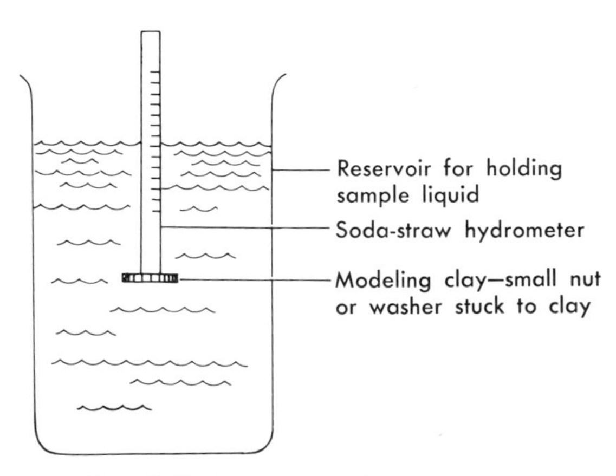

Fig. 2-8. Soda-straw hydrometer.

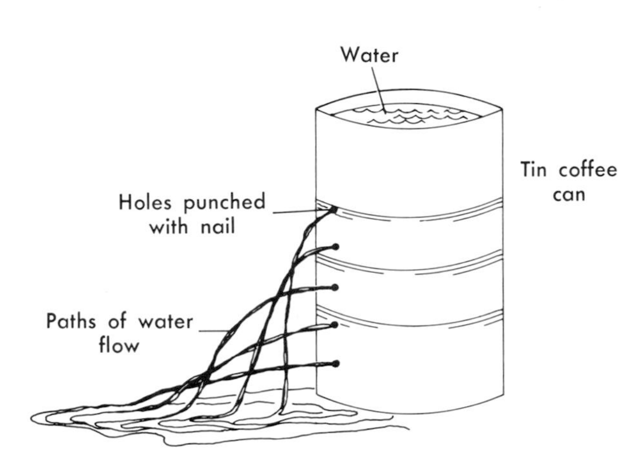

Fig. 2-9. Pressure demonstration device.

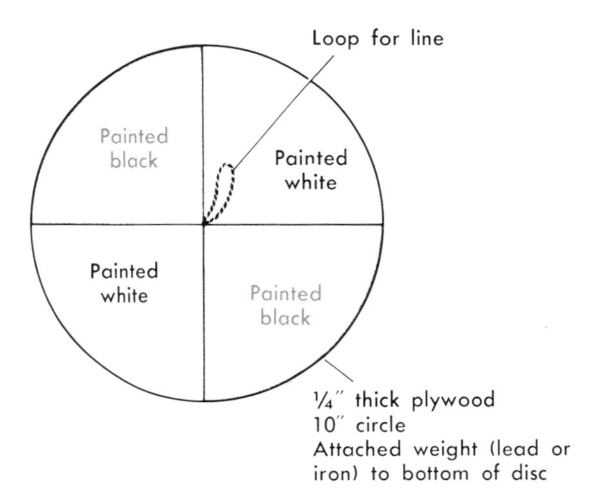

Fig. 2-10. Secchi disc.

Equipment instructions

Sounding line (Fig. 2-6). Use a string with snap swivel at one end for attaching lead or thermometer. Lower device into the water to desired depth. Read the depth by counting the knots on the string. To record temperature, lower the thermometer to the given depth, leave there for 3 minutes, then quickly raise the line and read temperature.

Conductivity tester (Fig. 2-7). Construct as shown in the diagram. Experiment to obtain proper meter range. Use as suggested in Lesson IX.

Soda-straw hydrometer (Fig. 2-8). Cut a plastic soda straw to a length of 5 inches. Plug one end with modeling clay. Attach a nut, washer, or other small weight to this end so that the straw floats partially submerged in a test tube of distilled water. Weight the straw so that it floats at a level between 1 and 2 inches from the upper end. Mark the water-level line on the straw. This is specific gravity 1.000. In brackish or salt water the soda-straw hydrometer will then float higher in the water sample. Other readings can be plotted against a commercial hydrometer, using various salt water solutions.

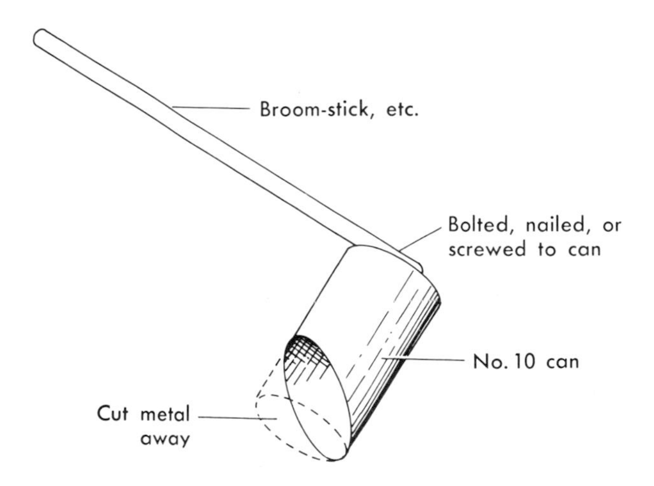

Fig. 2-11. Bottom sampler.

Pressure demonstration device (Fig. 2-9). This device is merely a coffee can with a series of nail holes punched in one side and covered with masking tape. By removing the tape from the holes, one by one from the top down, the effect of pressure, produced by water weight, can be seen dramatically.

Secchi disc (Fig. 2-10). To measure relative translucency of water, lower this 10-inch plywood circle into the water until black and white quadrants merge. Record this depth as an absolute number (no units). This is your "K" factor, or depth of visible light penetration as seen from the surface.

Bottom sampler (Fig. 2-11). Cut a No. 10 can into a scoop shape. Attach to a suitable handle. Use caution when carrying, to avoid being cut by a sharp metal edge.

Lesson II. In the classroom and at a water area—Mapping a body of water

Have each study group draw a sketch map of the water system being studied. Identify all input and output points and major landmarks.

Use compasses to determine direction. Draw maps roughly to scale. Consult a topographical map of your area for outline. (See Fig. 2-12 for a map of a hypothetical pond.)

When individual groups have completed their maps, transfer data gathered to a larger (approximately 24 inches × 35 inches) sheet of paper, using the most accurate data obtained.

Each study group should plot three data stations, using this large scale map and several compasses (for example, 4 groups = 12 stations). The groups should use the following procedure to locate stations as precisely as possible in the absence of specific landmarks:

1. Choose a potential station. While standing at that station take a compass bearing on an easily located landmark. If this bearing is 180° or less, add 180° to it. If the reading is between 181° and 360°, subtract 180° from it. The resultant will be *back azimuth* from the landmark to your station. It provides the compass direction *from* the landmark *to* your station.
2. Without changing location, repeat this procedure, using another landmark.
3. Now using your large map of the water system and a protractor, draw in the azimuth

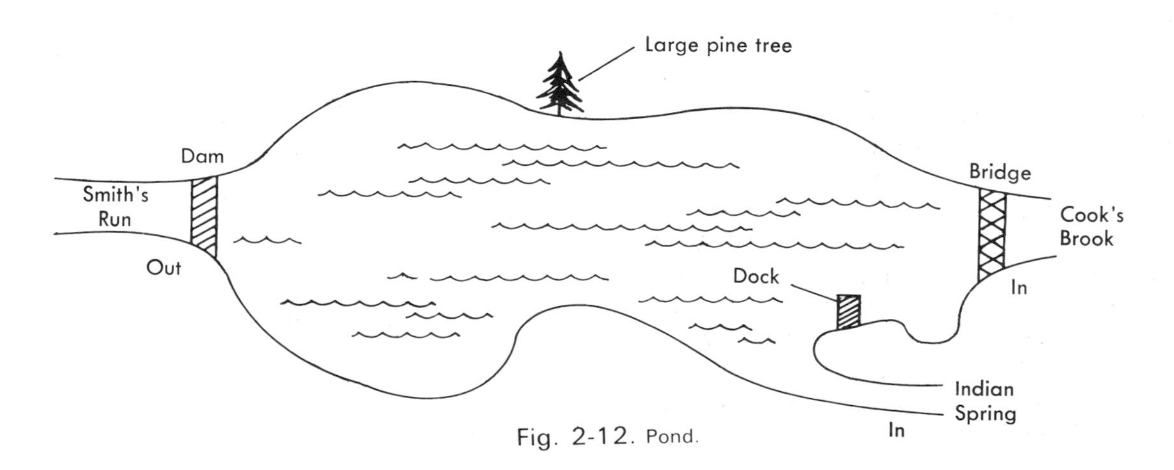

Fig. 2-12. Pond.

lines from each landmark. The point at which the two lines cross is your station location. Label this point Station 1. Repeat for each additional station. This method (which is used to determine the location of forest fires) is called triangulation and will provide fairly accurate results if done carefully.

Return to the classroom and prepare a copy of the large map for each group and one for data display.

This lesson requires quite a bit of time and may be spread over several class periods, but it will serve to emphasize the fact that data is useful only when its origin can be accurately fixed.

Lesson III. In the classroom—Water: the unique fluid

This should be an indoor discussion session during which the following topics are explored. (Each characteristic of water should be demonstrated in at least one respect. See bibliography.)

1. Conductivity
   a. Will water conduct electricity?
   b. Will water conduct heat?
   c. Does salt water conduct electricity better than fresh water?
2. Temperature and density
   a. What are the freezing and boiling points for fresh water?
   b. What is density? Specific gravity?
   c. How is density or specific gravity affected when water gets colder? Freezes? Gets warmer?
   d. Why is the unique behavior of freezing water important to life?
   e. How does temperature change generate water currents vertically? Horizontally?
   f. What is a "thermocline"?
3. Pressure
   a. Does water have weight? How is the weight of water related to its density?
   b. What is "pressure"? How is pressure related to depth? How may water pressure at different depths be computed? Develop some typical examples. (The pressure demonstration device may be used here.)
4. Color and transparency
   a. Does water have color?
   b. Where does this color come from?
   c. Why is the transparency of water important to life?
   d. How can we determine relative transparency?
5. Miscellaneous
   a. What is the speed of sound in water?
   b. What is "surface tension"?

Sources of answers to these and other questions raised are given in the bibliography. Encyclopedias and other reference works will be helpful. Encourage the students to locate the answers themselves when possible.

TEMPERATURE DATA SHEET

Station ____________	Date ____________
Air temperature ____________	Time ____________
Water temperature:	
Surface ____________	6 feet ____________
1 foot ____________	9 feet ____________
2 feet ____________	12 feet ____________
3 feet ____________	Bottom ____________

Lesson IV. At an aquatic environment—Temperature patterns

Our first attempts at qualifying certain aspects of the water system under study involve the determination of temperature profiles for each of the stations under consideration.

Each group should determine the following:

1. Air temperature
2. Surface temperature
3. Temperature at 1-foot depth
4. Temperature at 3-foot depth
5. Temperature at 6-foot depth
6. Temperature at 9-foot depth
7. Temperature at 12-foot depth
8. Bottom temperature

For use in this activity, have each group develop a data recording form such as the sample on p. 81. Record results in a notebook. Repeat these tests for each group's three data-collecting stations.

Where is it coldest? Warmest? How fast does the temperature change? Is the air or the water colder? Make a sketch or graph of the thermocline—the changes in temperature related to depth.

Lesson V. Indoors/outdoors—Specific gravity measurement

NOTE: This is an ideal short lesson that may be included with temperature determination or treated as a separate investigation.

At each of the stations being monitored, group members should obtain surface water samples in test tubes. Label each sample with the station number (see sample data sheet). Record the surface temperature and determine the specific gravity of each sample, preferably with a clinical hydrometer used for urine testing. (The urine-testing hydrometer, urinometer, is preferable because it uses a small water sample and provides accurate readings for the specific gravity range from 1.000 (distilled water) to 1.060 (above sea water limits). The homemade soda-straw hydrometers described in Lesson I may be used here and calibrated against the clinical hydrometers.

Return samples to the classroom, let samples reach room temperature, and again determine the specific gravity. Are there any differences? Are there any differences not attributable to temperature variation? How do you account for any other differences in specific gravity?

Record the results in notebooks for further use.

Lesson VI. In the classroom—The water cycle

NOTE: Consult any earth science text for background information for this discussion.

Although we have heretofore treated the body of water being studied as an isolated system, in actual fact it is a small part of a much larger hydrological system.

SPECIFIC GRAVITY DATA SHEET

Station No. ______________ Date ______________ Time ______________

Surface temperature ______________

Specific gravity in field ______________

Specific gravity in laboratory ______________

Trace the watershed system, of which your study area is a part, from its origin to its "zero level" at a larger river or an ocean. Indicate how water is cycled back to the upper reaches of the watershed. How does the water move?

With one or more of the audiovisual aids listed in the bibliography as a motivation device, a discussion of the water cycle should be undertaken, during which the position of the body of water under study should be determined in its relationship to the larger watershed.

Lesson VII. At a stream—Measurements of current

The students have discovered how water moves on land surfaces. Now let them determine how *fast* it is moving.

There are two major ways of measuring current velocity:

1. Lagrangian method. This method determines the distance covered by a fluid particle as a function of time:

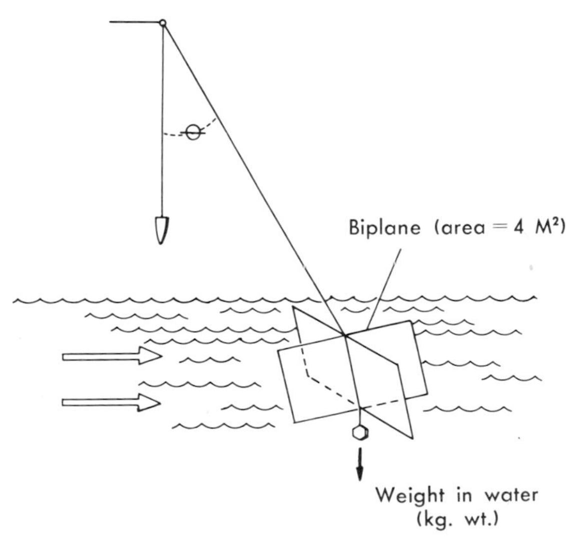

Fig. 2-13. Eulerian method of measuring current velocity.

$$s = \frac{d}{t}$$

It gives average current velocity over distance studied. The method is easy to use and is the basis for this lesson.

2. Eulerian method. This method provides a measure of the current velocity at a stated point in the fluid. It is rather complex and is offered as an option for advanced students. (See Fig. 2-13.) Weigh entire system in water by hanging the system on a scale.

Record weight (W) in kilograms ________.

Biplane area (A) in square meters is ________.

θ is ________°.

Tan θ is ________.

Velocity $(V) = 2\,\frac{W \tan\theta}{A}$, ________; V = ________.

The Lagrangian method can be readily adapted for student use, as in the following suggested instructions:

1. Go to the upstream portion of your study site.
2. Prepare two plastic bleach bottles (one empty, one containing enough water to make it float with only a small volume above water). Label the empty one A, the other B.
3. Place both bottles in the center of a water flow. How long does it take each drifting bottle to go 100 feet? A____ B ____In which direction do they float? Are there differences in either direction or time? How can you account for these differences?
4. Calculate the speed of the current in feet per second.
5. How long did it take bottle B to travel 100 feet? ____. Divide this number into 100 feet ____. Speed equals distance divided by time. Stream is flowing at the rate of

_____ feet per second. Why didn't we use bottle A?

6. Multiply stream velocity in feet per second _____ by 3,600 (60 × 60) to obtain feet per hour. Divide this figure by 5,280 to obtain stream velocity in miles per hour _____. Multiply result by 1.15 to obtain velocity in knots (nautical miles per hour) _____.

   Current velocity in feet per second

   _____ _____ _____

   Current velocity in knots

   _____ _____

7. Repeat above procedure on each side of center of stream.

   Left side: Time _____ sec. Distance = 100 ft.

   Speed = 100 divided by _____ sec. = _____ ft./sec.

   Right side: Time _____ sec. Distance = 100 ft.

   Speed = d(100 ft.) divided by t(_____ sec.) = _____ ft./sec.

$$s = \frac{d}{t}$$

8. List the three current velocities obtained:

   _____ ft./sec. on left side

   _____ ft./sec. in center

   _____ ft./sec. on right side

   _____ Add and divide by 3 to obtain average velocity of stream.

   _____ divided by 3 = _____ ft./sec. = average speed of stream.

9. Measure the width of the stream at five separate locations within your 100-foot velocity markers. Record your answers.

   Average width of stream within study area is _____ ft.

   _____ ft. Station 1

   _____ ft. Station 2

   _____ ft. Station 3

   _____ ft. Station 4

   _____ ft. Station 5

   _____ Add and divide the sum by 5 = _____

10. At Stations 1 and 5 make the following measurements: wade across stream in a straight line (or walk across on a log or other bridge) and measure the depth of the water in three places on that straight line.

	Station 1		*Station 5*
a.	_____ ft.	a.	_____ ft.
b.	_____ ft.	b.	_____ ft.
c.	_____ ft.	c.	_____ ft.

Add the results at Station 1 and divide by 3 to obtain average depth _____ .

Add the results at Station 5 and divide by 3 to obtain average depth _____.

Depth at Station 1 _____ ft. + depth at Station 5 _____ ft. ÷ 2 = average depth of stream _____ ft.

Average depth of stream within study area is _____ ft.

Average width was previously measured as _____ ft.

Average current velocity was calculated to be _____ ft./sec.

To compute cubic feet of water per second flowing within the study area, multiply depth _____ ft. × width _____ ft. × velocity _____ ft./sec. = rate of stream flow _____ cubic ft./sec.

One cubic foot of water contains approximately 7.5 gallons of water. A rate of flow of 1 cubic foot per second is equal to 448.8 gal./min.

To determine rate of flow in gallons per second, multiply rate in cubic feet per second by 7.5 = _____ gal./sec.

To convert to gallons per minute, multiply above result (_____ gal./sec.) by 60 (number of seconds in a minute).

Result = _____ gal./min.

Multiply rate of flow in gallons per minute times number of minutes in a day to determine gallonage of water per day in stream.

_____ gal./min. _____ minutes in a day =

_____ gal./day in stream

According to the U. S. Department of Agriculture, each person uses about 150 gallons of water per day. Divide gallonage per day by this figure to find out how many people this stream could provide water for.

_____ gal./day ÷ gallons per person per day = _____

Lesson VIII. Outdoor/indoor—Sedimentation

Each research team should be given a depth-sounding line, a bottom sampler, and a supply of plastic bags. Their task is to plot a cross section of the water system, locating channels (both primary and secondary), floodplains, and any other underwater features.

If a boat is available, it may be used. If this is not feasible, as much data as possible should be obtained from shoreline or bridge samplings.

Plot a transect line by taking a compass bearing across the water system between two easily located points. Take samples of bottom sediment every 10 feet or so along this line, recording the distance from landmarks and recording the depth at each sampling. Place sediment samples in plastic bags.

On returning to the classroom prepare a graph of the cross-sectional area of the water system, using data obtained. Label sampling locations. If this graph is plotted on a large piece of oak tag, it is possible to attach small plastic containers of sediment to the graph with arrows indicating the appropriate station. This will be a vivid portrayal of the bottom profile. Several students may wish to make a model of the area under study by using modeling clay or papier-mâché.

Lesson IX. In a variety of environments—Pollutants

By this time your students may have noticed that the water contains some things that reduce its quality. These may be termed pollutants. There are two basic types of pollutants: natural and man-made.

Natural	*Man-made*
Acidity from decaying vegetation and decomposed animal matter	Trash and garbage
Dissolved minerals	Sewage
Silt	Chemicals (detergents, dyes, and others)
	Odors (for example, hydrogen sulfide)
	Nonclimatic thermal changes

Two good indicators of pollution are relative pH readings and electrical conductivity readings. To indicate relative levels of electrical conductivity, it will be necessary to replace the flashlight bulb in the test device with a milliammeter. Try 0 to 1 or 0 to 10 ma. range to begin. The range of the meter will be dependent on conductivity level of water. Vary range of meter until an appropriate range is discovered. Accuracy will be influenced by such factors as corrosion of the electrodes and distance between electrodes and therefore only relative readings are obtainable. (See Lesson I for construction.)

At each station obtain a Secchi disc reading. Obtain three water samples from each station under consideration. Label each sample with the station number. Return samples to the laboratory.

To test for pH, place a strip of wide-range hydrion paper in one of the test tubes containing sample water. Allow the paper to remain for 1 minute, remove and compare the color of the paper with the indicator chart supplied to obtain pH value when testing acidity. A pH value of 7 is neutral, below 7 is acidic, above 7 is alkaline.

To test further, such chemical indicators as bromothymol blue, bromcresol green, phenol red,

SELECTED CHARACTERISTICS OF WATER BODIES
TRANSLUCENCY K FACTOR

		pH values according to			
	Conductivity	Hydrion paper	Bromothymol blue	Bromcresol green	Chlorphenol red
Distilled water					
Field sample 1					
2					

and chlorphenol red may be used as a double check. Add three drops of indicator to each sample being tested. Note color change (see accompanying chart).

By comparing the pH reading in an obviously unpolluted water sample (for example, distilled water) with field sample readings, a relative indicator chart can be constructed.

You have now used two of the three samples from each station. To test electrical conductivity, immerse electrodes of the conductivity test apparatus sample and note reading on the meter scale. Compare this reading with the reading obtained from each distilled water sample. Be sure to clean the electrodes after each test.

Additional investigations may be made with dissolved oxygen content, dissolved mineral content, etc. by using kits such as those obtainable from La Motte Chemical Corporation, Chestertown, Maryland, or Hach Chemical Corporation, Ames, Iowa, and following instructions supplied with kits or found in Strobbe's *Environmental Science Laboratory Manual.*

Sometimes one may observe visible pollution in samples by allowing a pint jar of the sample to sit untouched in the classroom for a few days. Use distilled water as a control. Look for colors or odors that may develop in the jar. Note any developing evidence of plant or animal life.

Record all observations on work sheets and in a notebook.

Lesson X. In the classroom—Interpreting and displaying data

"Data, data everywhere and not a time to think." Perhaps this has been one of your reactions to this series of experiences in environmental monitoring.

This final indoor lesson is suggested for sharing data, preparing display graphs and pictorial presentations, making posters, and otherwise pulling together the learning of the previous lessons.

Some suggestions for using the environmental data obtained during the lessons to help in the battle for environmental quality follow:

1. Prepare a complete report on the condition of the water body studies. If pollution is present, document its existence with photographs and graphs of chemical data. Forward this report to appropriate local and state authorities.
2. Using color slide photographs of the body of water and its physical and chemical con-

ditions, prepare a slide program with a tape-recorded narration to accompany the slides. Offer to present the program to interested civic and governmental organizations.

3. Conduct a panel discussion at a P.T.A. meeting or similar civic meeting, using a topic such as "Our Local Water Resources–Are They Well Used?" Invite local governmental officials to join students on the panel.
4. Conduct a regular ongoing monitoring program to ascertain the condition of the local water systems. (See Chapter 3.)
5. Invite the operator of the local waste-treatment facility or an official of local, state, or federal pollution control agencies to address the class on pollution prevention and abatement.

When the research has been interpreted, the presentations arranged, and the reports made, your students should have arrived at the realization that the price of environmental quality is constant vigilance and concerned questioning of attempts to "improve" our land, air, and water resources. By developing the ability to discriminate between ecologically sound planning and thoughtless development, your students may help to prevent a future of environmental poverty for our planet.

Remember, the students you have today will be the ecological arbiters of tomorrow. Guide them well.

Materials

Quantities listed are for one study research team.

- 2 No. 10 cans and handles
- 1 coffee can
- 2 compasses
- 10 plastic bags (sandwich size)
- 1 topographical map
- 1 measuring tape (50 feet)
- 3 empty plastic bleach bottles
- 1 Secchi disc (Lesson I)
- 1 set pH indicator chemicals or hydrion paper
- 4 hand lenses
- 1 stereo microscope
- 2 stream thermometers
- 1 dissolved oxygen analysis kit (Hach or La Motte Chemical Corp.)
- 100-200 feet of sounding line (Lesson I)
- 1 conductivity tester (Lesson I)
- 1 hydrometer (clinical, for urine testing)
- 1 hydrometer (homemade) (Lesson I)
- Miscellaneous test tubes and collecting bottles, labels, marking pencils, official notebook, work sheets

OBJECTIVES	APPROPRIATE LESSONS	OBJECTIVES	APPROPRIATE LESSONS
Cognitive		Affective	
1	III-V	1	I, II, IV, V, VII, VIII
2	II, VII, VIII	2	IX, X
3	VIII, IX	3	III-V, VII, VIII
4	VIII	4	I-III, V-VIII
5	IV, V, VII	5	I-III, V-VIII
		Generalizations	
6	III-V	1	IV
7	III-X	2	V
		3	III
		4	VII
		5	VIII, IX
		6	X

This list represents an ideal quantity of equipment. By judicious sharing of equipment, the lessons can be accomplished with much less. See Lesson I for further information.

Evaluation

Evaluation should be carried out in terms of the behavioral objectives stated. The chart on p. 87 indicates in which lessons evidence for each of the objectives and generalizations may be observed or collected.

This EEIP can be evaluated also by means of teacher-prepared tests covering the content of the various lessons. Do not neglect to evaluate the environmental concern developed by your students, for this is the real measure of success or failure of such lessons.

BIBLIOGRAPHY

Bowditch, Nathaniel: American practical navigator, Washington, D. C., 1968, U. S. Navy Hydrographic Office.

Davis, Kenneth S., and Day, John A.: Water: the mirror of science, New York, 1965, Harper & Row, Publishers.

Mason, Fred J., and Houdart, Joseph F.: Water quality monitoring manual, Browns Mills, N. J., 1970, CESC Press.

Milliken, Margaret, Hamer, Austin, and McDonald, Ernest: Field study manual for outdoor learning, Minneapolis, 1968, Burgess Publishing Co.

Prickard, G. L.: Descriptive physical oceanography, Oxford, 1963, Pergamon Press.

Rosenfeld, Samuel: Science experiments with water, Irvington, N. Y., 1965, Harvey House, Inc.

Shepard, Francis P.: Submarine geology, New York, 1963, Harper & Row, Publishers.

Strobbe, Maurice: Environmental science laboratory manual, St. Louis, 1972, The C. V. Mosby Co.

U. S. Department of Agriculture: Water. In the yearbook of agriculture, 1955, Washington, D. C., 1955, U. S. Government Printing Office.

FILMS

The Water Cycle, No. 979, 11 minutes, black and white, Encyclopaedia Britannica Films, Inc., 252 Christopher St., Upper Montclair, N. J.

Water-wealth or Worry for America, No. 543, 24 minutes, color, Modern Talking Picture Service, Inc., 1234 Spruce St., Philadelphia, Pa. 19107.

Wild Rivers, No. 1948, 28 minutes, color, Modern Talking Pictures Service, Inc., 1234 Spruce St., Philadelphia, Pa. 19107.

Rivers, an allegory, 11 minutes, color, International Film Bureau, Inc., 332 South Michigan Ave., Chicago, Ill., 60604.

Our Wealth of Water, 27 minutes, color, Interstate Commission on the Potomac River Basin, Transportation Building, Washington, D. C.

TRANSPARENCIES

Weathering and Water Cycle, Wards National Science, Inc., P. O. Box 1712, Rochester, N. Y. 14603—15 transparencies.

Work of Streams: the Erosion Cycle, Ward National Science, Inc., P. O. Box 1712, Rochester, N. Y. 14603—15 transparencies.

Creative Visuals, Big Spring, Texas—Conservation:
- Demands for Water
- A Water Treatment Plant
- Water Usefulness Affected by Adjoining and Upstream Uses
- The Hydrologic Cycle
- Water Has Many Uses

FILMSTRIPS

Popular Science Publishing Co.
- Water—a Most Unusual Substance, 40 frames, color
- Conserving Our Soil and Water, 40 frames, color
- How Rivers Are Formed, 40 frames, color
- The Life Cycle of Rivers, 40 frames, color
- Life and Death of Fresh Water Lakes, 40 frames, color

Harper & Row
- Rivers of Water and Ice, 42 frames, color
- The Story of Underground Water, 41 frames, color
- Underground Water, 41 frames, color

Encyclopaedia Britannica Education Corporation
- The Story of Rivers, 40 frames, color

Society for Visual Education
- Work of Ground Water, 47 frames, color
- Work of Running Water, 47 frames, color

3 MONITORING THE ENVIRONMENT

WHY MONITOR?

For students to make sound and mature judgments concerning environmental quality, they must have a knowledge of different environments, and firsthand study of immediate ones is both feasible and desirable.

It has consistently been demonstrated that experiential environmental studies significantly increase awareness of the diverse factors that influence the dynamics of a particular environment.

Through a series of monitoring activities students may observe and investigate a variety of environmental conditions. They may gather, analyze, and interpret data that reflect the relative quality and establish the rate of those changes.

Just as a change in the normal pulse rate or heartbeat of a medical patient is of significance to the doctor, a change in the amount of dissolved oxygen in a particular water system is significant to anyone concerned with maintaining its quality.

WHAT TO MONITOR?

Some teachers have been encouraging students to monitor certain environmental factors for a long time. When children make their own daily measurements of temperature, amounts of rainfall or snowfall, barometric pressure, wind direction, cloud cover, relative humidity, and the like, they are monitoring an environment. If they make comparisons of their information with weather data provided by the news media, the monitoring may become more intensified and sophisticated, and interest builds up.

If students are motivated to compare similar weather or climatic factors measured in the schoolyard with data measured in the nearby park or vacant lot, they will be developing descriptions of selected microclimates.

Some types of monitoring that youngsters at the elementary level have already carried out include the following:

1. Determining the qualities of selected constituents in local bodies of water, such as dissolved oxygen, phosphate and nitrate content, and degree of salinity (saltiness) and acidity
2. Determining the efficiency or desirability of local methods of solid waste disposal
3. Determining the amount of solid particles suspended in the air in selected locations
4. Measuring the amounts of carbon monoxide, sulfur dioxide, and hydrogen sulfide in selected locations
5. Determining local weather factors on a daily basis
6. Determining daily variations, in one or more selected locations, of one or more climatic factors such as air and soil tem-

perature, relative humidity, amount of precipitation, and wind direction

7. Surveying traffic to determine (a) daily variations in traffic density and direction, on a highway or at an intersection and (b) the number of passengers in automobiles at selected times of the day
8. Appraising the intensity of noise in locations such as classrooms, cafeterias, playgrounds, and streets in business or residential areas
9. Noting the dates of first and last flowering for trees or herbaceous plants
10. Recording the daily habits of one or more animals
11. Determining by survey the amount of land or beach erosion by water or wind
12. Determining dates and degrees of bird migrations
13. Making a cumulative record of the number and type of plants and animals in one or more selected small areas over a period of several years if possible

At the secondary level, many of these same activities may be engaged in, with greater sophistication in data-collecting techniques and greater intensity and span of data gathering. The following projects are of particular interest to students in the secondary schools:

1. Monitoring constituents of water, to include a determination of indicator microorganisms, and making a profile of an entire stream
2. Monitoring components of air, with special concern for polluting constituents around highways and residential and industrial areas
3. Making quadrat or transect studies of diverse environments over a period of years
4. Surveying local land use
5. Surveying an area for hazards such as gas tanks, high-voltage electric supplies, nuclear energy release, and others
6. Collecting data to compare capital investments and operating costs of abating pollution, provided by local industries *and* tax dollars from local, state, or federal sources
7. Providing presumptive pollution data for a statewide or regionwide data bank

FROM KNOWLEDGE TO ETHICS

Diverse environments are usually available for monitoring. Whenever possible, optimum environments should be compared with degraded ones because healthy environments provide standards with which to evaluate other, less favorable situations.

Students are well equipped for the task of environmental investigation. Their inherent curiosity and desire to explore and "pry into things" may be given meaningful direction by monitoring activities. As a result of direct observations, students may develop awareness of the interrelated factors that influence environments. Students may learn not only to discern the dynamics of selected environments of unequal quality but also to develop attitudes favoring the preservation of optimum environments and the improvement of despoiled ones.

TOWARD ECO-ACTION

Responsible social action can be a natural outcome of monitoring activities. If the students' investigations reveal adverse environmental conditions, their reports to proper local, state, or federal agencies can be the first step toward improvement.

Often environmental degradation may have taken place gradually and have gone almost unnoticed until severe damage has been done. Usually, if environments are subject to close scrutiny, early signs of deterioration may be detected, and more serious consequences avoided.

HOW TO GET STARTED—CHECKLIST

A general environmental-quality checklist or inventory is often a useful preparation for more intensive monitoring activities. Such a checklist can help to pinpoint the areas most appropriate for further investigation. In addition, the list serves to prepare students for making the careful observations that are a requisite for environmental monitoring.

The accompanying Community Checklist is probably best suited for junior high school level or above. However, it could easily be adapted for use at a lower grade level. Of course, checklists may also be designed for use in studying particular environmental factors or other environments.

COMMUNITY CHECKLIST

	YES	NO
1. Does your community provide specific areas for residential, industrial, and commercial development? List at least three other factors that should be taken into consideration in planning a city.	____	____
2. Does your community have open spaces that can be developed? How do you think these open areas could be best utilized?	____	____
3. What types of public transportation does your city have? What are the advantages in a well-developed public transportation system?	____	____
4. Is a wide range of races, colors, and creeds represented in your community? What contributions have the groups made to the community or to the nation?	____	____
5. Have any new housing units or developments been constructed in your city during the last year? In your opinion, do these new housing areas represent an improvement over other existing residential areas? What reasons do you have for your judgment here? Why is the lack of housing a critical problem in some cities today?	____	____
6. What signs of change does your community show? What reasons can you give for such changes?	____	____

COMMUNITY CHECKLIST—cont'd

	YES	NO
7. Are the residents of your community assured of an adequate supply of water for municipal and industrial purposes? What steps are necessary for communities to maintain a water supply of adequate quantity and quality?	____	____
8. Does your community have access to poison-control information? Why has poison control become so important in recent years?	____	____
9. Are educational opportunities available to all segments of the population of your community? Why is education so vital to the growth and development of cities?	____	____
10. Are adequate and varied recreational facilities available for all residents of your community? What recreational facilities do you believe should be improved or expanded in your city?	____	____
11. Are residents of your city exposed to a reasonably pollution-free atmosphere? How do you know? What steps are taken or should be taken to assure this?	____	____
12. Are adequate cultural advantages and opportunities available in your community? What other cultural areas would you like to see developed?	____	____

SOLID WASTES—CHECKLIST

Solid wastes are the castoffs of all facets of household, community, industrial, and agricultural life. They may include garbage, trash, abandoned automobiles, construction wastes, discarded furniture, or a host of other materials. Environmental degradation is hastened when these materials are discarded over various parts of the landscape.

In the last few decades the amount of solid wastes discarded by each person has probably increased threefold. This sharp rise has been brought about by sophistication in packaging and wrapping products of all kinds, especially foodstuffs. Rapid population growth has seriously aggravated the problem.

The long-term practice of throwing solid wastes in a pile at the outskirts of a community, often in an unused stream bed or wetland, is now grossly inadequate as well as environmentally unacceptable. Man is about to be engulfed by his own wastes.

It is important that students be provided with information as to the nature of the problem as well as suggestions for its improvement or, if possible, its elimination.

The amount of wastes generated in communities varies because of the population, complexity of the community, and nature of the effort to control or dispose of solid wastes.

Because of these variances, it becomes essential that students examine their immediate environment or community to determine how the problem affects them personally and how this community fits into the larger solid waste problem.

CHECKLIST FOR SOLID WASTES

	YES	NO
1. Maintain a record of solid wastes discarded by your family for a 1-week period. How much space would be required to bury this amount in a waste-disposal landfill of the conventional type?		
2. What percentage of the material could be recycled on your community at the present time?		
3. Are any recycling centers available for your community?	____	____
4. Are any industrial firms that will accept wastes for recycling available for your community?	____	____
If so, please list the industries.		
5. Are any returnable bottles collected by food stores in your community?	____	____
If so, please list names.		
6. Do any ordinances (laws) in your community prohibit or regulate the use of throwaway bottles or other containers?	____	____
7. Are there incinerators for burning paper in your community?	____	____

CHECKLIST FOR SOLID WASTES—cont'd

	YES	NO
If so, where are they located?		
Does your school incinerate, or burn, its wastepaper?	____	____
Are there ways of reusing such burned-up paper wastes?	____	____
8. How many items that could be recycled or disposed of, such as old TV sets or plumbing fixtures, are stored somewhere in your house or apartment?		
Why haven't these items been disposed of?		
9. Can you suggest any groups in your community who might be interested in receiving the information you have collected in this survey?	____	____
If so, please list.		

TEST ENVIRONMENTAL QUALITY—CHECKLISTS

Following are checklists to cover activities that can be conducted by students at various grade levels. The ages and abilities of the students should determine the depth of their investigations.

EROSION CHECKLIST

Select a few city blocks and other special environmental areas for this survey.

	YES	NO
1. Where does water go when it flows from rooftops, parking lots, or roadways?		
2. If your finding for item 1 above was into the sewer system, that runoff water is called *storm* waste or sewage. Is there a separate system for storm, or runoff, water?	____	____
3. Can you find traces of soil, or earth, material in the street gutters or on sidewalks and roadways?	____	____
4. Do any land areas where you are surveying have rills or gullies where soil has washed away?	____	____
5. Can you trace where the soil has gone by following any of the rills or gullies?	____	____

EROSION CHECKLIST—cont'd

	YES	NO
6. What relationship, if any, can you find between the size of the gullies and the slope of the land? Have you found any other situations that produce gully erosion?	____	____
7. Do you notice discoloration of the bodies of water in your community during or immediately after a rainstorm?	____	____
If so, please describe what you found.		
8. If there are pipes or culverts entering a stream or other bodies of water in your community, do you notice any earth material near the mouth of the pipe?	____	____
9. Do you think that soil erosion is a severe or significant problem in your community?	____	____
10. Are there any situations in which means have been employed to stop soil erosion by water?	____	____
11. Have you found evidence of soil erosion by wind anywhere?	____	____
If so, where?		
12. Are any means employed to prevent or check wind erosion in the areas you have surveyed?	____	____
If so, what means were used?		
13. If your community includes an open area bounded by an ocean, bay, or lake, you may wish to prepare a separate set of responses for such an environment.		
14. Can you suggest any groups in your community that might be interested in receiving the information you have collected in this survey?	____	____
If so, what are they?		

CHECKLIST FOR WATER QUALITY

	YES	NO
1. What is the source of water for most persons in your community?		
2. How would you describe the taste, odor, and color of your drinking water?		

CHECKLIST FOR WATER QUALITY—cont'd

	YES	NO
3. Do you believe that someone has already used the water you are now using?	____	____
Has all water been recycled at some time?	____	____
4. Can you identify any previous user of your water supply?	____	____
If so, please suggest names of previous users.		
5. What surface waters are in your community?		
6. Are there evidences that any of the waters in your community are polluted?	____	____
If so, how do you know?		
7. Waste water that comes from homes or public buildings is called "sanitary sewage." Waste water from industries is designated "industrial sewage." How and where is sanitary sewage disposed of in your community?		
8. Is industrial sewage treated separately?	____	____
If so, is industrial sewage treated by community sewage systems or by one or more private industry systems?		
9. How would you rate the quality of the surface water in your community?		
What reasons do you have for the opinions you have given?		
10. Do you think that the entire waste-water problem is handled adequately in your community?	____	____
If so, how do you know?		
11. Can you identify any situations in your community where water is wasted?	____	____
If so, please list them.		
12. Can you think of any ways in which individuals or groups, agencies, or industries might use less water than they are now using?	____	____
If so, please list them.		

CHECKLIST FOR WATER QUALITY—cont'd

	YES	NO
13. Do you know if any agencies or groups in your community might be interested in receiving the information you have collected in this survey?	____	____
If so, please list them.		

LAND-USE CHECKLIST

Obtain a map of your community and try to determine the answers to these survey items.

	YES	NO
1. With the map and some knowledge of your community, estimate the following:		
a. What percentage of the land is covered by buildings, roadways, and paved-over areas?		
b. What percentage of the land has soil at its surface?		
c. What percentage of the entire community area is used for parks and recreation?		
Do you consider the park and recreational areas adequate?		
How do you know?		
d. What percentage may be used for recreation?		
Do you consider the recreation areas adequate?	____	____
How do you know?		
2. What percentage of the community area is used for the following?		
a. Houses.		
b. Stores and other service areas.		
c. Public buildings.		
d. Industries.		
e. Recreation.		
f. Open space.		
Do you think these are desirable proportions?	____	____
3. Are there any unused areas?	____	____

LAND-USE CHECKLIST—cont'd

	YES	NO
Can you suggest any uses for these areas?	____	____
If so, please list.		
4. Are there any fertile farm fields now being used for other purposes?	____	____
If so, please describe.		
5. Are there any areas not being used for optimum purposes?	____	____
If so, please suggest possible changes.		
6. Do you know of any agency or groups in your community who might be interested in receiving the information you have collected in this survey?	____	____
If so, please list.		

INSTRUCTION PLANS FOR ENVIRONMENTAL MONITORING

Following are detailed instruction plans for involving students in the monitoring of important environmental parameters. These include weather, solid wastes, and air and water quality. Collecting data on the weather and solid wastes in the environment are suitable pursuits for middle-grade students; air and water quality are discussed with respect to junior and senior high school levels. The monitoring of water quality is discussed in considerable depth in this chapter, not only because of its major importance to our daily lives, but also because the technology is available, so that significant data can be accumulated without expensive equipment and special training. Therefore students can readily play a role in obtaining valid information on which to base environmental decisions.

PRIMARY GRADES—A PREPARATION

At the primary levels, monitoring the environment as described in the previous discussion is scarcely possible. Youngsters at this age have great difficulty in making written records in situations away from the classroom. It is difficult for them to write on clipboards or tablets when not seated at a desk or table. Similarly, primary youngsters are limited in their ability to make precise measurements.

On the other hand, environments away from the classroom provide many opportunities for counting, collecting data, sorting information into sets, reading thermometers, and measuring lengths of objects in feet and inches or in comparable metric units.

The environmental education plans in Chapter 2 provide examples of these activities.

Such measuring and counting can provide an indispensable readiness for more detailed environmental monitoring activities by middle-grade youngsters. Emphasis on more healthy environments for children at this age can provide a base of ecological knowledge and familiarity that can be a standard for comparison with more polluted or degraded environments. Above all, environmental study experiences can establish patterns of study suitable for environments away from the classroom. If and when polluted environments are encountered, class discussion can begin to develop an environmental ethic, which is probably the most desirable goal of environmental education.

MIDDLE GRADES—WEATHER

The possibilities for environmental-monitoring activities for youngsters who are able to work in small groups seem almost limitless. Two sets of plans are included to illustrate a variety of monitoring activities that have been found to hold high interest value for children in the middle grades. They may also be adapted for use in upper elementary or junior high school classes.

Weather is the universal environmental phenomenon. It influences the behavior and activities of people everywhere and provides dramatic evidence of cause-and-effect relationships. Weather is an environmental factor that affects virtually everything on earth. Weather is a constant topic of discussion because everyone experiences it daily.

Unfortunately, these continual direct encounters are seldom utilized effectively in a classroom study of weather. Yet observations of various weather factors may be collected in sufficient numbers to allow students to generalize inductively and, with suitable data and concepts, to make predictions. The study of weather is basic to many other environmental investigations; both air and water pollution, for example, are profoundly influenced by weather conditions. Discussions of weather are found in all major science textbook series. It seems highly desirable, then, to involve children in monitoring activities that will enable them to demonstrate increased interest and skill in making, recording, and interpreting weather observations.

A variety of inexpensive and reasonably accurate weather instruments may be constructed in

WEATHER INSTRUMENTS

Thermometer:	Measures the temperature in degrees.
Wind vane:	Indicates the direction of winds near ground level.
Barometer:	Measures air pressure.
Rain gauge:	Measures rain or any form of precipitation.
Hygrometer:	Measures humidity.
Anemometer:	Measures wind speed.
Nephoscope:	Indicates the direction of high winds.

BEAUFORT SCALE

BEAUFORT NO.	WIND SPEED (mph)	DESCRIPTION	OBSERVATION
0	0-1	Calm	Smoke rises vertically
1	1-3	Light air	Smoke drifts slowly
2	4-7	Slight breeze	Leaves rustle
3	8-12	Gentle breeze	Leaves and twigs in motion
4	13-18	Moderate breeze	Small branches move
5	19-24	Fresh breeze	Small trees sway
6	25-31	Strong breeze	Large branches sway
7	32-38	Moderate gale	Whole trees in motion
8	39-46	Fresh gale	Twigs break off trees
9	47-54	Strong gale	Branches break
10	55-63	Whole gale	Trees snap and are blown down
11	64-72	Storm	Widespread damage
12	73-82	Hurricane	Extreme damage

WIND CHILL CHART

Instructions: Find the wind speed in the left column and the temperature in the top line of numbers. The figure where the two rows intersect tells you how cold it seems to be.

WIND SPEED (mph)	TEMPERATURE IN DEGREES FAHRENHEIT										
—	35	30	25	20	15	10	5	0	−6	−10	−15
5	33	27	21	16	12	7	1	−6	−11	−15	−20
10	21	16	9	2	−2	−9	−15	−22	−27	−31	−38
15	16	11	1	−6	−11	−18	−25	−33	−40	−45	−51
20	12	3	−4	−9	−17	−24	−32	−40	−46	−52	−60
25	7	0	−7	−15	−22	−29	−37	−45	−52	−58	−67
30	5	−2	−11	−18	−26	−33	−41	−49	−56	−63	−70
35	3	−4	−13	−20	−27	−35	−43	−52	−60	−67	−72

RELATIVE HUMIDITY—MEASURING MOISTURE

Instructions: This chart is used to determine the relative humidity after taking readings from both the wet- and dry-bulb thermometer of your hygrometer. First fan the wet-bulb for 15 to 20 seconds, take a reading of it and the dry-bulb. Find the difference between the two readings; locate that difference in the first column to the left above. Follow that row out to the degree column closest to your dry-bulb reading. The number that you find in that column is your percent of relative humidity.

DIFFERENCE BETWEEN WET- AND DRY-BULB READINGS	TEMPERATURE OF DRY-BULB THERMOMETER							
	30°	40°	50°	60°	70°	80°	90°	100°
1	90	92	93	94	95	96	96	97
2	79	84	87	89	90	92	92	93
3	68	76	80	84	86	87	88	90
4	58	68	74	78	81	83	85	86
6	38	52	61	68	72	75	78	80
8	18	37	49	58	64	68	71	74
10		22	37	48	55	61	65	68
12		8	26	39	48	54	59	62
14			16	30	40	47	53	57
16			5	21	33	41	47	51
18				13	26	35	41	47
20				5	19	29	36	42
22					12	23	32	37
24					6	18	26	33

the classroom. It is extremely important to avoid allowing the construction of these instruments to become an end in itself. They are fun to build, and that is part of the charm of this monitoring activity. But no matter how well constructed and attractive they may be, the construction of the instruments themselves means little. Only their application to a responsible and carefully directed study of weather conditions that can develop the desired skills and interest is significant. Figs. 3-1 to 3-10 show how several weather instruments can be constructed and how they can be organized into a weather station. The weekly weather report permits the systematic recording of data that are the basis for the students' generalizations and predictions. A number of useful tables of information relating to weather conditions are also included.

Text continued on p. 102.

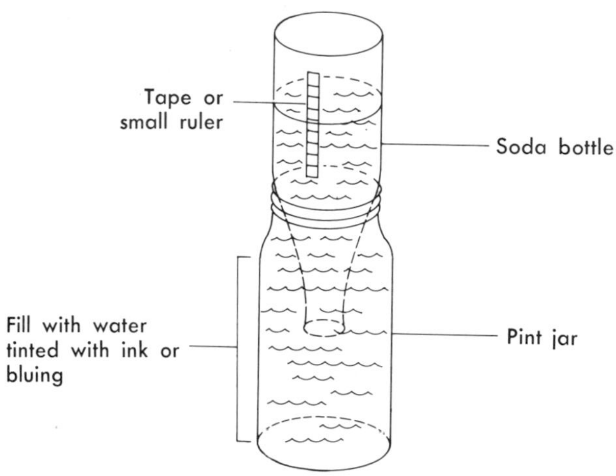

Fig. 3-1. Simple barometer. Fill a soft drink bottle two-thirds full and turn upside down inside a pint jar.

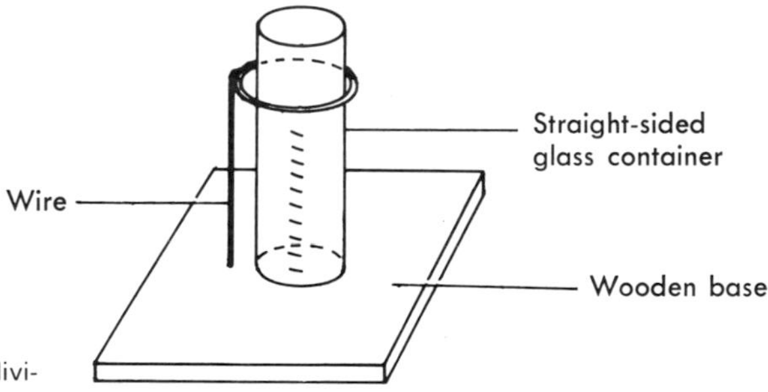

Fig. 3-2. Rain gauge. Mark ⅛-, ¼-, ½-, and 1-inch divisions on the glass container with a file, starting at the bottom. An alternative method is to use a funnel for collecting greater volumes of rainwater. In such a case, be sure to use a scale modified by the ratio of the squares of the radii of the funnel and collecting jar.

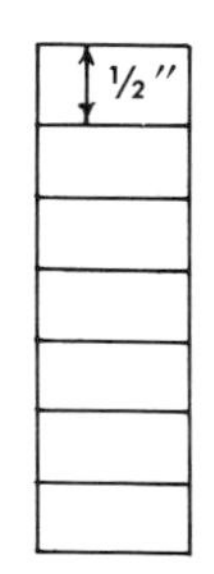

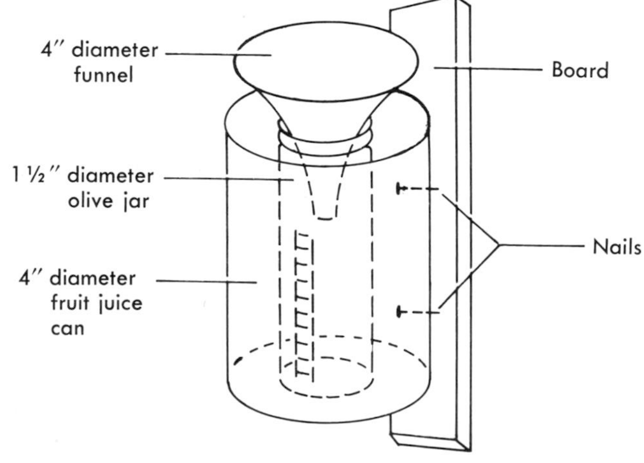

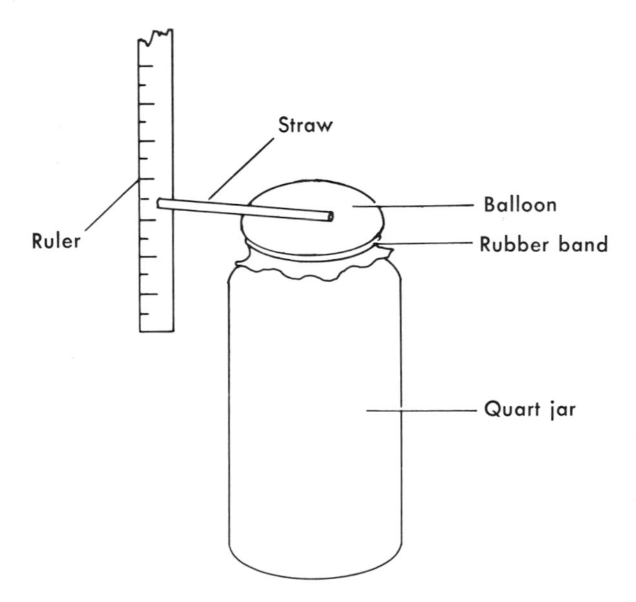

Fig. 3-3. Aneroid barometer. Glue a straw to the center of the balloon covering the jar.

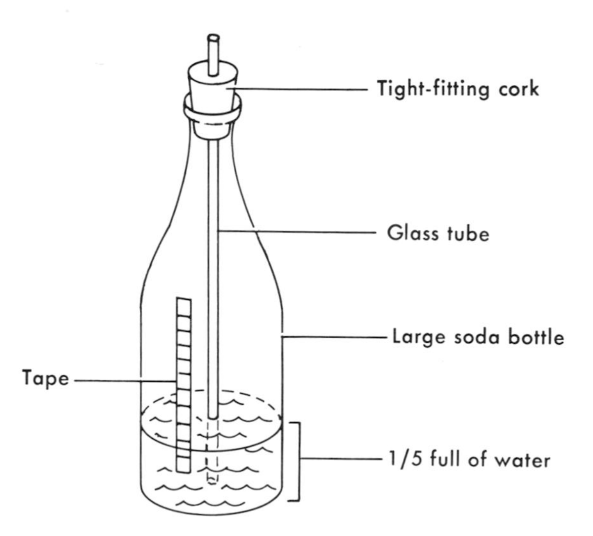

Fig. 3-4. Bottle barometer. Fasten the tape 1 inch below water level to about 3 inches above the top of the water level. Mark the tape in inches, quarter inches, and eighth inches. Provide calibration or index readings by comparing with an aneroid barometer or barometer readings from radio or television broadcasts.

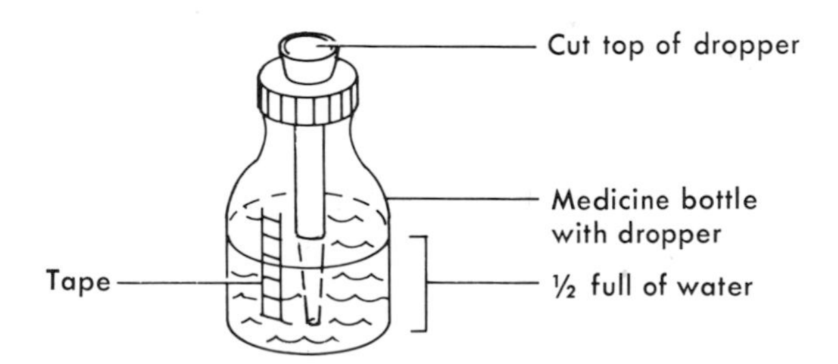

Fig. 3-5. Bottle barometer. Add a few drops of water from the top. Calibrate as in Fig. 3-4.

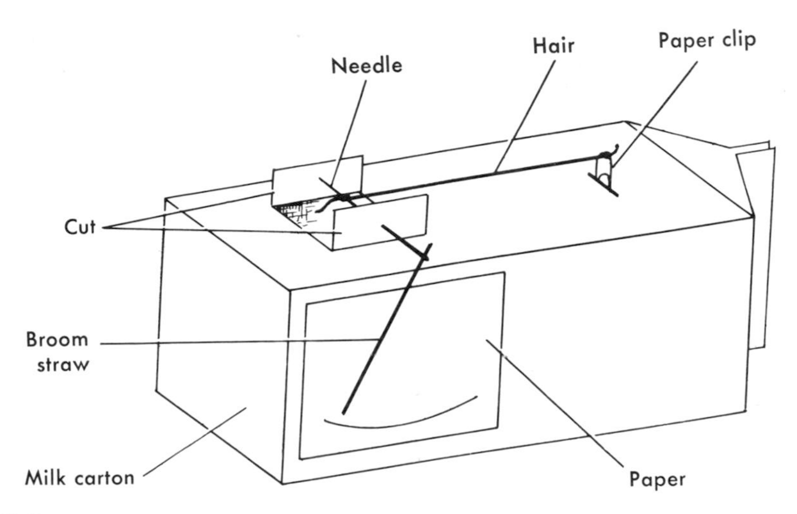

Fig. 3-6. Hair hygrometer. Wash the hair with soapy water or alcohol and rinse in clear water. Envelop the entire instrument in a warm wet towel for 10 minutes and mark the position of the pointer *10* (high relative humidity). Then place the instrument in a dry, warm place for 15 minutes and mark the pointer position *1* (low relative humidity). Divide and number the rest of the scale.

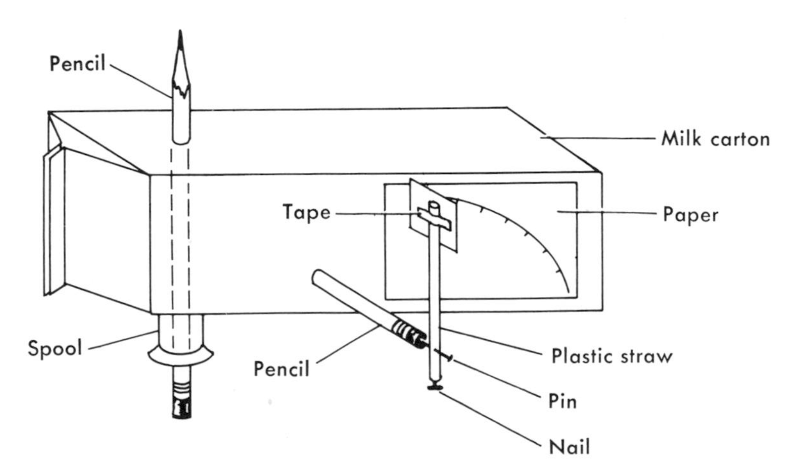

Fig. 3-7. Pressure-plate anemometer. Grasp the spool and hold outside the car window at 5, 10, 15 mph, and up, to put numbers on the scale.

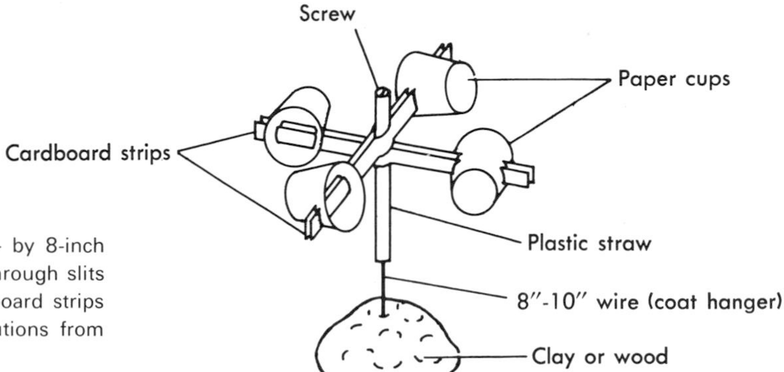

Fig. 3-8. Wind gauge, or anemometer. Fold 2- by 8-inch cardboard in half lengthwise and insert in cups through slits 1 inch from the tops of the cups, with the cardboard strips at right angles. Color one cup and count revolutions from the car window at different speeds to calibrate.

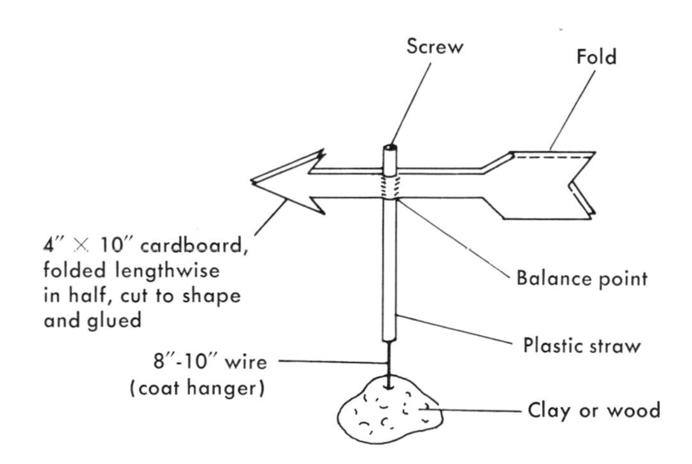

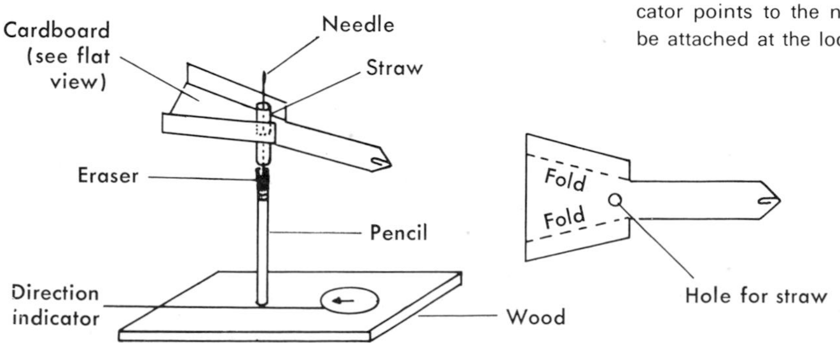

Fig. 3-9. Weather vane. It must move freely and will point to the direction from which the wind is blowing. The instrument must be placed so that the arrow of the direction indicator points to the north, or else a magnetic compass may be attached at the location of the direction indicator.

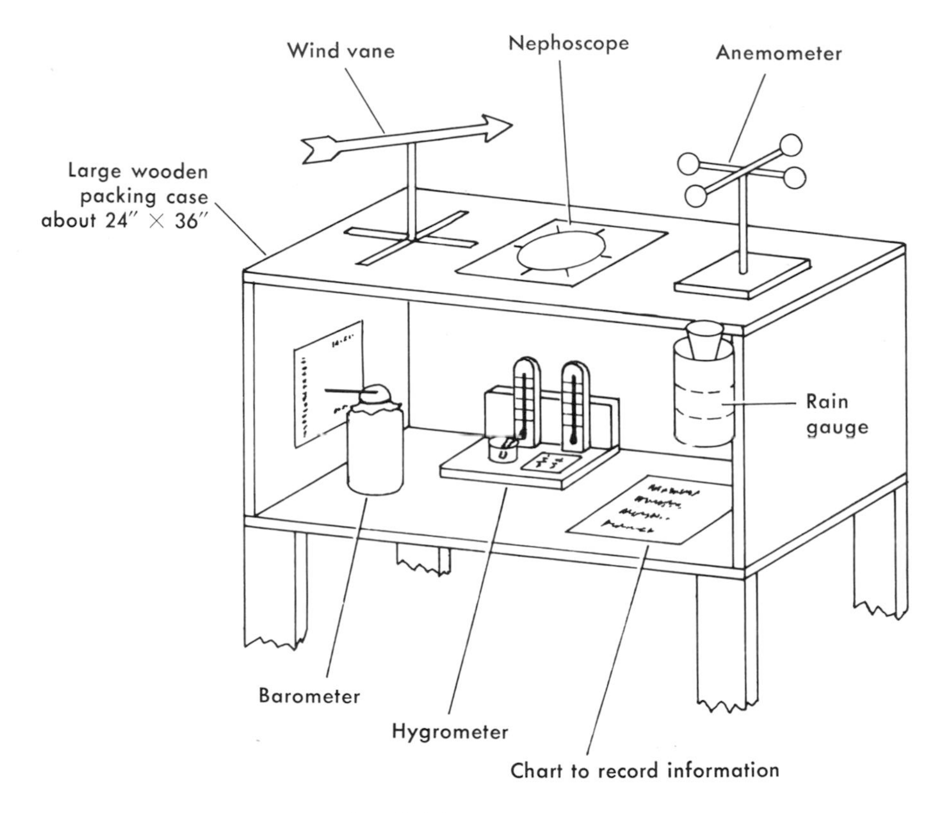

Fig. 3-10. Weather station.

MIDDLE GRADES—SOLID WASTE

The insult of litter is evident in many environments. It is only one of numerous indications that the esthetic and ecological functions of environments are being destroyed or degraded through present methods of solid-waste disposal.

If the problem presented by solid waste is enormous, so are the opportunities for purposeful monitoring. Almost no equipment is required, and yet the activities described are valuable for several reasons. They can indicate to the student the extent of trash and litter, which are the most commonly observed forms of solid waste. They can enable the student to calculate the cost of litter cleanup and evaluate the effectiveness of present solid-waste disposal practices.

More importantly, the student is challenged to rethink traditional attitudes toward solid-waste disposal and consider alternative approaches to the problem.

Following are some of the outstanding generalizations related to the problems of use and reuse of solid wastes:

1. The esthetic and ecological functions of environments are being destroyed or degraded through present methods of solid-waste disposal.

HOW MUCH DOES LITTER PICKUP COST?

Reporter ____________________

Date ____________________

	GLASS	PAPER	METAL	WOOD	RUBBER	PLASTIC	OTHER	TOTAL COLLECTED
Number collected								
Percent of total collected								

Area cleaned, in acres* ____________________

Time involved to clean it ____________________

Number of students involved ____________________

Formula to determine cost of cleaning up the roadside:

$$\frac{\text{Total number of pieces of litter collected} \times 23¢}{\text{Number of acres or square feet}} = \text{Cost per acre or square foot}$$

Example: $$\frac{180 \text{ articles} \times 23¢}{2 \text{ acres}} = \$20.70 \text{ per acre}$$

To find the percent for each category of the total collected, divide the total number of articles collected by the number of articles in each category.

*One acre contains 42,560 square feet.

2. Solid-waste disposal has become a national economic problem. Present-day society demands more elaborate packaging as well as an increasing number of disposable consumer products. The resulting waste products puts mounting pressure on already scarce areas available for waste disposal.
3. As available waste-disposal areas close to urban areas disappear, solid waste must be transported to more distant areas, at a much higher cost to the taxpayer.
4. Solid wastes may become a national resource when modern technology develops more efficient and less costly methods of reuse or recycling.
5. In disposing of the wastes of modern society, man's disregard for maintaining favorable environmental quality has frequently led to the serious impairment or total destruction of essential ecosystems.

It is often useful and instructive to have children do a survey of the amounts and kinds of solid litter in an area, possibly as part of a clean-up campaign.

Perhaps more significant than the actual clean-up is the computation of the cost of litter removal. The state highway department in New Jersey estimated that litter along major highways cost 23 cents per item to be removed by highway or park personnel. If this statistic in terms of tax dollars is reported to the citizens of a community and focused on one of the local areas, much might be done to begin the establishment of a more desirable ethic for the use and disposal of solid materials.

The data-collection form on cost of litter pickup (p. 103) has been used by students with much success.

The study of individual pieces of litter collected in a clean-up campaign or from any other source provides striking evidence of the dependence of all human societies on *distant* environments. The student work sheet below may be used for such a study.

Students may also wish to make a survey of the amount of trash and solid waste used by the families of the entire class. This figure may also be extended by the cooperation of other classes. From these data, a per capita solid-waste production statistic may be derived. The per capita waste production might be extrapolated to the entire city population and compared to figures obtained from the community sanitation department. Students may find the record-keeping chart on types and sources of solid waste on opposite page useful.

If a trip is made by the class to an area where solid wastes are being collected or disposed of, the students may collect information, using the data sheet on how much trash we accumulate (p. 106).

The value of solid materials may be computed by children (see example on p. 106). Although many recycling operations have been initiated, most solid materials are not being reused.

The *World Almanac* provides information on the wholesale cost of metals and certain other materials if local information cannot be obtained for the value of solid materials now being discarded.

UPPER ELEMENTARY/JUNIOR HIGH GRADES—AIR QUALITY

Both the monitoring activities just described for the middle grades may also be adapted for upper elementary levels if these activities have not previously been tried by the students.

Because of the recent attention focused on air pollution, the following ideas for activities are presented for use by students. Because of the difficulty obtaining adequate and representative samples of air, the results obtained by the activities

Text continued on p. 107.

WHERE DO SOLID WASTES COME FROM?

LITTER ITEM	LOCATION	ORIGINAL OR PREVIOUS USE(S)	NATURAL RESOURCES USED TO PRODUCE	PROBABLE MEANS BY WHICH LITTER GOT TO SITE

TYPES AND SOURCES OF SOLID WASTE

Recorder ____________________ Date ______________________

Group members______________ Time of arrival _______ Departure _____ Total time _____

Location ________ Size in acres _____ Was operation ongoing at time of visit? _____

Type of operation (describe how waste is being disposed of): ______________________________

____

CATEGORIES OF SOLID WASTE OBSERVED	TYPES	SOURCES
Household ____________	Cesspool cleanings ________	Demolition, construction _____
Commercial ____________	Dead animals ____________	Trees and landscape ________
Industrial ____________	Junked vehicles __________	Appliances, furniture, bulk ___
Agricultural ____________	Chemical wastes __________	Tires ______________
Institutional ____________	Waste oil ______________	Sewage-plant solids ________
	Incinerator ashes __________	

TYPES OF SOLID WASTE IN EVIDENCE: Glass _______ Wood _______ Plastic ____________

Paper ________ Aluminum______ Other metals _______

Total population being served by this operation ________ Record number of community disposal trucks observed ______________

Can you explain why this site was selected for waste disposal? ___________________________

____

Are environments being affected by this operation? _____ Immediate area? Yes _____ No_____

Are more distant areas affected? Yes _______ No _______

Are distant areas sources of supply for these wastes? Yes _______ No _______

Please explain your answers on the reverse side of this sheet.

HOW MUCH TRASH DO WE ACCUMULATE?*

Name ______________________ Week ______ Number in family: Adults ____ Children ____

TYPE	MON.	TUES.	WED.	THURS.	FRI.	SAT.	SUN.	TOTAL
Glass (bottles, jars, etc.)								
Plastic (milk cartons, bags, etc.)								
Aluminum (cans, wraps, etc.)								
Other metals								
Styrofoam								
Paper								
Wood								
Other								

*Count should be kept by weight whenever appropriate or possible

HOW MUCH ARE SOLID WASTES WORTH?

MATERIAL	PREVIOUS USE OF PRODUCT	VALUE PER TON FOR RECYCLING
	Examples:	
Paper	Newsprint	$
Aluminum	Old lawn furniture	
Steel	Old tub	
Tin	Cans or roofing	
Copper	Wire	
Iron	Pipe	
Lead	Storage batteries	
Rags		
Other		

described can indicate what is happening only in a limited area. The detection of air pollutants, with the exception of a survey of solid particles falling from the air, must be made by means of commercially obtained test equipment. Sources of supply for this equipment are indicated with each activity.

Ever since early man learned to modify his environment by burning fuels, the problem of air pollution has plagued his settlements and communities. With the increasing sophistication of technology and the burgeoning growth of population, the by-products of human living have mushroomed. The pressing problem is to implement a nationwide cleanup of the air. By federal legislation, limits and standards have been set for the quality of air to be attained by 1975. Each state has been required to submit plans to implement these air-quality standards. Their plans are subject to approval of the federal Environmental Protection Agency.

The job of cleaning up the air is a complex one requiring the combined efforts of many agencies, officials, and the general public. Because the sources of pollutants are diverse and numerous, inspection of emissions to determine violations will be a tremendous job. An informed and active group of students could assist their communities by monitoring the quality of air in their area in a general way. Monitoring activities then become a valuable learning tool, both as direct experience with the concepts involved in the study of air pollution and as a real involvement in ecoaction.

For upper elementary students activities can focus on sharpening observational skills and strengthening the use of the mathematical processes of percentage and density. A comparison of various odors, both natural and man-made, will serve to increase olfactory acuity. Many city children become accustomed to the variety of odors around them and often ignore the dangerous ones.

Monitoring activities may include the following:

1. Observing and describing various man-made and natural odors, including pollutants
2. Measuring amounts of dustfall with microscope slides and adhesive such as petroleum jelly or double sticky tape
3. Measuring windblown particles, with a jar mounted several feet above the ground and covered with sticky paper
4. Measuring effects of smoggy air on fabrics, building materials, and metals, by suspending samples of different objects in an area exposed to the air

Junior high school students can perform these activities and also determine gaseous pollutant levels, using commercially produced spot detectors and gas-detecting tubes. Although each test is a bit expensive, preliminary analysis can be made to indicate necessary action that public agencies may choose to take.

It is crucial that during these monitoring activities meteorological data also be taken. Wind speed and direction as well as precipitation levels affect pollution accumulation. For example, the expectation of an air pollution episode is based on a prediction from the weather service of a temperature inversion expected to last at least 36 hours.

If accurate records of the activities are kept, data should be reported to concerned agencies at a local and even state level.

Where local agencies make air pollution information of very specific kinds available to the public, such as the telephone messages concerning air quality available in Philadelphia, students may take advantage of these resources for their records.

Following are some significant generalizations related to the study of air quality:

1. The air we breathe is not infinite. The troposphere has limits and boundaries.
2. Changes in the quality of our air are not easily detected with the unaided senses because the comparisons involve differences of only a few parts per million, and some pollu-

WHAT PARTICLES ARE IN OUR AIR?

Student's name ____________________ Date ____________________

Teacher ____________________ Hour ____________________

A. DUST DRAG (SEMIQUANTITATIVE)

	HEIGHT IN A STRAW TUBE	LOCATION	INTERPRETED MEANING
Trial 1			
Trial 2			
Trial 3			
Trial 4			
Trial 5			

B. MICROSLIDE PARTICLE COLLECTION (QUALITATIVE)

	LOCATION	DESCRIPTION	INTERPRETED MEANING
Slide 1			
Slide 2			
Slide 3			
Slide 4			
Slide 5			
Slide 6			

C. WEIGHT OF PARTICLES (QUANTITATIVE) USING HIGH-VOLUME SAMPLER

	FILTER			FLOW RATE				
	WEIGHT BEFORE SAMPLING (IN GM)	WEIGHT AFTER SAMPLING	NET WEIGHT OF PARTICULATE MATTER	START MANOMETER	LITERS/MIN.	FINISH MANOMETER	LITERS/MIN.	AVERAGE FLOW RATE
Trial 1								
Trial 2								
Trial 3								
Trial 4								

WHAT PARTICLES ARE IN OUR AIR?—cont'd

C. WEIGHT OF PARTICLES (QUANTITATIVE) USING HIGH-VOLUME SAMPLER—cont'd

	AREA OF COLLECTION	SAMPLING TIME	CONCENTRATION OF SAMPLE* (MCG./M.^{3}/MIN.)	INTERPRETED MEANING
Trial 1				
Trial 2				
Trial 3				
Trial 4				

*Concentration = change in filter weight (average flow rate × sampling time)

Note: 1 gram = 10^6 mcg.
1 liter = 10^3 cm.^{3}
1 meter^3 (m.^{3}) = 10^6 cm.^{3}

Sample calculation for advanced groups†

If net gain of filter = 0.300 gm. for 4 hours at an average flow rate of 1,500 liters per minute:

$$\text{Concentration of particulate matter} = \frac{(0.300\text{ gm.}) \qquad (10^6\text{ mcg./gm.})}{\left(\frac{1{,}500\text{ liter}}{\text{min.}}\right)\left(\frac{(10^3\text{ cm.}^3)}{\text{liter}}\right)\left(\frac{(1\text{ m.}^3)}{10^6\text{ cm.}^3}\right)\left(\frac{(4\text{ hr.} \times 60\text{ min.})}{\text{hr.}}\right)} = 833\text{ mcg./m.}^3$$

†Source of calculation: Gordon, David, editor: Eduquip Air Pollution Study Program Manual, Boston, 1971, Eduquip, pp. 8-10.

tants such as carbon monoxide are invisible and odorless.

3. Pollutants in the air originate from two main sources: man's use of fossil fuels for heating, transportation, and production and, to a smaller extent, natural sources such as volcanoes and pollination.
4. When fossil fuels such as coal, petroleum, or gas are burned without a sufficient supply of oxygen, oxides of sulfur, nitrogen, and carbon are formed. Heating and industrial plants discharge these by-products into the air. These chemicals react with each other and with water vapor to form corrosive acids or smog.

Dustfall or particulate matter

Students may also collect particles that have fallen from the air ("dust drag"). To collect and measure particles on the site, start with several large plastic straws. Tape one end closed and attach a paper funnel to the other end of each. Now place a small magnet in a plastic bag. Drag the bag over the ground. Shake collected particles into the funnel, taking notes or marking the straw to indicate amount collected on first and second run. Compare depth of particles in each straw. (See p. 108.)

Particles may, of course, be collected directly from the air. Have each team select an area of the school to survey for air particles. Cut oak tag into 8- × 10-inch sheets. Staple heavy transparent plastic wrap to the oak-tag sheets. Coat each transparent sheet with petroleum jelly. Leave room at the top for collector's name, date, and collection site. Hang seven sheets next to each other on the windows or along the wall of a specific location. Take one down each day for a week. Spray each completed panel with plastic fixative or hair spray. The results should reveal an arithmetical progression of particle concentration, other things such as wind condition being equal.

Extending the study of particulates. Microscope slides make very suitable particle collectors for windblown particles when the slides are covered with a transparent grease such as petroleum jelly. A slide can easily be suspended with a pinch-type clothespin from anemometers, wind vanes, fence-post stakes, or clothesline.

1. Use microscope slides with paper labels (for date and location) and covered with petroleum jelly.
2. Set out the slides in many different locations around town. (See later suggestions.) Use pinch-type clothespins to suspend the slides vertically from small branches, weather vanes, anemometers, poles, or other supports.
3. The slides should be kept outside for seven days, then collected and covered carefully with another clear, clean slide for protection or sprayed with a plastic fixative such as Krylon or Artist fixative.

Students should be encouraged to plan an air-quality study in their own community, using a street map. They will need to consider, for placement of the slides, which areas of town might have the most or the least particles, so that interesting contrasts and comparisons may be discovered. Consider the following factors: (1) topography—mountains, waterways, valleys, etc., (2) traffic flow patterns, (3) sites of industrial plants, incinerators, and power plants, and (4) prevailing wind patterns.

Nonparticulates—noxious gases and odors

More elaborate air samples may be taken and analyzed if a high-volume sampler is obtained from a supplier such as Eduquip, Inc., or National Environmental Instruments, Inc. (addresses follow). A homemade sampler may be constructed from a vacuum cleaner, but the volume of air pumped must be measured. Materials for the detection and measurement of noxious gases such as carbon monoxide, nitrogen dioxide, and sulfur dioxide are available from the following suppliers:

National Environmental Instruments, Inc.
Fall River, Mass. 02724

Eduquip, Inc.
1220 Adams St.
Boston, Mass. 02124

Mine Safety Appliances Co.
201 N. Braddock Ave.
Pittsburgh, Pa. 15208

Test Fabrics, Inc.
55 Vandam St.
New York, N. Y. 10013

Instructions for conducting the various tests are usually included with the materials and are further detailed in Strobbe's *Environmental Science Laboratory Manual.* Students can do all kinds of studies such as comparing exhaust emissions from different makes of cars and comparing air pollution parameters in selected localities, for example, factories, shopping centers, residential areas (p. 108).

A relatively simple and yet meaningful exercise in the development of a classification for pollution odors. Certain materials can be obtained such as vanilla, lemon, pine needles, turpentine, gasoline, marsh gas (methane), and sulfur dioxide (very diluted) and their smells classified into sweet, sour, pungent, bitter, burnt, and other categories. Extreme caution must be exercised to train students to smell all substances by wafting gases with their hands from an open container. *Students should never sniff gases directly from the container.* This rule is especially important for pollutants such as sulfur dioxide, nitrogen dioxide, and organic solvents.

From what they have learned about the effects of smog and air pollution, have the students consider what special measures and controls will be necessary to reduce particulate concentrations, for example, sharing transportation, closing down factories, reducing electrical usage. (Recent news stories about inversion problems in Birmingham, Alabama, and New York City should provide ideas.) Have students prepare a list of helpful actions for individuals, industry, and community agencies.

JUNIOR/SENIOR HIGH GRADES—WATER QUALITY

For many Americans, a crisis of water quality is already at hand. Lakes and rivers are in jeopardy or already have been turned into open sewers filled with municipal, industrial, and agricultural wastes. Pollution has closed lakes and rivers in recreational areas where until a few years ago millions of Americans enjoyed swimming, boating, and fishing. Pollution is now threatening to contaminate surface and groundwater sources. Municipalities, agricultural operations, and industries, in some areas, are finding it increasingly difficult to obtain enough water to meet their demands.

The problem of water quantity and availability is difficult for many to comprehend. Three fifths of the earth's surface is covered by water, nature's most abundant natural resource. But what must be realized is that only a fractional portion of the total water supply is available for man's use.

The world's supply of water is contained within the hydrological cycle. About 97% is salt-laden ocean water and thus unavailable for consumption directly by man, animals, or plants. An additional 2% is held in ice caps and glaciers. Only 0.6% of the world's water is in the underground reserves of all continents and only 0.3% is held in the atmosphere.

Some of this water is used in situ (the place where it exists or originates) for recreational fishing and wildlife. The remainder is withdrawn from a source, to be used for agriculture, industries, and municipalities. This withdrawal of water for use can be grouped into two classes, consumptive and nonconsumptive use. Consumptive use refers to those uses of water which make it unavailable to others in the immediate area. Nonconsumptive use means that which does not prevent future utilization. Nonconsumptive use may, however, cause a deterioration in the quality of the water for future users. The major portion of intake or withdrawn water throughout the world is used for nonconsumptive purposes. It has been predicted that by 1980 water demand for all purposes will be 600 billion gallons per day in the United States. In view of increasing demands and the current inefficient utilization of the supply, the demand may very soon exceed the supply. We are now at the point of being forced to prevent and control pollution to guarantee an ample water supply for the future.

The term *pollution* has now been legally defined as the "presence of substances in water in such quantities and of such quality that the water's value to other users is unreasonably impaired." This expanded definition covers the multiple uses of water—not only as drinking water.

Pollution results from both natural and man-centered activities. Some pollution in our streams results from organic matter from plants, animals, and soil, which naturally reaches the stream but can be tolerated easily. The natural purification process—the breakdown of organic pollutants by microorganisms—requires oxygen. The time required for an equilibrium to be reached is commonly referred to as a stream's "recovery time." When an excessive amount of organic material is added to a body of water, the breakdown process results in a rate of dissolved oxygen demand greater than the supply and replenishment rate in the stream, lake, or other body of water. The limited supply of oxygen is thus rapidly depleted, and the decay cycle of the organic matter enters an anaerobic (without oxygen) phase. In the absence of oxygen, the bacterial decay process results in the production of hydrogen sulfide, a noxious gas.

Under these conditions the body of water can soon be considered "dead"—devoid of oxygen and most living things.

The additional wastes polluting the water result from increased population, greater industrial use of water, disposal of complex wastes, and expanded farm irrigation, Among the wastes being dumped into our waters every day are included sewage and other waste waters from cities, industries, and shipping; phosphates and nitrates; pesticides and herbicides; oil; salts; disease-causing bacteria; radioactive wastes; heavy metals; and thermal, or heated, discharges of water.

These wastes have placed serious strains on our waste-treatment systems, as well as on our waterways. Some of the materials can be rendered harmless through conventional treatment, but many are difficult to remove. These materials find their way back into our water system in greater concentrations and continue to pollute water that must be reused. Approximately 80% of the water presently used by humans comes from surface water. This surface water is being polluted at an alarming rate. As a result, the treatment of water is becoming not only increasingly difficult, but also increasingly necessary, to meet minimum standards for reuse.

America's massive clean water program took form with the passage of the Water Quality Act of 1965. The Act is intended "to enhance the quality and value of our water resources and to establish a national policy for the prevention, control, and abatement of water pollution." The clean water program called for states to determine the uses of their water resources. Each stretch of interstate and coastal waters was designated for specific uses such as drinking, recreation, navigation, industry. Any water user must return water to the stream at the highest standard designated for that stream. Once the states had determined uses for water, certain criteria, or limits, were established. These criteria referred to ranges or levels of such substances as dissolved solids, dissolved oxygen, bacteria, and heat sediment that were legally allowed in the water. After the criteria were adopted by the states and approved by the Secretary of the Interior, the standards became federal standards, subject to federal enforcement.

In 1966 the Clean Water Restoration Act authorized appropriations for construction grants to help build sewage-treatment plants, for grants to state water-pollution control programs and for research into estuarine pollution, manpower and training needs, natural costs of pollution control, watercraft pollution, and financial incentives to industry. This Act also specifies that each state must develop plans for improving existing facilities and developing new facilities as needed to achieve and maintain water quality according to the prescribed standards and to prevent pollution of its waterways.

The Water Quality Act of 1965 and the Clean Water Restoration Act of 1966 established the Federal Water Quality Administration in the Department of the Interior as the federal watchdog over water quality. These pieces of legislation are only the beginning of a major effort to combat and control water pollution in the United States. The need today is for nationwide involvement at the local level. It is at the local level where our educational system enters the program against water pollution.

Students may be involved in the environmental struggle by serving as environmental monitors. Our vast national educational system contains great resources for studying and learning about the environment. A network of environmental monitoring stations should be established within this educational system. This network could be of vital assistance to those federal and state agencies that are concerned with building statistical descriptions of environmental resources. Students, organized similarly to the Ground Observer Corps of World War II, could provide statistics, which would then be channeled to state or local public health agencies, county planners, or local governments for appropriate action.

The first step in the introduction of such a program into a classroom is to train students to recognize, monitor, and record information about water pollution problems within their own community. The information they obtain should then be transmitted to the various governmental departments. If the purchase of equipment for such environmental monitoring programs is considered unfeasible for some districts with limited funds, the help of civic organizations and industry should be enlisted. When schools actively seek such support and students participate in the campaign for funds, they readily see how economics, government, community institutions, and education can work together to bring about a world worth living in—a lesson that cannot be gleaned from any textbook.

Surveying the water system

What is a water system? Since water occurs in so many different forms and is conducted from place to place in such a varied manner, the opportunity to study this natural resource is present in nearly all geographical regions.

Whether the local body of water is called a pond, lake, stream, bay, river, bayou, or impoundment, it affords an opportunity for monitoring the effects of natural and man-related processes on the quality of the water.

An efficient way to analyze any of the bodies of water mentioned is by looking at each of them in terms of a systems analysis. Each one has at least one point of water input and one of output, often several of each. By locating and identifying all input and output points and determining those which are of consequence in the purifying or polluting process, a systems diagram for study of the water system can be constructed. This systems diagram will be a schematic plan of the body of water and will serve to locate places of sewage or other input and their relationship to observed conditions at stream-sampling locations.

For the purposes of this manual, the water systems discussed will be bodies of fresh water above the head of high tide. Although most of the activities to be discussed are applicable to brackish, or salt water, areas, there are enough modifying characteristics of salt water, such as high chloride content, to justify the preparation of a salt water supplement to this guide. Therefore any discussion of naturally high salt content waters will be postponed until such a supplement can be made available.

Adoption of a particular water system as the subject of a survey and monitoring program should be based on a consideration of the following items:

1. Geographical proximity of the water system to the school or group headquarters
2. Accessibility of important potential sampling stations
3. Time period available for conducting the study
4. Personnel available to conduct the study
5. Importance of the water systems available for study

Once these points have been discussed and the possible choices have been narrowed to two or three, a field inspection of the alternatives may help to make the final decision as to the site. The time period and personnel available may make it necessary to select a small portion of the entire body of water as the system to be monitored. If this be the case, the section of the stream, river, lake, or other body should be treated as if it were the entire body of water. Input and output quality should be observed and documented, and then monitoring of subsequent changes in these levels of quality should be correlated with the analysis of effluent discharge into the system.

Defining the system. Regardless of the type of water system chosen, there is a standard procedure for preparing the systems diagram that will be the basis of the study program.

First obtain any maps or charts available for the particular body of water under study. These may be obtained from local, county, and state offices or from the U. S. Department of Coast and Geodetic Survey. These maps will help locate important input, output, and modification points on the water system.

Locate the major input of the water system, either the actual water source or any convenient starting point along the body of water. Locate this point on your systems diagram and label it Station 1. Use arrows to indicate the direction of flow. (See Fig. 3-11.)

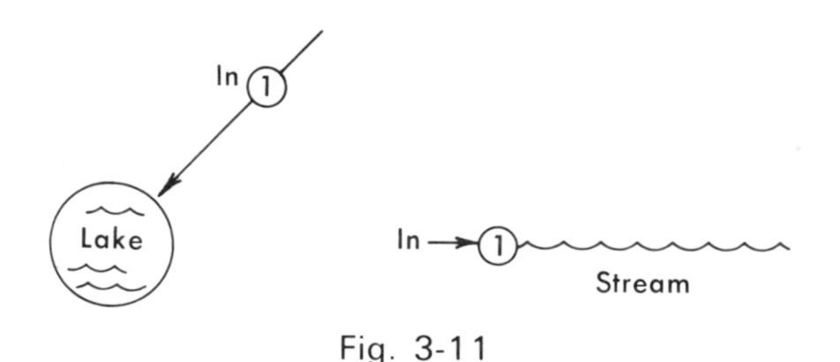

Fig. 3-11

Locate the major output point, either the mouth of the body of water or an arbitrarily established point for the water study. Locate this point on your diagram but do not assign a numerical label as yet. (See Fig. 3-12.)

The next step is to locate on the diagram all other input and output points of importance, especially effluent inputs and areas of water removal for various uses. Label all inputs and outputs. Assign numerical labels. (See Fig. 3-13.) Select repre-

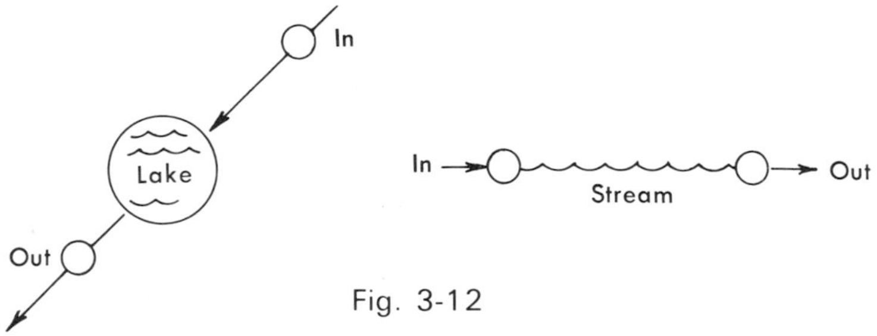

Fig. 3-12

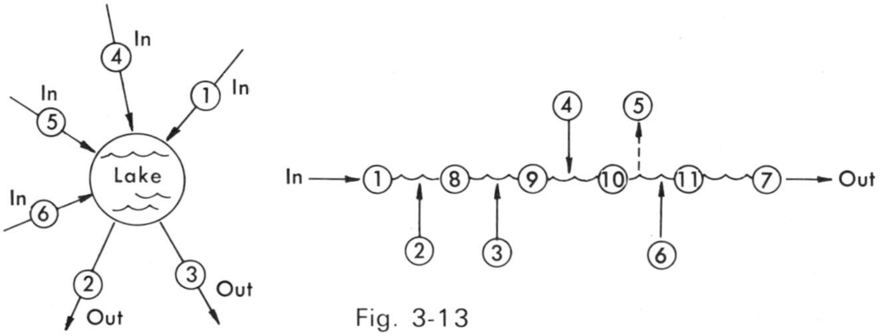

Fig. 3-13

sentative sampling stations and follow the same procedure.

Prepare a descriptive list of the stations selected, with station locations noted as precisely as possible. Although in certain situations the input of direct rainfall and the output of evaporation may be of importance, in general these may be neglected in the preparation of the systems diagram.

It will usually be of value to prepare a large-scale map that parallels the systems diagram and relates the schematic systems diagram to the actual geographical setting.

Planning the survey. To conduct a field study of a given water system effectively, a judicious amount of planning is necessary. The plan developed should provide adequately for (1) defining the objectives of the study, (2) researching available records, and (3) preparing for the logistics of the study. Let us consider each of these topics briefly.

Defining the objectives. Before the initiation of a plan of study, the general objectives of that study should be decided on and listed.

Following are some sample objectives:

1. Ascertaining the natural condition of the water system in the absence of pollutants
2. Obtaining information that will aid in the selection of appropriate measures needed to protect the quality of the water system for legitimate uses
3. Determining the effects of present levels of waste discharge on water-system quality
4. Identifying possible polluters and obtaining evidence useful in pressing for pollution abatement

Researching available records. Once you have obtained the maps suggested for preparation of the system diagram, a research team should be charged with the task of obtaining any other printed material bearing on the water system under study. This group should also be given the assignment of acquiring data on waste-treatment processes in effect, legal criteria established for the water system, and any or all plans for the future development of the water resource.

Preparing for the logistics of the study. Once the form of the survey has been decided on and the remainder of this or a similar manual has been read to ascertain necessary equipment and procedures to be used in the survey, an equipment list should be prepared. Equipment ought to be gathered and checked to make sure all necessary items are in place. Personnel should be instructed in the objectives and plan of the survey, and each person involved should be instructed as to his exact assignment. A team needs to be chosen to perform the chemical determinations of water samples. This will be the "laboratory crew." Transportation for personnel and equipment should be obtained. Laboratory crews should be alerted to receive samples and perform necessary laboratory determinations. The crew should be instructed as to the amount of work load to be expected, so that they may make necessary preparations.

1. Make preparations.
2. Double-check preparations.
3. Conduct the survey.

Conducting the survey. Survey procedures should be based on American Public Health Association (A.P.H.A.) standard methods and follow the general outline suggested here.

1. Stream samples should be taken above and below each major source of waste input and at each point of water use.
2. Tests to be made can be selected from those listed on pp. 116 and 117.
3. Sampling methods should be those recommended later in this chapter.
4. All samples should be labeled immediately and accurate records kept.
5. Before initiation of the survey, a team should be appointed to accept all data and to prepare a report on the survey.

Reporting the results of the survey. Results

obtained from the various tests conducted should be plotted on graphs to a convenient scale as soon as the laboratory analysis is completed. By plotting concentration levels of selected constituents against a lengthwise enumeration of sampling stations, one can obtain a simplified portrayal of water-system quality. This type of visual display will provide a dramatic presentation of data, which can be interpreted easily.

Polaroid photographs can serve to depict clearly conditions extant at the various stations.

A preliminary water-system survey should include at least the following information:

1. Description of water system
2. Diagram of water system
3. List of sampling stations
4. Description of survey procedure
5. Results of survey
6. Conclusions and recommendations for further study

Other data, such as process and treatment-plant information, should be appended to this report. For further information, consult the sections on recording and reporting later in this chapter.

Using the survey as a guide for routine monitoring. Once the survey has been completed and a report has been prepared, the school or other group can begin to plan for a continuing program to monitor water-system quality against possible deterioration from careless use.

An environmental monitoring station can be established, permanent stream stations set up, and a regular sampling schedule maintained. Sampling stations should be chosen in accordance with the results of the preliminary survey and the principles enumerated in the discussion on selection of sampling stations (pp. 124 and 125). Frequent reports should be prepared. The assistance of interested citizens and groups ought to be solicited and technical help sought from available governmental agencies.

The study of water quality achieves its maximum value only when the information obtained is put to use in a continuing program for the prevention or abatement of pollution of water resources.

Tests for water quality

For comprehensive analysis of typical water or waste-water samples, tests indicated in section A of the following outline should be routinely conducted. *The tests for temperature, pH, dissolved oxygen, and hydrogen sulfide should be made in the field at the sampling station.* All other listed determinations may be performed in the laboratory.

Depending on the results of the preliminary survey, the students may need to test routinely for such materials as chlorine, copper, sulfates, and detergents. Two tests that should be conducted if laboratory facilities and necessary equipment are available are coliform bacteria counts and biochemical oxygen demand (BOD). Detailed discussion of these analyses can be found in *Environmental Science Laboratory Manual** and *Standard Methods for the Examination of Water and Waste Water.*†

For recommended concentration limits for the various contaminants of water, see "Desirable Criteria for Fresh Water Supplies" in the Appendix to this chapter or consult the Drinking Water Standards of the United States Public Health Service.

A. Suggested determinations
   1. Temperature
   2. Odor
   3. pH
   4. Dissolved oxygen
   5. Chloride
   6. Hydrogen sulfide

---

*Strobbe, Maurice A.: Environmental science laboratory manual, St. Louis, 1972, The C. V. Mosby Co.

†Standard methods for the examination of water and waste water, New York, 1965, American Public Health Association.

7. Phosphate
8. Nitrite
9. Nitrate
10. Total hardness

B. Other desirable determinations
1. Coliform colony count
2. Chlorine
3. Biochemical oxygen demand
4. Sulfate
5. Detergents

C. Possible additional tests
1. Color
2. Turbidity
3. Ammonia
4. Arsenic
5. Boron
6. Cadmium
7. Chromium, hexavalent
8. Copper
9. Fluoride
10. Lead
11. Manganese
12. Mercury
13. Silver
14. Uranyl ion
15. Zinc
16. Carbon chloroform extract
17. Cyanide
18. Methylene blue–active substance
19. Oil and grease
20. Pesticides
21. Herbicides
22. Phenols
23. Radioactivity

Detailed procedures for these tests can also be found in *Environmental Science Laboratory Manual,* and *Standard Methods for the Examination of Water and Waste Water.*

Supplies and equipment to perform the various determinations suggested may be obtained from a variety of distributors and manufacturers:

Hach Chemical Co.
P. O. Box 907
Ames, Iowa 50010
LaMotte Chemical Products Co.
Chestertown, Md. 21620
Millipore Corp.
Bedford, Mass. 01730

Consult their catalogues for available equipment and supplies. Whenever possible, select procedures that minimize handling of dangerous liquid chemical reagents such as concentrated sulfuric acid and sodium hydroxide. A self-contained, plastic-enclosed coliform testing unit is now available from the Millipore Corporation. The unit, called the Coli-count water tester, catalog No. MC-00-000-24, is used *without* sterilization procedures.

Temperature

Significance. The temperature of a particular sample from a water system, measured at the site, will provide useful data only when compared with the air temperature, water temperatures of surrounding areas, and the temperature of any effluent being discharged into the water system.

The temperature of the water will have a direct effect on its capacity to retain certain gases, on the chemical reactions taking place, and on biological and bacteriological activities. Perhaps the most significant effect of temperature is on the ability of the water to retain dissolved oxygen at 100% saturation. At low temperatures the dissolved oxygen (D.O.) level in parts per million at 100% saturation is high; at high temperatures D.O. value at saturation is reduced (approximately 8 ppm). This relationship between temperatures and dissolved oxygen may, for example, determine the number and species of fish in a given area.

Aside from the aforementioned relationships, the most important discovery that can result from temperature sampling of a water system is an indication of the possibility of thermal pollution. This thermal discharge can be highly detrimental to the aquatic life present in the water system and can add to an already existing pollution load.

Temperature should be recorded and reported in degrees centigrade if possible. Temperature graphs may be plotted and unusual situations then subjected to further analysis.

TABLE 1. Fahrenheit to centigrade conversion

DEGREES FAHRENHEIT	DEGREES CENTIGRADE	DEGREES FAHRENHEIT	DEGREES CENTIGRADE
30	−1.11	61	16.11
31	−0.56	62	16.67
32	0.00	63	17.22
33	0.56	64	17.78
34	1.11	65	18.33
35	1.67	66	18.89
36	2.22	67	19.44
37	2.78	68	20.00
38	3.33	69	20.56
39	3.89	70	21.11
40	4.44	71	21.67
41	5.00	72	22.22
42	5.56	73	22.78
43	6.11	74	23.33
44	6.67	75	23.89
45	7.22	76	24.44
46	7.78	77	25.00
47	8.33	78	25.56
48	8.89	79	26.11
49	9.44	80	26.67
50	10.00	81	27.22
51	10.56	82	27.78
52	11.11	83	28.33
53	11.67	84	28.89
54	12.22	85	29.44
55	12.78	86	30.00
56	13.33	87	30.56
57	13.89	88	31.11
58	14.44	89	31.67
59	15.00	90	32.22
60	15.56		

Procedure. Temperature readings may be obtained by two methods: (1) measurement in the water system at the sampling site and (2) measurement in the sample bottle immediately after sampling. Of the two, the first is the recommended "standard" method. Immerse the thermometer at an appropriate depth in the flowing water long enough to obtain a constant reading, then raise the thermometer to the surface and read immediately. Of course, this technique is applicable only at the surface or in shallow water.

For making readings under other circumstances, more complex equipment (for example, a recording thermometer) is required and instructions for use are usually furnished with the equipment.

Readings should be made with a good centigrade thermometer and results recorded as precisely as possible. Avoid rough handling of the thermometer, since breakage occurs readily. Temperature readings should be taken regularly with each sample.

If a Fahrenheit thermometer must be utilized,

TABLE 2. Odor—qualitative descriptions*

CODE	DESCRIPTION
A	Spicy odor
Ac	Cucumber-like odor
B	Flowery
Bg	Geranium-like odor
Bn	Nasturtium-like odor
Bs	Sweetish
Bv	Violet-like odor
C	Industrial or chemical smell
Ce	Chlorine
Ch	Petroleum odor
Cm	Medicinal odor
Cs	Rotten eggs—hydrogen sulfide
D	Disagreeable
Df	Fishy odor
Dp	Pigpen smell
Ds	Sewage odor
E	Damp earth
Ep	Peaty odor
G	Grasslike odor
M	Rotting straw
Mm	Moldy—damp cellar
V	Root vegetable odor

*Adapted from Standard methods for the examination of water and waste water, New York, 1965, American Public Health Association.

Table 1 will provide convenient conversions to centigrade temperatures.

Odor

Significance. Disagreeable odors in water are frequently the result of decaying organic matter, decomposition of sewage or industrial waste, or by-products of the life processes of certain microscopic organisms.

The tests for odor are highly subjective in nature and therefore lack scientific precision. However, they serve to identify some types of possible pollution or contamination and thus are included.

Procedure. Odor tests should be conducted as soon as possible after the sample has been obtained. Many odors are due to dissolved gases, which will be lost as the sample ages.

The sample should be obtained in a 60 milliliter (ml.) glass-stoppered bottle. Fill to the 30 ml. mark. The sample should be collected according to the methods enumerated in the section on sampling methods, pp. 125 to 127. If it is necessary to store the sample, it should be refrigerated in an odorless area. Plastic containers should not be used to store samples for odor testing.

TABLE 3. Odor—quantitative descriptions*

NUMERICAL VALUE	TERM	DEFINITION
0	None	No odor perceptible
1	Very faint	Odor that would not be detected ordinarily by average consumer, but that could be detected in laboratory by experienced observer
2	Faint	Odor that consumer might detect if his attention were called to it, but that would not otherwise attract attention
3	Distinct	Odor that would be detected readily and that might cause water to be regarded with disfavor
4	Decided	Odor that would force itself on one's attention and that might make water unpalatable
5	Very strong	Odor of such intensity that water would be unfit to drink (term to be used only in extreme cases)

*From Manual of instruction for water treatment plant operators, Albany, N. Y., New York State Department of Health.

To obtain a qualitative description of the odor of the sample, remove the glass stopper from the bottle after first shaking the sample. Sniff the odor lightly. Record the code letters from Table 2 that best describe the odor noted. For most reliable results, sample should be at a temperature of approximately 20° C. or 68° F.

pH

Significance. The term *pH* is used to describe the instantaneous hydrogen ion activity in a given water sample. This value may also be interpreted as an indication of the balance between acids and and alkalies in the sample. The pH scale ranges from 0 to 14, a value of 7.0 being neutral. Readings below 7.0 are acidic, whereas those above 7.0 are alkaline solutions.

Natural values of pH in fresh-water systems are commonly in the range from 5.5 to 8.0, whereas the pH of ocean water is usually around 8.0 and is slightly alkaline. Pollution from various sources may extend these ranges, with lows of around 2.0 occurring in acid mine drainage and highs of 9.0 to 10.0 in alkaline discharge areas. The pH value is readily responsive to changes in water quality and, as such, is an excellent indicator of possible water pollution.

Procedure. Since pH may change significantly in a matter of a few moments as a result of chemical and biological processes in the sample, this test should be performed in the field as soon after sampling as possible.

Decant a portion of a well-mixed water sample into a test tube. Using a wide-range pH indicator paper, immerse a piece of the indicator paper in the sample. Observe the color change and within 30 seconds compare the color of the test paper with the color chart supplied with the paper. Record the pH value of the sample.

Repeat the same procedure with a short-range paper encompassing the value obtained in the first test. Record the result as accurately as possible.

Various chemical indicators and electrometric instruments are available that will further increase the accuracy obtained in this test. Consult equipment catalogs for additional information.

Note: For the sake of safety and convenience, we recommend that the following chemical analyses be carried out with dry reagents. Such materials are available in premeasured, prepackaged form from Hach Chemical Company, Ames, Iowa. The reagents are marketed as kits and are particularly convenient and appropriate for student use. (Somewhat comparable materials can now also be obtained from LaMotte Chemical Products Company, Chestertown, Maryland.) Instructions for these analyses are included with the kits and are further detailed in Strobbe's *Environmental Science Laboratory Manual.*

Dissolved oxygen

Significance. The atmosphere that we breathe and that comes into repeated contact with our water resources contains approximately 21% oxygen by volume. Some of this oxygen is absorbed by the water supply in a process called aeration and can be measured by test as ppm D.O., or parts per million dissolved oxygen. Adequate dissolved oxygen levels are necessary for the maintenance of a normal aquatic ecosystem, and any effluent that lessens D.O. available may drastically reduce chances of fish survival.

Dissolved oxygen measurements are routinely made in all water-quality surveillance programs and should be part of the analysis of each series of water samples. Graphs of D.O. values, when properly correlated with temperature conditions, can be of utmost importance in documenting instances of water-quality degradation. Dissolved oxygen is the only test universally listed in all water-quality criteria, federal, state, and local.

Dissolved oxygen levels are inversely related to water temperature levels, that is, high temperatures generally mean low D.O. values, whereas

TABLE 4. Approximate 100% saturation values for dissolved oxygen at sea level*

TEMPERATURE (°C.)	DISSOLVED OXYGEN (ppm)
0	14.6
1	14.2
2	13.8
3	13.4
4	13.2
5	12.8
6	12.4
7	12.2
8	11.8
9	11.6
10	11.4
11	11.0
12	10.8
13	10.6
14	10.4
15	10.2
16	10.0
17	9.8
18	9.6
19	9.4
20	9.2
21	9.0
22	8.8
23	8.6
24	8.5
25	8.4
26	8.2
27	8.0
28	7.9
29	7.9
30	7.6

*Computed from Rawson's Nomogram to the nearest 0.2 ppm where possible.

levels of D.O. at low water temperatures usually are 11 to 12 ppm in unpolluted waters. D.O. values of 3 to 5 ppm are generally considered to be the lowest limit that will permit survival of fish over an extended period of time. Refer to Table 4 for 100% saturation values for D.O. at various water temperatures.

Notes on procedure. Since oxygen reactions continue to occur in the sample bottle, it is imperative that the sampling procedure outlined in sampling methods on pp. 125 to 127 should be rigidly adhered to.

Whenever possible, D.O. determinations should be carried out in the field. If not, the sample should be fixed in the field for later determination in the laboratory. "Fixing" is the addition of chemical reagents to stop all oxygen reactions in the sample. See instructions supplied with reagents for further information.

It is suggested that the high range test be carried out first. This test gives readings to the next highest ppm. For low D.O. levels or high accuracy the low range test may be used.

Other chemical and electrometric methods for obtaining D.O. values may be found in the science equipment catalogs in the APHA's *Standard Methods.*

Chloride

Significance. Chloride concentration in water systems is a measure of the presence of the dissolved salts: sodium chloride, magnesium chloride, calcium chloride, and others. Water with a moderately high chloride concentration (250 ppm) may or may not taste salty, depending on which metallic salt composes the majority of the chloride compounds present. Most public water supplies in the United States obtained from surface water sources have a chloride concentration of less than 25 ppm. The U. S. Public Health Service has set 250 ppm as the recommended limit for chloride in public water supplies.

Since chloride passes through the human system unchanged, it is to be expected that discharges from municipal waste-treatment plants would tend to be high in chloride content as compared to the normal water supply in the area under study. This will be demonstrated easily in any sampling series above and below such effluent discharge points. This property of chloride then makes it a very useful indicator for tracing such wastewater through the water system. High chloride content is detrimental to metal pipes and is an important factor in the corrosiveness of water.

Notes on procedure. Chloride concentration is usually measured by titration of a prepared sample with a silver nitrate solution. Begin the analysis with a low range test and move to the high range if the concentration of chloride requires an excessive amount of reagent.

For the low range test, one drop of indicator solution equals approximately 7.6 ppm of chloride. Other methods are fully discussed in the APHA *Standard Methods* and similar works.

Hydrogen sulfide

Significance. Hydrogen sulfide (H_2S) occurs in some water systems as a result of the decomposition of wastes by bacteria at low oxygen levels. This anaerobic decomposition results in the liberation of a gas having the characteristic "rotten egg" odor of H_2S. Hydrogen sulfide should not be present in water of good quality, and any indication of its presence signifies potential pollution.

Notes on procedure. Since hydrogen sulfide is a dissolved gas, the test for its presence should be performed in the field as soon as possible after sampling. Avoid aerating sample. See p. 126 for sampling methods for dissolved gases.

Phosphate

Significance. Phosphorus, in the form of phosphate, is one of the primary nutrients and is essential for the growth of plants and animals. Its importance in water-quality measurements is due to its action as a fertilizer in promoting algal blooms and the attendant difficulty of reducing its concentration in water to a desirable level.

Phosphates may enter water systems from direct contact with high-phosphate soils, from agricultural runoff of phosphate fertilizers, from organic wastes, and from phosphate-based detergents.

Phosphate-based detergents are the major contributor of phosphate to water supply systems. Phosphate concentration will be found to be very high in domestic wastewater and some industrial effluents. Graphs of phosphate levels along a stream will dramatically pinpoint pollution problems from such sources.

Most natural waters contain 0.01 to 0.05 ppm of phosphate during periods of significant productivity. The average concentration in weak wastewater is 5 ppm; in medium-strength wastewater, 15 ppm; and in strong wastewater, 30 ppm. Certain types of tertiary treatment of domestic wastewater can significantly reduce phosphate concentration but are seldom utilized because of expense to the communities involved for the purchase of necessary chemicals.

Substitutes for phosphates in detergents are being actively sought currently, and research may provide an effective laundering substitute for this powerful polluter. The majority of communities utilize a primary treatment of sewage wastes. This treatment removes the material that floats or will settle out in sewage. Screens catch the heavy matter and filter it out, whereas settling tanks accumulate the material that will settle. The effluent is usually chlorinated to kill infectious germs.

Few communities employ a secondary treatment, in which bacteria consume the organic parts of the wastes. This is accomplished by bringing the sewage and bacteria together in trickling filters or in an activated sludge process.

Tertiary treatment is the utilization of additional chemical or electrochemical processes to purify further the effluent from a secondary treatment stage. These processes may effectively remove up to 98% of the organic matter present in the effluent plus some chemicals such as salts and phosphates.

Notes on procedure. Testing should begin with the lowest range test, moving to the next dilution range only if the color produced is too intense to be measured accurately. Phosphate and most other determinations should be made within 12 hours of sampling, if possible, since phosphate may assume various forms as a result of chemical study, and some of these forms are not measurable by the recommended method.

Nitrite

Significance. Water containing nitrogen in the nitrite state (NO_2^-) is the result of an intermediate step in the complex decomposition by bacteria of wastes containing organic nitrogen. Ammonia compounds are transformed by these bacteria under aerated conditions into nitrites. Under unaerated conditions, bacteria may also reduce nitrates to nitrites.

Nitrite concentration in unpolluted surface water is usually very low. Presence of significant quantities of nitrite may indicate possible contamination of the water supply by wastewater sources.

High nitrite concentration in drinking water may cause death from a reaction called methemoglobinemia, a condition that interferes with the ability of blood to carry oxygen.

In high-quality water, nitrite should be virtually absent, but whenever high concentrations of nitrate are detected in polluted water, some nitrite will also be found.

Notes on procedure. If more than a trace amount of nitrite is present, it will be necessary to dilute the sample volume with demineralized water. The following dilution volumes and corresponding dilution factors would then be in effect:

RANGE	SAMPLE VOLUME	TO OBTAIN NITRITE, MULTIPLY SCALE READING BY:
0-0.3 ppm	5 ml.	0.003
0-3 ppm	0.5 ml.	0.03
0-30 ppm	0.05 ml.	0.3

Note: Test results with the recommended kit are obtained in ppm of nitrite-nitrogen (N). To convert results to ppm of nitrite (NO_2), multiply test results by 3.3 and record as ppm of NO_2.

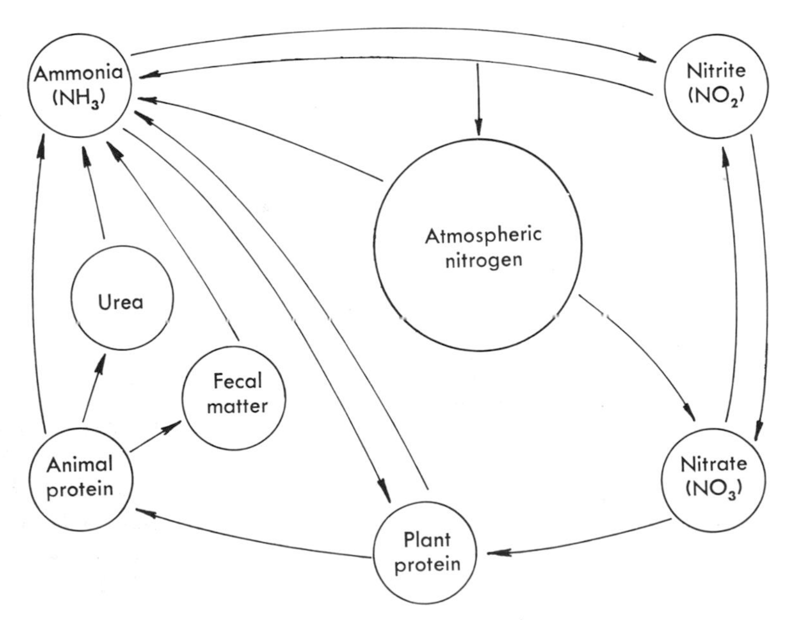

Fig. 3-14. Nitrogen cycle.

Nitrate

Significance. Nitrate occurs in water systems as a product of the bacteriological oxidation process of nitrites. It may also be present because of runoff from agricultural areas that have been treated with nitrate-rich fertilizer. Electrical storms in the atmosphere convert significant amounts of atmospheric nitrogen to nitrate (NO_3^-).

Nitrate is a nutrient in water and, with phosphorus, contributes to excessive algal growth, which in turn clogs streams and lakes and hampers recovery of the water system from pollution loads.

Nitrate, nitritc, and ammonia are forms resulting from oxidation and reduction processes involving atmospheric nitrogen. They comprise the interrelationship referred to as the nitrogen cycle, a simplified version of which is shown in Fig. 3-14.

High nitrate levels are especially dangerous in drinking water that is to be consumed by infants. Infants' stomachs are not highly acidic and, as such, may permit bacterial reduction of nitrate to nitrite, causing methemoglobinemia. (See nitrite as previously discussed.)

Notes on procedure. Samples to be tested for nitrate concentration may be collected in the usual manner. If, however, it will not be possible to analyze them promptly on return to the laboratory, it is necessary to take precautions to retard biological activity within the sample bottle. Two methods are suggested. If no test for detergents is to be performed on the sample, the addition of 1 ml. of chloroform per 100 ml. of sample to the sample bottle prior to the introduction of the water sample should suffice to inhibit biological processes. If a detergent test involving chloroform extraction is to be made, an alternative method of sample preservation is to freeze the sample.

The recommended test kit determines nitrate- and/or nitrite-nitrogen (as N). To obtain only ppm of nitrate-nitrogen (as N), one must subtract the result of the nitrite test from the total obtained in the nitrate test. To express results as ppm of nitrate, multiply results by 4.4 and record as ppm of NO_3^-.

Total hardness

Significance. Hardness of water is a measure of the presence of ions of calcium and magnesium in the water sample. It may also be defined in terms of the ability of the water to use up soap. Water of high quality usually has a hardness level of less than 250 ppm. The primary significance of water hardness is in its effect on the economics of water use. Water supplies of an extreme hardness level are unsuitable for many industrial and domestic purposes, and such water must undergo a softening treatment prior to use.

Quantitative range descriptions of relative hardness are as follows:

0-60 ppm	Soft water
61-120 ppm	Moderately hard water
121-180 ppm	Hard water
Above 180 ppm	Extremely hard water

Water with a hardness level of above 120 ppm (such as calcium carbonate) is usually subjected to treatment to reduce this level before use. The determination of excessive hardness is especially important in water to be used for laundry purposes.

Notes on procedure. Water hardness levels may be measured by a simple drop-count titration process with an accuracy of plus (+) or minus (−) 5%, using the Hach Chemical Company equipment. Instructions are supplied with the equipment, and tests are simple and straightforward. Results are obtained in grains per gallon. Multiply the result by 17.1 to report as parts per million (EDTA).

Selection of sampling stations

Type, location, and number of stations. In general, sampling stations should be selected according to the following considerations: stream stations, input stations, and output stations.

Stream stations. A station should be at the initial input of the stream, at the mouth or output point of the stream, above and below each major effluent input, and at such other points as may be indicative of the quality change of certain stream sections. Such natural landmarks as bridges, major landforms, and confluence points will also indicate possibilities for the location of sampling stations.

The number of stations to be established will be subject to such variables as the number of man-hours available, length of the water system under study, important areas of water use, sources of pollution, available equipment, laboratory resources, and other factors judged important to the success of the program.

Choose stations that are both accessible to the survey team and indicative of the quality of the stream.

These criteria are equally valid for stations in lakes and ponds, although it will be necessary in such cases to make current determinations to establish the direction of flow.

Input stations. Any source of additional streamflow shall be considered an input station. Following are the two major types of inputs:

1. Feeder streams: Small branches of the watercourse. They may be sampled prior to confluence with the main watercourse. Any evidence of low quality would indicate the necessity of additional stations along such a feeder, until the source of pollution is noted.
2. Effluent stations: Any outfall pipe or similar device that allows treated or untreated effluent from any source to flow into the water system should be a sampling point. Obtain the sample prior to its mixing with the main water system.

Output stations. Any location where water is withdrawn for use should be considered in choosing the location of sampling stations. Obtain the sample at the point of withdrawal.

Evaporation and precipitation. The input from rainfall into the system may usually be ignored in considering the system as a whole. However, certain subsystems such as extremely shallow bodies of water may indicate the need for establishment of stations to measure precipitation and evaporation. In such a case, consult the literature of the field of hydrology for methods of making such measurements.

Indications of preliminary survey. When selecting sites for and number of stations for a monitoring program, it would be wise to consult the results of your preliminary water-quality survey to assist in selecting those stations that appear to yield the most indicative data with the least expenditure of effort.

Stations that were shown to reveal little meaningful increase in useful data should be discontinued, and the position of other stations should be shifted or left intact as indicated by the survey results.

Response to changing conditions. Because of the ever-increasing pressure on our water systems resulting from new residential and industrial development, it may be occasionally necessary to revise or expand the number and/or location of monitoring stations. To assist in making such decisions, regular comprehensive water-quality survey reports should be prepared as often as possible for the monitoring program. These reports, then, can be consulted for possible recommendations.

Sampling methods

General sampling notes. Although some determinations require unusual methods in their handling and collection, the following discussion will prove to be of value in deciding on a standardized sampling procedure.

Labelling of samples. All samples should be labelled immediately on collection, and pertinent data should be permanently logged on the appropriate record sheet. It is advisable to collect all samples in a collecting bottle inscribed with a code number, which can be referred to on the data sheet. The collecting bottle may be of glass or plastic, depending on the chemical test being conducted. (See instructions for the various types of samples, as described previously.) The identifying code number should be written in indelible ink. Waterproof felt pens are suggested for marking plastic bottles.

Sample volume. For most purposes a sample volume of 500 ml., or approximately 1 pint, should be sufficient.

Preservation of samples. All determinations should be made as soon as possible after collection of the sample. Samples for dissolved gas determination should either be field tested or field fixed. (See the procedure for dissolved oxygen, pp. 120 and 121.) If more than 12 hours will pass before analysis of general chemical samples can be made, it is desirable either to refrigerate the sample at a low temperature to retard biological activity or to suppress such activity by the addition, prior to sampling, of 1 ml. of chloroform per 100 ml. of sample. Do not add chloroform to bacteriological or detergent samples, since this substance will interfere with the test procedures.

Sample temperatures should be raised to the range of 20° to 27° C. before tests are conducted.

Compositing samples. For sampling stations at which there is little mixing, it may be necessary to sample a cross section of the stream and to composite the sample for chemical determinations. Sampling the four quadrants around the station will also assist in ensuring representative samples.

The following discussion includes additional compositing techniques.

Stream samples. Wherever possible, stream samples should be taken in a thoroughly mixed section of the water system at each station. To obtain samples, the following procedures are recommended: general chemical samples, dissolved gas samples, bacteriological samples, effluent samples, sewage wastes, and industrial wastes.

General chemical samples. Rinse a plastic collecting bottle two or three times with the water to be collected. This lessens the possibility of contamination from previous samples. Lower the sample bottle into the water with the neck of the bottle facing the direction of streamflow, allow the water to fill the bottle and flow over it for a short period of time, place the cap on the bottle, and remove from the water. Refrigerate if necessary for preservation.

Dissolved gas samples. Rinse a 60 ml. glass-stoppered bottle two or three times with the water to be tested. Obtain sample as before. Insert the glass stopper underwater, taking care to avoid entrapping air bubbles. Remove from water. Fix sample immediately by following instructions in appropriate test kit.

Bacteriological samples. Coliform tests should be initiated at the sampling stations by filling the MPN presumptive test tube under the surface of the water. A test tube holder may be used to avoid contact with possibly polluted water. Incubate sample immediately. If Millipore filters and equipment are available, the direct colony count is more feasible. Instructions for these tests may be found in Strobbe's *Environmental Science Laboratory Manual.*

Effluent samples. Since most effluent-producing processes vary according to time, it will often be necessary to take special precautions to ensure representative samples from these sources.

Sewage wastes. Sampling should be conducted round the clock for a 24-hour period, to ascertain the variation in effluent constituents and flow rate. To obtain a sample, place the appropriate sample bottle under a discharge pipe, allowing the effluent to fill the bottle and overflow for 2 or 3 minutes. It may be desirable to wear rubber gloves during this operation, to prevent contact with possibly contaminated water.

Industrial wastes. Industrial wastes vary according to the process cycle followed. Either a 24-hour or a compositing technique may be used, with the assistance of a process description, if obtainable. Collection techniques are the same as for sewage wastes.

• • •

Remember that the object of any sampling method is to secure a water sample indicative of the quality of the water system at a particular location and at a particular time. Any technique that ensures such representative samples is acceptable.

Recording data

Importance of accurate recording. Even the gathering of veritable mountains of raw data would have little meaning to most people if the results obtained were not digested into some form of report. The first step in the preparation of such a report is the accurate recording of all data obtained in both field and laboratory studies.

Immediate recording of such data will ensure that the memory of the observer does not substitute figures with the passage of time.

The degree of accuracy required in the various tests is dependent on the ultimate objectives of the proposed water-quality study program. For a research program designed to establish records of the present condition of a water system, a high degree of accuracy is required, and the highest possible care should be taken in reading instruments and recording results. For a general monitoring survey of a stream with the intent to point out possible pollution sources, it is not quite so important to record precise absolute values. Instead, it may be sufficient to record whether or not a certain maximum concentration is being exceeded.

Strive to record as many significant figures as possible, while keeping in mind the purpose of the study and the percentage of possible error in the particular test being conducted.

General instructions for data recording. In general, data obtained should be recorded in the following manner:

1. Immediately and on suitably prepared forms, which are bound into a permanent or semipermanent cover.
2. In ink, except when recording under field conditions, when pencil should be used to avoid the possibility of losing records by the contact of ink with water.
3. Legibly, concisely, and permanently. Draw a diagonal line through errors. Do not erase! You may discover it was not an error after all.
4. Completely, including all items that serve to amplify, delimit, or define the readings obtained. Identification codes or numbers for samples, sampling stations, sampling bottles, and the like should always be listed.
5. Scientifically, using metric and centigrade measurements whenever possible. Data obtained in other systems of measurement should be converted to metric or centigrade equivalents or both.

Data recording should be done by a person designated as the recorder for the survey team. All data should be given to the recorder as soon as it is obtained.

Methods of recording. Two useful methods for recording both field and laboratory data are described in the following sections. Both methods are in keeping with the suggestions in the preceding discussion.

Water-Quality Data Sheet. A Water-Quality Data Sheet such as the accompanying sample will be of value in reducing the amount of time spent on record keeping and transferral of data from field notes to permanent records. This form may be used for determinations carried out in the field. The Water-Quality Data Sheet may then be returned to the laboratory for completion of remaining analyses and finally filed in an area where it is readily available for further reference.

WATER-QUALITY DATA SHEET

Environmental monitoring station ______________________________

Reporter ______________________

Water system ______________________ Location ______________________

Station No. ____________ Sample No. ____________ Bottle No. ____________

Sampling station location ______________________________

Date ______________ Time ______________ Depth ______________

Flow level: High ____________ Intermediate ____________ Low ____________

1. Temperature: Water ______ Air ______
2. Odor: Code ______________
3. pH ______________
4. Dissolved oxygen ____________ ppm
5. Chloride ____________ ppm
6. Hydrogen sulfide ________ ppm
7. Orthophosphate ________ ppm
8. Nitrite ________ ppm
9. Nitrate ________ ppm ______
10. Total hardness ________ ppm ______

Visible pollutants: 11. (In sample) ______________________________

12. (At site) ______________________________

Other tests: 13. Coliform count or MPN value ______________________ /100ml.

14. Biochemical oxygen demand ______________________ ppm

15. ______________________________

16. ______________________________

17. ______________________________

18. ______________________________

19. ______________________________

20. ______________________________

Under no circumstances should a completed data sheet be mailed, carried, or otherwise removed from the data file area. If copies are desired, they can be made by a photocopy or similar process to ensure accurate reproduction of the original data. Copies thus produced may be made available to persons or agencies interested in reports on the quality of individual water samples.

The Water-Quality Data Sheet is designed to record information that will provide a meaningful indication of the quality of a particular water sample, obtained from either stream or effluent sampling stations. A separate data sheet must be completed for each sample collected.

The blanks on the Water-Quality Data Sheet should be filled in as follows:

Environmental monitoring station: List the name of the school, club, or other organization sponsoring the water-quality study.

Reporter: Fill in the name of the person actually completing the data sheet.

Water system: Give the proper name of the water source being studied.

Location: List the city, county, or other governmental subdivision in which the water system is located.

Station No.: List the code number or letter assigned to the sampling station where this sample was collected.

Bottle No.: Sample bottles should be numbered consecutively, beginning with *1* and indelibly marked with the assigned number. List the number of the bottle used to collect this sample.

Sampling station location: Provide an exact geographical description of the location. Use latitude and longitude if possible. Consult geological survey maps for this information.

Date: Record the date of sampling.

Time: Record the local time, using 24-hour system. List the time zone. For example, 1:52 P.M. eastern standard time would be recorded as 1352 EST.

Depth: Record the depth from which the sample was obtained. If the sample was obtained at the surface of the water, write *surface* in the space.

Flow level: This parameter may be recorded quantitatively in cubic feet per second, gallons per minute, or in a convenient metric unit. A qualitative measurement may be recorded simply by placing a check mark in the appropriate space.

Temperature: List both water and air temperatures in degrees centigrade.

Odor: Record the most appropriate odor code from Tables 2 and 3 on p. 119.

pH: Record pH units as accurately as possible.

Dissolved oxygen: Record the test results in parts per million D.O.

Chloride: List the result of chloride determination in ppm of chloride, after first taking into account any necessary conversion factors.

Hydrogen sulfide: Record the result obtained from the test to the nearest tenth of a part per million.

Orthophosphate: List the results in parts per million.

Nitrite: Record the results of the test in parts per million. Specify whether the unit is ppm of N or ppm of NO_2.

Nitrate: Record the results in ppm of nitrate nitrogen (N) or ppm of nitrate (NO_3). Specify which recording unit is used. If the test measured nitrates plus nitrites, do not forget to subtract the nitrite value obtained in the previous test.

Total hardness: Give the result in parts per million by the EDTA method or in ppm of $CaCO_3$.

Visible pollutants:

In sample: Describe any evidence of foreign matter observed in the sample.

At site: List pollutants observed at the location of the sampling station.

Other tests:

Coliform count or MPN value: If coliform determination is made, record the *most probable number* value per 100 ml. of sample. Consult tables provided with the test equipment for this value. If a direct colony count is made, record the number per 100 ml. of the sample.

Biochemical oxygen demand—List the results obtained in parts per million. For additional tests, list the type of test performed and the result obtained.

Notebook recording. An alternative to the tabular form of record keeping represented by the Water-Quality Data Sheet is the system of keeping records in narrative or seminarrative form in a bound notebook. This method is perfectly acceptable if the criteria enumerated in the general instructions for data recording are observed.

Material should be indexed, so that all data are readily retrievable.

Data-processing systems. For schools or agencies that have access to a computer storage and retrieval system, the data obtained in the various monitoring and survey activities may be processed for storage in such a system. This would provide excellent exposure to modern data-processing techniques.

Reporting on water quality

Importance of reporting. Raw data, regardless of where or how they are recorded, have little value unless they are used as the basis for a report that aims to correct instances of water-quality abuse. Unreported information in a filing system is useless until it is given life, through the processes of digestion, analysis, and drawing of conclusions. These processes form the skeleton of all reports, no matter what the objective of a report may be.

Data made available to appropriate agencies may serve to provide further impetus for active pollution-abatement programs. Accurately recorded and reported, these data may serve to establish present status ratings or present pollution problems for water systems. This type of rating may serve then as a base line against which to measure the effects of modification in wastewater-treatment processes.

Reporting to agencies. Environmental monitoring stations, whether sponsored by schools or by other community agencies, should immediately establish the reporting of water-quality levels to local governmental agencies. Contacts should be made with the appropriate persons in each agency to ascertain what types of data are desired, how they should be reported, and to whom they should be channeled.

A reporting team should be established to maintain liaison with the interested agencies. Two-way avenues of information should be the chief goal of this team.

Following are some suggested agencies that may be interested in receiving data on water quality:

A. Local
   1. Public health officer
   2. Commissioner of sanitation (or equivalent)
   3. Councilmen (or equivalent)
   4. Planning board
   5. Environmental protection agencies
   6. Municipal wastewater or sewer authority
   7. Municipal board of health
   8. Department of public works

B. County
   1. County planning board
   2. County health department
   3. County sewer authority
   4. Department of public works

C. Regional
   1. River basin commissions
   2. Soil and water conservation districts
   3. Federal water pollution control administrations

D. State
   1. State health agency
   2. Department of conservation (or fish and game)
   3. Department of environmental protection

E. Federal
   1. Federal Water Quality Administration

Methods of reporting. Three formats are suggested as possible means of reporting: water-quality report, water pollution report, and narrative reports.

Water-Quality Report Form. Under certain circumstances it may be valuable to record data on both the previously described Data Sheet and on a simplified data-retrieval card such as the accompanying sample form. This simplified form would be of great value to persons conducting research on a particular water system. Once criteria have been set for desired ranges of any tested material or condition, data obtained that falls outside these ranges can be readily encoded and retreived by this simple data-processing system.

In general, a water-quality report should include the following:

Environmental monitoring station: Insert the name of the agency or institution conducting the monitoring program.

Reporter: List the name of the person completing the report form.

Phone: List phone number(s) at which the reporter may be contacted.

Water system: List the name of the body of water under study.
Sample No.: List the serial number of the particular sample being reported on.
Sampling station number and location: List the coded station number and briefly describe it.
Date: Record the date of sampling.
Time: Report the local time, using the 24-hour system (for example, 0930 EST).
Depth: Record the depth at which the sample was taken.
Flow level: Record H for high flow, M for moderate flow, L for low flow.

Determinations made:

1. *Temperature*—Record for water and air, in degrees centigrade.
2. *Odor*—Record appropriate codes.
3. *pH*—Record in pH units.
4. *Dissolved oxygen*—Record in parts per million.
5. *Chloride*—Record in parts per million (after conversion).
6. *Hydrogen sulfide*—Record in parts per million.
7. *Orthophosphate*—Report in parts per million.
8. *Nitrite*—Report in parts per million of nitrite nitrogen.
9. *Nitrate*—Report in parts per million of nitrate nitrogen.
10. *Total hardness*—Record in parts per million (EDTA).

WATER-QUALITY REPORT FORM

Environmental monitoring station ______ Reporter ______ Phone ______

Water system ______ Sample No. ______ Sampling station No. and location ______

Date ______ Time ______ Depth ______ Flow level ______

DETERMINATIONS MADE:

1. Temperature: Water ______ Air ______ 2. Odor ______ 3. pH ______

4. Dissolved oxygen ______ 5. Chloride ______ 6. Hydrogen sulfide ______

7. Orthophosphate ______ 8. Nitrite ______ 9. Nitrate ______ 10. Total hardness ______

VISIBLE POLLUTANTS:

11. (In sample) ______ 12. (At site) ______ 13. Coliform MPN value ______

14. B.O.D. ______

OTHER TESTS:

	TYPE	RESULT		TYPE	RESULT		TYPE	RESULT
15.	______	______	17.	______	______	19.	______	______
16.	______	______	18.	______	______	20.	______	______

Remarks: ______

1	2	3	4	5	6	7	8	9	10	11	12	13	14	15	16	17	18	19	20

Visible pollutants:

11. *In sample*—List any observed.
12. *At site*—List any observed.
13. *Coliform count*—Record in number of colonies per 100 ml.
14. *B.O.D.*—Record in parts per million.

Other tests—Record type of test and determinations (15-20) made.

Remarks—Provide any pertinent descriptive information.

After recording the above data, any items that do not fall within established limits for the water in question should be identified by punching out the marginal space alloted to that constituent with a paper punch. For example, thermal pollution would be indicated by punching out box 1 on the bottom of the form.

To utilize this simplified form as such a data storage and retrieval system, first complete all items as described in the preceding section, compare readings obtained with the particular standard ranges established by local or state authorities for the water system, punching out the numbered boxes corresponding to any items whose levels are outside these ranges. After collecting the cards, take a coat hanger and cut a section of it to a length of 6 to 8 inches. Bend a 2-inch handle into one end as in Fig. 3-15. Insert the probe into code item 1 of a stack of properly aligned report forms. Shake the cards vigorously. Any report form with an anomalous temperature reading will fall out. These items may then be subjected to additional study.

Repeat this procedure for all encoded categories.

Water Pollution Report Form. For a less technical type of report form, the accompanying Water Pollution Report may be used. This narrative-type report may be sent directly to interested agencies, to polluters, or to interested representatives of the news media. It is designed to point out visible evidences of possible pollution and should, whenever possible, be buttressed by such additional evidences as water-quality data sheets, photographs, and detailed or specific descriptive data on existing conditions.

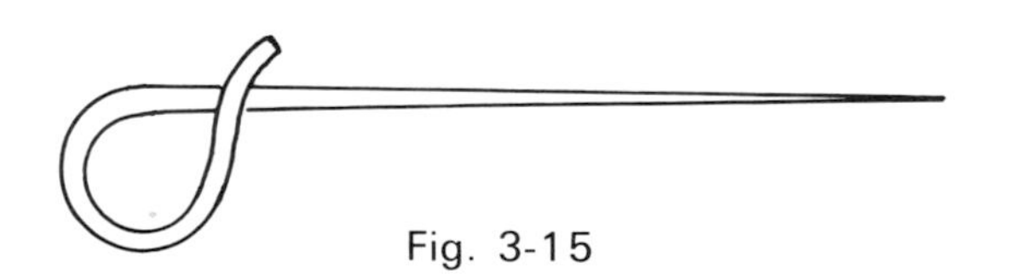

Fig. 3-15

Reporter: List the name of the person completing the form.

Address: List the address at which this person can be located. Provide more than one address if necessary.

Phone: List the phone number(s) of the previously named person.

1. *Location of observed pollution:* Provide as precise a location as possible; refer to nearby landmarks to aid in defining location.
2. *Date and time observed:* Record local time in the 24-hour system (for example, 0930 EST).
3. *Nature of pollutant:* Identify or describe the offensive substance observed.
4. *Appearance (color, odor, etc.):* Describe as accurately and completely as possible what you observed.
5. *Fish or wildlife affected:* List the types of each affected and give an approximation of the number afflicted.
6. *Source of pollution, if located:* Provide a complete description of such a source or suspected source.
7. *Name and address of alleged polluter:* Provide all identifying information available.

Attach any other evidence that may be available.

Narrative reports. Most activity in the field of water quality is directed toward the control and abatement of existing conditions of water-quality abuse. Narrative reports aimed at specific audiences serve to develop environmental awareness and an attendant readiness for programs of action aimed at restoring esthetic, chemical, and bacteriological acceptability of our water systems.

The goal of any reporting system can be expressed best with the motto "Clean Water for a High-Quality Environment!"

Give a complete report but use as few words as possible. Include illustrations when available. Re-

WATER POLLUTION REPORT

Reporter ______________________________

Address ______________________________

Phone ______________

1. Location of observed pollution ______________________________

____

2. Date and time observed ______________________________

3. Nature of pollutant ______________________________

____

4. Appearance (color, odor, etc.): ______________________________

5. Fish or wildlife affected (estimate numbers): ______________________________

____

6. Source of pollution, if located ______________________________

7. Suspected source of pollution ______________________________

8. Name and address of alleged polluter ______________________________

____

____

Please attach any additional available evidence such as copies of water-quality analysis forms and photographs.

member the old adage about a picture's equalling a thousand words.

Write at the level of your intended audience. They will not help you if they can not understand you.

For a more complete discussion of the preparation of such narrative reports, refer to the earlier section on surveying the water system.

In general, narrative reports should be (1) readable, (2) dynamic, (3) factual, and (4) concise.

APPENDIX
DESIRABLE CRITERIA FOR FRESH SURFACE WATER SUPPLIES*

Temperature: No thermal discharge that will detrimentally affect the natural aquatic biota should be present. This is especially dangerous in the summer.

*Based on The Report of the National Technical Advisory Committee on Water Quality Criteria to the Secretary of the Interior, 1968, and other sources.

Odor: Offensive odors should be absent.
pH: 6.0 to 8.5.
Dissolved oxygen: 4 ppm minimum; saturation is desirable.
Chloride: 250 ppm maximum; less than 25 ppm is desirable.
Hydrogen sulfide: Should be absent.
Phosphate: Less than 0.05 ppm is desirable. The average concentration in weak wastewater is 5 ppm, in medium wastewater is 15 ppm, and in strong wastewater is 30 ppm.
Nitrite and nitrate: 10 ppm (as N) maximum; absence is desirable.
Total hardness: Less than 120 ppm.
Coliform MPN value: Less than 100/100 ml. is desirable.
Biochemical oxygen demand: 15 ppm or less is desirable.
Copper: 1 ppm maximum; absence is desirable.
Iron. 0.3 ppm maximum; absence is desirable.
Sulfate: 250 ppm maximum; less than 50 ppm is desirable.
Ammonia: 0.5 ppm (as N); less than 0.01 is desirable.
Lead: 0.05 ppm; absence is desirable.

SURFACE WATER CRITERIA FOR PUBLIC WATER SUPPLIES*

Two types of criteria are defined as follows:

1. *Permissible criteria:* Those characteristics and concentrations of substances in raw surface waters that will allow the production of a safe, clear, potable, esthetically pleasing, and acceptable public water supply that meets the limits of drinking water standards after treatment. This treatment may include, but will not include more than, the processes described above.
2. *Desirable criteria:* Those characteristics and concentrations of substances in the raw surface waters that represent high-quality water in all respects for use as public water supplies. Water meeting these criteria can be treated in the defined plants with greater factors of safety or at less cost than is possible with waters meeting permissible criteria.

*From Report of the Committee on Water Quality Criteria, April 1, 1968, Federal Water Pollution Control Administration, Washington, D. C., p. 20.

CONSTITUENT OR CHARACTERISTIC	PERMISSIBLE CRITERIA	DESIRABLE CRITERIA
Physical		
Color (color units)	75	<10
Odor	Narrative	Virtually absent
Temperature*	Narrative	Narrative
Turbidity	Narrative	Virtually absent
Microbiological		
Coliform organisms	10,000/100 ml.†	<100/100 ml.†
Fecal coliforms	2000/100 ml.†	< 20/100 ml.†
	(mg./L.)	(mg./L.)
Inorganic chemicals		
Alkalinity	Narrative	Narrative
Ammonia	0.5 (as N)	<0.01
Arsenic*	0.05	Absent
Barium*	1	Absent
Boron*	1	Absent

*The defined treatment process has little effect on this constituent.
†Microbiological limits are monthly arithmetic averages based on an adequate number of samples. Total coliform limit may be relaxed if fecal coliform concentration does not exceed the specified limit.
‡As parathion in cholinesterase inhibition. It may be necessary to resort to even lower concentrations for some compounds or mixtures.

CONSTITUENT OR CHARACTERISTIC	PERMISSIBLE CRITERIA	DESIRABLE CRITERIA
Cadmium*	0.01	Absent
Chloride*	250	<25
Chromium, hexavalent*	0.05	Absent
Copper*	1	Virtually absent
Dissolved oxygen	≥4 (monthly mean) ≥3 (individual sample)	Near saturation
Fluoride*	Narrative	Narrative
Hardness	Narrative	Narrative
Iron (filterable)	0.3	Virtually absent
Lead*	0.05	Absent
Manganese (filterable)*	0.05	Absent
Nitrates plus nitrites*	10 (as N)	Virtually absent
pH (range)	6-8.5	Narrative
Phosphorus*	Narrative	Narrative
Selenium*	0.01	Absent
Silver*	0.05	Absent
Sulfate*	250	<50
Total dissolved solids (filterable residue)*	500	<200
Uranyl ion*	5	Absent
Zinc*	5	Virtually absent
Organic chemicals		
Carbon chloroform extract (CCE)*	0.15	<0.04
Cyanide*	0.20	Absent
Methylene blue active substances*	0.5	Virtually absent
Oil and grease*	Virtually absent	Absent
Pesticides		
Aldrin*	0.017	Absent
Chlordane*	0.003	Absent
DDT*	0.042	Absent
Dieldrin*	0.017	Absent
Endrin*	0.001	Absent
Heptachlor*	0.018	Absent
Heptachlor epoxide*	0.018	Absent
Lindane*	0.056	Absent
Methoxychlor*	0.035	Absent
Organic phosphates plus carbamates*	0.1‡	Absent
Toxaphene*	0.005	Absent
Herbicides		
2,4-D, 2,4,5-T, plus 2,4,5-TP*	0.1	Absent
Phenols*	0.001	Absent
	(Particle count per liter)	(Particle count per liter)
Radioactivity		
Gross beta*	1000	<100
Radium 226*	3	<1
Strontium 90*	10	<2

Several words used in the table require explanation in order to convey the subcommittee's intent:

Narrative: The presence of this word in the table indicates that the subcommittee could not arrive at a single numerical value that would be applicable throughout the country for all conditions.

Absent: The most sensitive analytical procedure in *Standard Methods for the Examination of Water and Wastewater* (or other approved procedure) does not show the presence of the subject constituent.

Virtually absent: This term implies that the substance is present in very low concentrations and is used where the substance is not objectionable in these barely detectable concentrations.

BIBLIOGRAPHY AND SUGGESTIONS FOR FURTHER READING

Books and pamphlets

Baldwin, Helene L., and McGuiness, C. L.: A primer on ground water, Washington, D. C., 1963, U. S. Department of Interior Geological Survey.

Community action program for water pollution control, Washington, D. C., 1967, National Association of Counties.

Dworsky, Leonard, B.: Water pollution control, Audubon Nature Bulletin Series 30, No. 3 Revised, New York, 1966.

Forman, Jonathan, and Fink, Ollie E.: Water and man—a study in ecology, Columbus, Ohio, 1950, Friends of the Land.

Information kit—water pollution control, Pittsburgh, Pa., Calgon Corp.

It's time we face America's water problem, Peoria, Ill., 1967, Caterpillar Tractor Co.

Know your river basin, No. 256, Washington, D. C., 1958, League of Women Voters.

Leopold, Luna B., Davis, Kenneth S., and the editors of *Life:* Water, Life Science Library, New York, 1966, Time, Inc.

Office of Science and Technology: A ten-year program of federal water resources research, Washington, D. C., 1966, U. S. Government Printing Office.

Paulson, Edgar G.: Water pollution control, Pittsburgh, Pa., Calgon Corp.

Raffo, John D.: Water—the waste of plenty, Browns Mills, N. J., 1969, CESC press.

Salinger, Richard, and West, Wallace: Conserving our waters and clearing the air: student manual, New York, 1968, American Petroleum Institute.

Soil Conservation Service: Conservation and the water cycle, Washington, D. C., 1967, U. S. Department of Agriculture.

Soil Conservation Service: Sediment, Publication No. 325, Washington, D. C., 1967, U. S. Department of Agriculture.

Soil Conservation Service: Water facts, P.A. 337, Washington, D. C., 1964, U. S. Department of Agriculture.

Soil Conservation Service: What is a watershed? P.A. 420, Washington, D. C., 1969, U. S. Department of Agriculture.

Standard methods for the examination of water and wastewater, New York, 1965, American Public Health Association.

Strobbe, M. A.: Environmental science laboratory manual, St. Louis, 1972, The C.V. Mosby Co.

Swenson, H. A., and Baldwin, H. L.: A primer on water quality, Washington, D. C., 1965, U. S. Department of Interior Geological Survey.

Water, The Yearbook of Agriculture 1955, Washington, D. C., 1965, U. S. Department of Agriculture.

Water in industry, New York, 1965, National Association of Manufacturers.

Welch, Paul S.: Limnological methods, New York, 1948, McGraw-Hill Book Co.

Whittemore, Suvia P., et al.: The big water fight, Brattleboro, Vt., 1966, League of Women Voters.

Periodicals

American City, 757 Third Ave., New York, N. Y. 10017.

Journal of the Sanitary Engineering Division, American Society of Civil Engineers, 345 E. 47th St., New York, N. Y. 10017.

Journal of the Water Pollution Control Federation, 3900 Wisconsin Ave., Washington, D. C. 20016.

Public Works Magazine, 200 S. Broad St., Ridgewood, N. J.

Water and Sewage Works, 35 E. Wacker Dr., Chicago, Ill. 60601.

Water Works and Wastes Engineering, 466 Lexington Ave., New York, N. Y. 10017.

FILMS

Dry Spell 4, 14 minutes, 16 mm. black and white film, produced by National Water Institute Management Association, free loan, Sterling—Movies U.S.A., Inc., Operations Center, 46 W. 61st St., New York, N. Y.

It's Your Decision—Clean Water, 14½-minute color animated film, presented by the Soap and Detergent Association and the League of Women Voters of the United States, free loan,

Association Films, Inc., Regional Film Center, 600 Grand Ave., Ridgefield, N. J. 07657.

Renaissance of a River, 16 mm. sound, color film, free loan, Interstate Advisory Committee on the Susquehanna, 2101 N. Front St., Harrisburg, Pa.

The Year of Disaster, 28 minutes, 16 mm. sound, color film, free loan, Caterpillar Dealers and Caterpillar Tractor Advertising Division, Peoria, Ill.

Water Bill U.S.A., 27 minutes, 16 mm. color film, free loan, Motion Picture Library, U. S. Department of Agriculture Soil Conservation Service, 7600 W. Chester Pike, Upper Darby, Pa. 19082.

Wild Rivers, 28 minutes, 16 mm. sound, color film, presented by Humble Refining Corp., free loan, Modern Talking Pictures Service, 3 E. 54th St., New York, N. Y. 10022.

4 HUMAN COMMUNITIES—CASES FOR ENVIRONMENTAL STUDIES

The study of man's use of environments is related to many fields of study, thus requiring an interdisciplinary approach from the broad realms of social and natural sciences. The impact of man on the environment is most significant in and near cities and smaller communities because environmental degradation is most evident in areas of high population density. Therefore these are the environments most deserving of study; collectively they illustrate practically all of man's environmental problems.

A number of communities may be designated as fruitful examples of most of the diverse environments in the United States. These communities are indicated on the map in Fig. 4-1. A detailed case study of each of these environments and the factors or problems relating to their use by the resident populations illustrates the concerns significant for environmental quality today.

A hierarchy of three community types has been selected, to reflect the relative immediacy of environmental conditions for the community inhabitants. The small *site-oriented* community is immediately dependent on one or more environmental factors. At the other extreme are larger communities, called *situation-oriented,* whose life is sustained by the activities and services provided by the population, and which is, in turn, sustained by materials and inputs from more distant environments. A group of communities, intermediate in size and transitional in environmental relationships, has also been suggested.

To illustrate this relationship, sixteen communities have been placed on a grid chart (Table 5) with the vertical component designating community size. The more familiar science-classified resources form the horizontal component. Each environment is thereby classified.

For each community, many of the unique environmental relationships and difficulties are listed. For example, Atlantic City was chosen because it illustrates the environmental problems of both a resort and a coastal city. Other coastal and resort communities undoubtedly have problems similar in kind and varying in degree. Although each of the selected communities has many problems relating to the use of its immediate environment, it also has unique advantages and special distinctions or achievements.

Each of the sixteen communities is discussed briefly with respect to those factors that make it distinctive, such as historical, environmental, and economic. Following this is a detailed study of the Atlantic City, New Jersey, area to give a complete example of how one of these sample communities, or your own, might be developed for study. By utilizing the case study method, interesting and relevant in-depth studies will provide the basis for students to conduct direct studies of scientific

Text continued on p. 142.

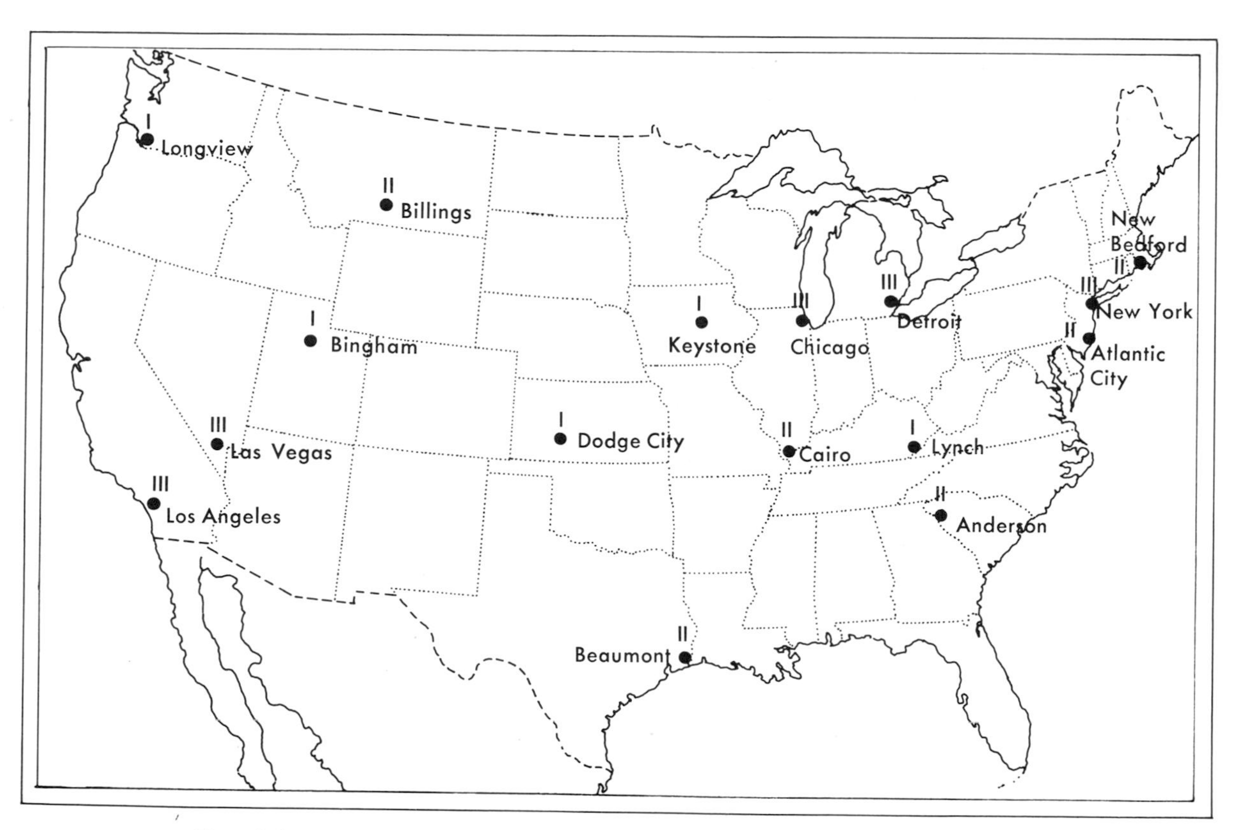

Fig. 4-1. Distinctive environments. **I**, Site-oriented; **II**, transitional; **III**, situation-oriented.

TABLE 5. Sixteen communities with distinctive environments

	SOIL, WATER	WILDLIFE	NATURAL COMMUNITIES	MINERALS, AIR
I. Site-oriented (functions of community directly related to local environment)	Keystone, Iowa—corn belt environment Soil Water and climate Pesticides New Bedford, Mass.—New England environment	Dodge City, Kan.—plains environment Plains Indians Cattle industry Overgrazing Cattle drives Homesteading Wheat production Minerals	Longview, Wash.—northwest forest environment Forest resources management Transport to market	Lynch, Ky.—Appalachian coalfield environment "Island of poverty" Desolation Strip and auger mining Destruction

Continued.

TABLE 5. Sixteen communities with distinctive environments —cont'd

	SOIL, WATER	WILDLIFE	NATURAL COMMUNITIES	MINERALS, AIR
	Forest industries Textiles Tourism Fishing Wildlife Soil	Disturbances and succession Predator-prey relationships Bison slaughter Elk range management	Utilization of water Sensitivity to building Industry-exports Soil Wildlife Natural forests Beaumont–Port Arthur, Tex.— Gulf coast environment Petroleum industry Offshore oil problems Mothball fleet Gulf lowlands, natural communities Swamps, bayous	of forests Cultural impoverishment Soil destruction and reclamation Fossil fuel formations Bingham Canyon, Utah—mountainous mining environment Seasonal grazing Copper ore mining Mining town—company housing National park area and use disturbances and succession
II. Transitional (community developed to point of being less dependent on immediate resources)	Anderson, S. C.—piedmont environment Changing agricultural patterns Attraction of textile industry Soil of southeast piedmont Waterpower National parks	Cairo, Ill.—midwest environment River port—growth in relation to "Egypt" region's transportation and development Soil Passenger pigeon extinction Beaver Central flyway Muskrat	Atlantic City, N. J.—mid-Atlantic coastal environment Changing evaluation of possibilities of sandbars, local pollution Saltwater industries Relationship to industrial revolution Public vs. private	Billings, Mont.—arid mountain environment Precious metal mining Sugar beet irrigation Alfalfa Range management Glaciation Disturbances and succession

TABLE 5. Sixteen communities with distinctive environments—cont'd

	SOIL, WATER	WILDLIFE	NATURAL COMMUNITIES	MINERALS, AIR
			recreational land Use of tidelands Pesticides Estuarine community	
III. Situation-oriented (function of community oriented to distant environments)	Los Angeles, Calif.—Mediterranean-type environment Historical development Changing agriculture Impact of urbanization vs. environment Throw-away economy Freeways Mexican-American culture Soil Water Agriculture Air Smog Minerals Irrigation Fragile environments	Las Vegas, Nev —desert environment Lack of natural resources base Importance of politico-cultural factors Accessibility to Los Angeles Water National recreation area Detroit, Mich.—midwest industrial river-port environment Auto and steel industries Cars, billboards "Motown" cultural phenomenon, landscape pollution	Chicago, Ill.—metropolitan lake-port environment Rail center and lake port Great Lakes economy Migration objective for southern blacks St. Lawrence Seaway Iron mining and transportation Water Lake ecology—pollution Disturbances and succession	New York, N. Y.—northeast megalopolitan environment Politics of urban crisis Communications and cultural center "Top-heavy" city—need for decentralization Decentralization of industry Water Air

and social aspects of their own community environments.

In the study of any community, a number of direct experiences with some aspect of the environment may be provided. These experiences give the student an opportunity to observe, measure, or monitor certain aspects of his own local environment illustrating the relationships or problems under consideration.

Because man is the only being that attempts to understand and communicate about environments, a consideration of the way in which people feel about, react to, and act on their environments, constitutes a significant innovation as an approach to environmental study.

The activity suggestions are the student's direct invitation to self-guided learning. Many of the activities may be carried on *without* a formal field trip by the entire class and the teacher. What matters most is that the teacher communicate his or her interest and enthusiasm for the observational inputs developed by the youngsters. Work and effort in these activities should "count" as much as or more than formal class discussion, tests, or other traditional activities by which children's progress is evaluated. Many of the case study communities suggested will be far removed in distance and character from the environments in which the children and school are situated. These activities are designed to provide a *direct* and *relevant* connection between the child's world and the special community environment selected for case study.

The most favorable behavioral outcome of the use of these activities and approach might be a classroom climate that (1) encourages children to suggest new relevant investigations, (2) rewards them for asking penetrating questions, (3) brings students to devise original or individual methods of investigating questions that they have raised, and (4) reflects an increasing concern for the quality of the total environment by both students and teachers.

ANDERSON, SOUTH CAROLINA—PIEDMONT ENVIRONMENT

Anderson is a farming center and textile-manufacturing community located in the foothills, or piedmont, of South Carolina. Although Anderson is the county seat of Anderson County, it has not experienced the rapid growth characteristic of many administrative communities.

The community developed as a supply center for agricultural industry. The crops of the area are varied, ranging from fruits such as peaches, apples, and grapes to truck garden vegetables and, of course, hay and cotton. The wide variety of crops produced is a result of the relatively mild climate and the well-developed, originally fertile but highly erodible soils of the southern piedmont area. Altitude is 500 to 1,000 feet above sea level. Annual rainfall is well above 40 inches a year, and colder winter temperatures do not remain below the freezing point for more than a few days at a time.

The entire piedmont of South Carolina is typified by a number of streams that flow into the Atlantic Ocean. The most notable of these is the Savannah River, which flows southeastward to the coast at Charleston, the principal city of South Carolina. Anderson is situated in the headwaters of the Black River, a tributary of the Savannah. The abundant rainfall and the numerous streams of the area provide much potential for hydroelectic power; such development of low-cost electricity has characterized the South Carolina piedmont since the twenties.

Anderson today is still greatly shaped by two environmental influences—availability of waterpower and a sloping topography that receives abundant rainfall.

The town has not grown so rapidly as its neighbor, Greenville, which is now the most urban of centers in the area. For Greenville, the transition from an agricultural to a textile-manufacturing economy is nearly complete, whereas Anderson is still significantly influenced by both of these economic factors. To native South Carolinians, Anderson is still a pleasant country town—a supply center for surrounding agricultural industry and a slowly developing textile industry.

West of Anderson lies the curve of the Blue Ridge Mountains as they change from a southern to a western sweep along the boundaries of North and South Carolina and Georgia. Some of the mountainous lands are in public ownership, in state or federal jurisdiction. The Nantahala National Forest is close to Anderson, and further west is the Great Smoky Mountains National Park, the most frequently visited park in the United States.

To simulate some of Anderson's environmental influences and problems in any community, students might consider such questions as the following.

Electricity

1. What sources of electricity are available to our community?
2. How does the cost of "our" electricity compare with that produced in the vicinity of Anderson?
3. Which is less polluting for the local environment—Anderson's hydroelectric power or the electricity-generating methods used in our community? What is our community planning in regard to future sources of power?

Soil erosion. Soil erosion has always been a serious problem throughout the piedmont of the Eastern coastal United States.

1. What evidences of erosion can students find on the school grounds or lands?
2. How is soil erosion influenced by steepness or length of slope?
3. Are some soils more erodible than others?
4. What factors might influence erodibility?
5. Is there a soil conservation district in your community, county, or parish? If so, how do its services help to control soil erosion? What are some means used to curb soil erosion?
6. Do any rivers in your vicinity have the names of colors? If so, is there any relation between the color names and soil erosion?

Agriculture and industry

1. Why does a farming supply center grow less rapidly than an industrial center? Will the need for agricultural and industrial employees change these population relationships in the near future?

Topography and climate

1. How should the topography and climate of an area be used to plan the most favorable environments for the future use of that area?

BEAUMONT–PORT ARTHUR, TEXAS—GULF COAST ENVIRONMENT

Beaumont, an industrial city and inland port, is located 25 miles from the Gulf of Mexico and is approximately 85 miles east of Houston, Texas. Port Arthur is 9 miles from the Gulf and 16 miles southeast of Beaumont. In the 1840s speculators made it the southern terminal of the Kansas City Southern Railroad and had a deep-sea channel dredged to connect it with the Gulf. In 1901 oil was discovered at Spindletop, a few miles from Port Arthur. Since then, the area around Beaumont and Port Arthur has specialized in the refining and export of petroleum products. The metropolitan area has also functioned as a center for the production of chemicals and synthetic rubber and for ship building.

Industry abounds in the area. Beaumont has become a center for the manufacturing of oil field equipment, serving as a good example of a secondary industry whose development was influenced by an earlier industry. Large mills process the rice grown within the country, with the aid of mechanical harvesters and aerially sprayed pesticides.

Sulfur mining is another important source of income in this area.

Pulp, paper, and plywood are produced here from the southern pine forests; the marketable timber is operated as small privately owned woodlots. Larger corporations contract with owners of woodlots for the production of wood. This dual community complex is an example of farmers discovering that, in an area of rather poor soil, the most productive crop can be trees.

Following are some environmental questions that might be investigated in the students' home community:

Woodlots. Visit woodlots or forests with single species and mixed stands of timber in your home community.

1. How are woodlots managed to produce a usable crop in a period of twelve to twenty years? Is this practice helpful in maintaining environmental quality?
2. Are woodlots or forests planted with one species more or less susceptible to biological or other environmental hazards?

Oil

1. What would be the effect on your home community if oil were discovered there now or in the near future?
2. What other sources of fuel do we have if oil sources and reserves run out?

Inland ports

1. What are the advantages in having a port removed several miles from a bay or ocean?
2. What are the disadvantages?

Mineral-extracting industries

1. What mineral-extracting or earth material industry is nearest your community? Try to visit it. What significance does it have for the economy of your area? How does this industry affect the environmental quality of the surrounding district?

Pesticides. The class may determine what pesticides are used in farm fields or forests in your area or in control of mosquitoes.

1. What are the advantages in using these chemicals?
2. What effects have these substances had on (a) birds, (b) other wildlife, (c) the quality of locally raised meats, and (d) plant life?

BILLINGS, MONTANA—ARID MOUNTAINOUS ENVIRONMENT

Billings is located in the south central part of Montana. It lies east of the backbone of the Rocky Mountains on the Yellowstone River, a tributary of the Missouri River. With a population of approximately 50,000, it is the third largest city in Montana.

Sagebrush and arid Rocky Mountain slopes make up the scenery surrounding Billings. This is an area of wide temperature variations; summers are dry and hot, whereas winters bring blizzards and subzero days.

Billings is indeed a western town. Although more modern than their ancestors, cowboys and Indians still walk the downtown streets. Rodeos and tribal fairs are highlights of every year. Lonely prospectors still head into the hills looking for "strikes," but most mining is now done on a large scale, using modern technology. Silver, gold, lead, copper, and zinc are among the metals most frequently mined in the vicinity of Billings.

Sugar beets and alfalfa can be grown on this land if irrigation is provided; Yearly rainfall, especially during the summer growing season, will not support good crops. Unirrigated land is used as grazing range for cattle and sheep. Therefore ranching still comprises a large part of Billings' economy. Many are the motorists who have found themselves trapped in the middle of a herd of cattle or sheep moving slowly down the highway.

Billings also supports a lively tourist industry. One of the main roads leading to Yellowstone National Park passes through Billings. It is near Custer Battlefield National Monument and the

700 square mile Crow Indian Reservation. Living glaciers can also be reached with ease.

The questions listed with the following topics can provide students with direct experience investigations to compare and contrast their own community environments with that of Billings.

Rainfall

1. How much rainfall is there in your local community? How does this affect your environment in regard to (a) water supply, (b) farm or forest crops, and (c) hydroelectric power?
2. How much rainfall in or near your community is wasted or reduced by (a) extensive paving of parking areas and (b) improper management of forest, shrub, or grassy areas?

Range management

1. When the soil cover is eaten for food by herds of animals, what precautions must be taken to ensure the preservation of this environment? How can steep slopes be protected from destruction by grazing animals?
2. What is the importance of keeping a grass cover on the lawns of all private homes? How can the valuable resource of grass cuttings be used to greatest advantage?

Irrigation

1. What problems develop with soils that are irrigated for raising crops? For maintaining lawns in suburbs and cities?
2. Irrigation water in dry states or areas sometimes comes from rivers that rise in neighboring states. Laws to guarantee each person a fair share are called *riparian rights.* What riparian rights are guaranteed for your community? For individuals in your community? Should every citizen have a "riparian" right to a clean and beautiful stream to pass through or near his community?

Glaciation. Many northern states have had their topography and soil affected by the action of a continental ice sheet, or glacier.

1. If the area of your community was once affected by glaciation, describe the effects. How did glaciation positively or adversely affect environmental quality in your community?

Disturbance and succession. In each living environment, plants and animals grow together, live together, and sometimes feed on each other. When these communities of plants and animals change or are changed, the modification is known as succession. When the land surface is disturbed by mining, agriculture, grazing, home building, floods, industry, or war, environmental changes occur, often lowering the quality of the original environment. In Billings and vicinity, disturbance is produced by mining and grazing.

1. What disturbances of the environment are occurring in your community? How have these disturbances affected environmental quality?
2. What measure can be taken to minimize the environmental problems produced by disturbance?

BINGHAM CANYON, UTAH—MOUNTAINOUS MINING ENVIRONMENT

Bingham Canyon is really a man-made hole in the earth produced by the Kennecott Copper Company to obtain metal ores from the plateau section of north central Utah. Approximately circular in shape, with many steplike levels progressing downward to its narrow base, Bingham Canyon's size is most misleading at first glance. It is, however, deep enough so that the world's tallest buildings could be accommodated with ease inside its boundaries.

A considerable smelting process is also carried on at Bingham, extending to the eastern edge of Great Salt Lake. This has produced great mountains of waste rock (slag), which emit choking fumes of oxides of sulfur gases until they have cooled. The area of Bingham Canyon can be located from Salt Lake City by its characteristic umbrella of yellow haze.

Bingham Canyon epitomizes environmental

problems related to open, or strip, mining and the smelting of sulfurous metal ores. How can resource materials be extracted from the earth's surface or near the surface without destroying the quality of the land forever?

The following questions point up the environmental impact of many mining and smelting industries.

Ore supply and recycling

1. Will the supply of ore in this location and others be adequate for the future needs of society?
2. How much of the present supply of copper and other minerals can be recycled with profit? If there is an increased cost for necessary recycling, who should bear the cost?

Disturbing fragile environments

1. What special dangers are there in disturbing the surface of a fragile environment (fragile with respect to plant and animal populations and their low annual water supply)?

Solid-waste disposal. Slag is a solid waste material with high volume.

1. How does your community dispose of solid wastes? What problems is your community experiencing?
2. Is recycling necessary, even if not economically profitable at present?
3. What creative or new ideas can you suggest as a means of providing for desirable environmental quality in an area where great mountains of slag are being produced? Discuss the accident that occurred in Aberfan, Wales, in the fall of 1966 and what that town has done toward resolving the problem.

Control of air-polluting gases

1. How can those industrial corporations conducting large-scale smelting operations control the air-polluting gases that issue from the open dumping of molten slag?
2. In what ways should the increased costs for this environmental improvement be met?

CAIRO, ILLINOIS—MIDWEST ENVIRONMENT

Cairo, Illinois, is located at the confluence of the Ohio and Mississippi rivers. Because this area resembled the fertile area of the Nile with the joining of two great rivers, the new community was called Cairo, and the area, Little Egypt. The founding fathers, including hopeful investors, anticipated that Cairo, Illinois, would become a thriving and prosperous port city like Cairo, Egypt.

Unfortunately, the area proved unsuitable for the dream. The land is low and swampy, making it undesirable for building, whereas shifting sandbars make it costly to maintain as a river port. At one time Cairo was the target of a land speculation scandal because eager land investors did not investigate the geography of the location.

Cairo, with an extremely mild climate, produces cotton, which it ships from its existing ports. The city, population 8,000 to 10,000, is now buttressed against flood danger by levees.

Hunters are attracted to lowlands near Cairo, which is considered the goose-hunting capital of the world. Hunters and other tourists are also attracted by a flourishing "strip" that offers gambling and other related activities.

Unemployment has been a continuing problem in this city. The population is approximately 60% black, and many white employers have been unwilling to employ black workers. For the past several years the town has had severe racial problems.

Following are some environmental problems related to Cairo that may be researched or considered by students.

Community growth projection

1. Why did Cairo fail to develop as a significant river port, since it is located at the junction or confluence of two of the largest rivers in North America?
2. In addition to providing a good anchoring place for boats and ships, what other ad-

vantages does a port need to encourage growth?

3. What constellation, or grouping, of environmental factors is needed for any community to grow?
4. Make a list of the most favorable and unfavorable environmental influences in Cairo, Illinois.
5. If employment is not available for many Cairo residents, is this a factor in environmental quality? How do you justify your response?
6. What ecological environmental knowledge or factors should community planners take into account before proposing a new community or an addition to an older one?

Soil. Much of Illinois, especially in the central and southern sections of the state, is chiefly concerned with agriculture.

1. How do Illinois soils compare with contrasting soil types of other agricultural areas in the United States?

The mixture of the Mississippi and Ohio River waters does not occur at once. This can be seen because the Ohio River water on the east bank seems to be much more clear than that flowing in the Mississippi.

2. What can you deduce about the relative intensity of agriculture in the Ohio River valley as compared to the valleys drained by the Mississippi River? Is all soil erosion caused by human land use?
3. In which river would you expect to find more polluting materials derived from agricultural fertilizers? (Fertilizers are washed into streams through water runoff.)
4. What are the chief stream pollutants produced by this fertilizer loss?

Wildlife. The Mississippi River valley is associated with the tragic history of the extinction of the passenger pigeon. Many human activities and improper land use have created environmental problems that led to the actual or impending extinction of many plants and animals.

1. Obtain an updated listing of animals or plants now endangered.
2. Discuss the relative importance of the following factors with regard to the loss of living species by extinction: (a) the building of cities, (b) highway building, (c) sport and game hunting and fishing, and (d) commercial hunting and fishing.
3. What advantages and disadvantages for the maintenance of environmental quality are represented by sport-hunting activities, including (a) operation of state game farms and fish hatcheries, (b) licensing of hunters and fishermen, and (c) hunting clubs and clubs for the owners of hunting dogs?

CHICAGO, ILLINOIS—METROPOLITAN LAKE-PORT ENVIRONMENT

Chicago's metropolitan area, second in population only to the Atlantic megalopolis, is an excellent example of the influence of natural transportation corridors on urban development. As the logical transportation-distribution center for the rich agricultural area west and northwest of the Great Lakes, Chicago has long functioned as a packing, wholesaling, and distribution center for this general area. As an example of its significance in this field, its Board of Trade occupies the premier position in the financial aspects of the agricultural markets, ranking in importance with Wall Street in this respect.

An historical rivalry between Chicago and New York City has always existed—a rivalry in terms of resource bases, levels of economic development, and productivity. In recent years the growth of Los Angeles on the west coast has brought that city into competition also. This economic rivalry can be used in contrast with a community such as Keystone, Iowa, where a general concern for the conservation of agricultural land, use of chemical fertilizers and pesticides, and the changing agricultural economy is needed. Chicago, of course, as the second largest metropolitan area in the United States, has its share of the major urban problems that need to be considered.

The following topically organized questions are designed to focus on some of these problems.

Transportation. Chicago is not only a preeminent railroad center but also the largest lake port in the United States.

1. For what environmental considerations did Chicago become an important rail center?
2. List at least a dozen commodities (raw materials, agricultural products, or manufactured materials) that move to or through Chicago. Which, if any, of these are processed or changed by workers at Chicago.
3. If unemployment becomes a more severe problem for Chicago, what means could be used to alleviate the problem?
4. How did the development of the St. Lawrence Seaway affect Chicago's development and economy?

Population and races

1. Why did so many black people migrate to Chicago from the south in the last century?
2. What is the present population of Chicago?
3. Is the proportion of rural to other migration changing?
4. Is unemployment among blacks in Chicago higher than among nonblack residents?
5. Is there an optimum size for communities?
6. Is the southwestern shore of Lake Michigan already overpopulated?
7. Is the number of persons that can be accommodated in a land area limited?
8. What suggestions can be made for urban planning in the future to avoid the decay of many neighborhoods in our large cities?

Water quality. Both Chicago and Milwaukee, Wisconsin, are on the western shores of Lake Michigan, with Hammond and Gary, Indiana, on the southern shore. No large cities are located on the eastern shore, which has some unique sand dunes.

1. Since Lake Michigan is being used both for water supply and as a receiving water body for processed sewage, what measures are needed to ensure the quality of Lake Michigan water?
2. Are Chicago's sewage-treatment processes adequate to ensure water quality in Lake Michigan?
3. Why is Lake Michigan not so polluted as is Lake Erie?
4. Is the western shore of Lake Michigan suitable for recreation for large numbers of people?
5. What means are being employed to ensure the recreational use of Lake Michigan on its western shore?

DETROIT, MICHIGAN—MIDWEST INDUSTRIAL RIVER PORT ENVIRONMENT

Detroit provides an opportunity to relate that city-region to man's use and misuse of the Great Lakes system and also to highlight the role that the automobile industry has played in American social and economic life. Detroit is our example of a midwestern inland waterway situation with raw material transportation supporting heavy industry. It is also the largest metropolitan area to be dominated to such an extent by one industry—the automobile industry. Approximately 28% of the metropolitan labor force is engaged directly in automotive manufacturing. This dependence on one industry, of course, has had consequences, both social and economic, for the entire metropolitan area.

Detroit will also provide a study of industrial location and inertia. The meaning of inertia in this context is that industry, once situated in a particular location, has a vested economic interest in maintaining that location; this interest is maintained despite changes in the economic factors that led to the selection of that location in the first place. Detroit may also be analyzed in terms of its being a center of urban black subculture, for example, the "Motown records" phenomenon and its devastating race riots of the 1960's.

A study of Detroit's environment and problems may include some of the following considerations.

Automobile and steel industries

1. What environmental factors influenced the development of the automotive industry in Detroit?
2. What influences can be found to account for the extreme concentration of all the large American automobile companies in Detroit?
3. With such a concentration of automotive industry now in Detroit, why are there automobile assembly plants in other parts of the United States or in foreign countries?
4. What would happen to the economy of the state of Michigan if Detroit's automotive industry were forced out of existence?
5. Discuss or evaluate the influences of the automobile on the following aspects of the biophysical or social environments:
   a. Amounts of raw iron ore used annually
   b. Air pollution
   c. Utilization of petroleum
   d. International tensions related to obtaining petroleum
   e. Building of roads and superhighways
   f. Access to hitherto rarely visited environments
   g. Spread of residential suburbs
   h. American customs and mores
   i. Billboard advertising and visual quality of the highway landscape
   j. Solid-waste disposal
   k. Recycling products made with metal materials
6. How has the steel industry and its locations been affected by the concentration of automobile manufacturing in Detroit?
7. For what reasons would automobile manufacturers resist moving a major portion of their activity to a location other than Detroit?

Motown and culture

1. What factors account for the development of a distinctive black subculture in Detroit rather than in Chicago, Philadelphia, Los Angeles, Newark, or New York?
2. How has the black community of Detroit gone about rebuilding itself after the devastating riots of the 1960's? Where did the money as well as the incentive come from? How does this influence black culture in Detroit today?
3. What environmental influences, social or biophysical, can be detected in "Motown" records and culture?
4. What is the relative power and influence of the automotive and steel workers' labor unions on (a) utilization of resources, (b) the national economy, and (c) workers' attitudes toward society, education, and environmental quality?

Environmental resources

1. How do the environmental characteristics of the rest of the state of Michigan compare to the immediate vicinity of Detroit with respect to (a) population density, (b) types of industry, (c) recreational potential, and (d) industry based on immediate environmental resources?
2. Can you suggest any environmental factors to account for the fact that Michigan is among the pioneers in developing direct studies of the environment by school children? Or that some of the first forests set aside as areas for school classes and individuals to study were here? These special educationally dedicated wooded areas are known as "school forests."

DODGE CITY, KANSAS—PLAINS ENVIRONMENT

Dodge City is a farm and livestock center today, but it represents a link with a colorful environment of the past—the western plains. With fewer than 15,000 population, Dodge City is not large, as many American communities are today, but fewer than twenty communities in the entire state of Kansas have a greater population. It is a "people center" in the "wide-open space" environment.

Museums and a restoration of a frontier-town street, Old Front Street, maintain Dodge City's link with the past and also suggest the environmental problems which that age developed.

The cattle drives to the rail center at Dodge City are associated with present and past problems of overgrazing. A consideration of warfare with the Plains Indians may invoke a new consideration of the "western land and resource ethic" that produced a head-on collision with a people whose hunting and fishing "land ethic" contrasted so markedly.

Today the environmental impact of Dodge City is linked to wheat production, range management for domestic or wild stock, and the extraction of minerals. Perhaps the most serious long-range environmental problem is the use of semiarid lands for the production of food or livestock. An organized study question outline for these problems is presented here.

Location and general description. Dodge City is situated on the Great Plains, west of the 100th meridian—flatlands with less than half of the water supply of the central lowlands. It is a town with some historic significance.

Statement of problems

1. How may an economy be stabilized with either wheat farmers or herdsmen on land receiving less than 20 inches of rainfall each year?
2. What predator-prey relationships should be maintained in this environment?
3. Can the land ethic typified by homesteading in the last century be maintained in the late twentieth century?
4. Should Natural Grasslands be extended as are our present National Parks?

Natural setting. The landforms of Dodge City include open, semiarid areas, ancient rock formations, containing zinc and limestone as valuable minerals, and gently rolling topography.

Climate. Dodge City has a semiarid, treeless landscape with cottonwood (aspen) trees along a water course.

Man's present evaluation of the natural setting

1. Can Dodge City maintain itself as it has in the past century?
2. What new land ethics might be adopted for Dodge City and vicinity?
3. What are the chief hazards for environmental quality now present in Dodge City?
4. What is the maximum population (carrying capacity) that can be accommodated in the Great Plains?

What is it like to live here?

1. What recreational opportunities are available to residents of the Great Plains?
2. Does tourism have a significant effect on the economy of the area?
3. What are the cultural benefits or disadvantages in the Great Plains?
4. Would this be a good place in which to relocate a family?

"Direct experience" student activities

1. Study of predator-prey relationships, for example, hawks and owls and their prey or foxes and weasels and their food supply.
2. Visit to a livestock reception center, abattoir, or meat-packing center.
3. Study of plant growth in vacant lots or sandy areas with some groundwater supply.
4. Study of microclimates.

5. Visit to game-management area or center from which animals are released by the state for hunting.

KEYSTONE, IOWA—CORN BELT ENVIRONMENT

Keystone, Iowa, is an example of a community that could not exist other than where it is. It is located in an area with some of the richest soil in the world. Suitable for low population density and high-yield farming, this town has about 520 residents. The corn belt, in general, boasts no large communities.

Yet Keystone represents what its name implies—an indispensable link between people and the life-giving soil—a soil with often more than 20 inches of topsoil. For these reasons Keystone deserves a long, hard look, for it epitomizes a worldwide dilemma.

Despite its abundantly rich resources of soil, water, and favorable climate, this area has such drawbacks as cultural sterility, the tendency of persons to leave farmland, and the need to operate large land tracts as farms to produce a profit. Keystone agriculture also points up the problems related to the use of pesticides, fungicides, and large amounts of chemical fertilizers. Can the quality of life for any living beings be maintained if Keystone continues to function as it is now doing? Answers to these questions will provide information to assist student inquiry.

Statement of problems and generalizations sought

1. How did people decide to utilize the corn belt environment in these special ways?
2. What factors attracted settlement here and resulted in the present land use pattern?
3. How have people exploited the natural environment?
4. What is it like to live here?

Natural setting. To understand the relationships among physical and human environments, study must start with the land—how this area came to be so flat to gently rolling (slightly dipping sedimentary rocks underlie the area, the effects of glaciation).

Climate—Continental climates; severe winters, hot summers. Distribution of precipitation—thunderstorms, hailstorms, tornadoes; "The Hailbelt." Hail insurance cost vs. chances of damage.

Keystone soil is fertile. It has high organic content; the mineral plant nutrients are not washed out by rainfall percolating downward through the soil, that is, it is unleached. How is soil formed from earth materials and rock?

Relationship to natural vegetation

1. Was the natural grassland really natural? At one time Indians burned the grasslands and forest borders. What effect did this have on the vegetation of the plains?

Changing agricultural economy

1. What crops are grown in Keystone and vicinity?
2. How did the crop choices influence the pattern of early settlements here?
3. How did the following technological innovations affect the Keystone area—railroads, barbed wire, agricultural machinery?
4. Why is the size of farms continually increasing? What does the term *agribusiness* mean? How much land is enough? How does new agricultural machinery affect farm size?
5. What are farm subsidies?

Rural depopulation

1. Discuss the relationship of some of the following: (a) changing ratio of labor to acreage; (b) decay of the smallest farms; (c) service towns; (d) the influence of changing times; (e) distance to market; (f) problems of providing diverse services to a small, scattered population; (g) commuting to jobs in larger towns; and (h) the attempts at industrialization in farm areas such as Keystone.

Present interaction of physical and human environments

1. How have the following factors affected environmental quality in the Keystone area?
   a. Feeding corn and soybeans to cattle and hogs
   b. Dairy cattle—radiation in milk
   c. Equating chicken and egg production to farm factories
   d. Computerized feed mixing and rationing for all livestock
   e. Use of chemical pesticides and fertilizers
   f. The shift in location of slaughterhouses to great centers like Chicago
   g. Discontinuous land holdings in the same farm operation
2. What are the effects of federal agricultural programs on farm areas such as Keystone?

Is the quality of the land declining?

1. What do we mean by the land ethic?
2. In agricultural terms, what is meant by *soil mining? Erosion* and *fertility?* How does soil mining affect soil?

What is it like to live here?

1. How do population density, the distance between homes and towns, and the special neighborliness contribute to the lack of broad cultural interchange with the rest of the world?
2. Can people in a Keystone type of environment comprehend the different pressures and problems of different environments?
3. Why is basketball the Midwest sport? (End of the crop season.)
4. What are the effects of selective migration on an area such as Keystone?

Direct experience student activities

1. Study of local soil types.
2. Testing local soil samples for acidity, organic content, and mineral nutrients.
3. Influence of local topographies.
4. Interpreting local annual-climate charts.
5. Developing daily citizen-activity tables or logs.
6. Interpreting local census data.
7. Getting newspaper information concerning land use and population activity changes (5, 10, 25, 50 years ago today).
8. Collecting information from older residents or historical society and cemetery studies.

LAS VEGAS—DESERT ENVIRONMENT

Las Vegas' rapid population increase from 64,405 in 1960 to an estimated 275,000 in 1967 illustrates the ultrarapid growth of a southwestern city, whose chief assets are desert climate, a position astride transcontinental routes, and accessible water, available because a dam was partly financed by public funds through the U. S. Bureau of Reclamation. Las Vegas' phenomenal growth in relation to a rather limited natural resource base provides perhaps the best example of the significance of human factors, that is, economic, social, and political factors, in the selection of a site for community development, not necessarily related to the physical environment. Being in a desert oasis, having the closest location in Nevada to the population center of Los Angeles, enjoying Nevada's liberal laws on gambling, and capitalizing on the desire for gambling and entertainment by part of the rather fluid society of Los Angeles—all these factors have played a part in promoting the growth of the gambling and entertainment center of Las Vegas.

Of all the metropolitan areas in the United States, it is the most dependent on tourism and is thus highly vulnerable to changes in disposable income and unemployment rates, particularly for the nearby southern California metropolis. Like Los Angeles, it is also a twentieth century city in terms of its major period of growth. Unlike Atlantic City, it has no natural resource focus for visitor interest. It is almost entirely a creation of the social rather than the physical world.

Some local environmental studies that may be undertaken to provide additional understanding of the problems of a Las Vegas type of environment may include the following.

Life support resources

1. What is the source of your community water supply? In what ways have state or federal funds been used to extend or protect the water supply?
2. What life support resources are provided by the environment of your community?
3. Which life support resources used by your community come from an environment distant from the community?
4. What life support resources used in your community are most vulnerable to destruction or interruption of delivery? Are there any alternate or back-up resources?

Tourism

1. What proportion of people's income-producing activities are derived from tourism in your home community?
2. What means are used to attract tourists to your community?
3. What hardships would be brought about if tourism were to stop altogether in your community?

LONGVIEW, WASHINGTON—NORTHWEST FOREST ENVIRONMENT

Longview is situated in the valley of the Columbia River just east of the coastal mountain ranges in southwest Washington and northwest Oregon. The broad flatlands leading to the inland waters of Puget Sound run northward, making the "long view."

Southwestern Washington has the advantages of a plentiful water supply, a forest timber resource, and a harvest of fish from the bountiful Columbia River, as well as low-cost transportation on that river.

Longview's economy is sensitive to fluctuations in the building trades, especially those using lumber and other forest products. The chief lumber trees are Douglas fir, white pine, ponderosa pine, hemlock, and spruce.

Among the environmental problems that must be dealt with in this northwest forest environment are maintenance of a continuing and harvestable supply of forest trees without soil erosion, the avoidance of water pollution in the Columbia River, and the maintenance of water supply and soil fertility in the great agricultural valley east of the coastal mountain ranges.

Following are some simulation activities and questions.

Direct student experiences

1. Studies in soil composition, soil erosion, and the maintenance of soil fertility.
2. Ecology and stabilization of forest communities.
3. River-port development, maintenance of adequate open space, and environmental quality at the river's edge.
4. The development of forest products and industries.
5. Maintaining adequate environments for wildlife in areas with increasing agriculture, lumbering, and industrialization.
6. The influence of large dams on the essential development of ocean fish in the river:
   a. Effect of excess nitrogen produced by river water cascading over spillways, producing nitrogen disease or bends in fish
   b. Effects of temperature increase of river water produced by lakes impounded behind dams
   c. Effect of dams disrupting natural spawning grounds

River industry pollution

1. What pollutants, if any, are being produced

by (a) paper industries, (b) agricultural industries, and (c) others?
2. What must be done to improve air quality from industries producing air pollutants such as sulfur dioxide by the paper industry?

LYNCH, KENTUCKY—APPALACHIAN COALFIELD ENVIRONMENT

Lynch is an excellent example of a company coal town that is suffering from a malaise affecting that entire area. The town is located in Harlan County, Kentucky, in the heart of the Cumberland Mountains. By 1920 it was the largest of the Kentucky coal towns, with a population of 10,000. Better built than most of the company towns, Lynch suffered along with other neighboring communities during the continuing depression of the coal industry in Appalachia. The depression began with the collapse of the coal market after World War I and continued until World War II; it soon returned in the late 1940's. The population of Lynch dropped to 3,810 by 1960. Native-born whites compose 80% of the population, with blacks representing less than 1% of the total.

Harlan County's peak population, 75,000, was reached during the coal boom of World War II; it had decreased approximately one third by 1960. By relying on heavily mechanized underground equipment and on strip mining and by employing progressively fewer men per ton of coal produced, the coal industry has managed to survive. The 1960 unemployment rate in Harlan County was 13% for males and 5% for females. This high rate of unemployment reflects the general lack of diversification of industry and the related attraction of "parasitic" industry seeking cheap female labor, a situation common in the Appalachians. The disastrous effects of primitive agricultural methods and the lack of land and soil conservation on the part of the coal-mining and lumbering industries in Appalachia provide ample opportunity to discuss conservation practices and objectives.

Some environmental studies that may be undertaken with regard to Lynch might include the following.

Environmental desolation

1. What kinds of blots on the landscape, or ugly places, are to be found in or near your community? What caused the ugliness to be located where you have found it?
2. How does strip mining as it has been commonly practiced exert an influence to mar landscape beauty?
3. The landscape of eastern Kentucky is characterized by many narrow valleys closed in by steep-sided hills. Why is it that many communities in the vicinity of Lynch are only two or three streets wide and several miles in length? Why are the driveways, or approaches, to many persons' homes across bridges?
4. What threats of stream pollution are posed by many strip-mining operations?
5. What suggestions can you locate or create to reduce the great piles of coal slag and waste rock debris that occur in strip-mining areas?
6. What, if anything, is being done to reclaim the lands destroyed by strip mining?

Cultural diversity and poverty

1. Why does an area with only a single dominant or significant industry tend to have depressed salaries and a lower standard of living?
2. What industries employing lower-cost female labor have been attracted to eastern Kentucky?
3. What areas in the vicinity of your community or in your state have lower salaries and often lower living costs? What factors can account for this discrepancy?
4. What differential is there in your community between the industrial salaries of men and

women? Are there any industries in your area dominated by female labor? What factors attracted the industries that employ a majority of females to your area?
5. Why is the section of Appalachia in which Lynch is located known as an "island of of poverty"? Discuss the health and safety hazards of mine work, as well as government regulations and their effectiveness.
6. Why were so few black people influenced to migrate to areas like eastern Kentucky?

LOS ANGELES, CALIFORNIA—MEDITERRANEAN-TYPE ENVIRONMENT

Los Angeles, founded in 1781 by the Spanish, was not located on the seacoast, an interesting contrast with the location that would have been chosen by the more commercially minded British or Americans. Its population in 1850 was 1,610, illustrating the very slow growth of the city up until that time. In mid-nineteenth century California, Los Angeles was a backwater, a distinctly inferior area compared to central California, which had the financial and commercial center of San Francisco, the educational center of Berkeley, and the state capital of Sacramento.

Los Angeles' rapid growth came mostly within the twentieth century, which helps to account for the dominance of the motor car in the transportation system of that city. The estimated population of Los Angeles County in 1970 was 7,223,235, which respresents a smaller numerical gain over 1960 than for the period 1950 to 1960 and the lowest percentage increase since the depression years of the late 1930's. Los Angeles' devotion of space and other resources to the automobile is nationally recognized and presents us with the best region for surveying urban sprawl and the environmental deterioration associated with motor vehicles.

The gradual deterioration of the fragile Mediterranean environment may be illustrated by the effects of smog on vegetation, both natural and agricultural, in the Los Angeles basin. The citrus yields, for example, have been cut in half during the period of greatest smog development, and approximately a million ponderosa pine trees in the San Bernardino National Forest have already been destroyed by smog. This region is one of the best examples of the importance of amenity in regional growth; the major inducement for population growth and the greatest attraction for industrial development is climate, rather than any significant natural resource base other than petroleum. Los Angeles may be considered as an example of the direction in which urbanization in the United States seems to be moving.

Some environmental considerations related to the study of a community such as Los Angeles might include the following.

Mediterranean-type (fragile) environment

1. What are the climatic characteristics of the Los Angeles area?
2. How does the Los Angeles environment resemble that of eastern Spain, the origin of Los Angeles' first settlers?
3. Are any large Spanish cities located in a fundamentally waterless area, such as Los Angeles?
4. What technological influences favored the growth of Los Angeles in the twentieth century after its long, slow growth for more than a century?
5. What are some environmental hazards that have destroyed many homes in the vicinity of Los Angeles?
6. What characteristics of the Los Angeles environment make it a fragile one?
7. Has concern for the maintenance of environmental stability been a major consideration in the development of the Los Angeles area? How can you account for this?
8. What local environmental resources, if any,

directly contribute to the life support of Los Angeles?

9. What environmentally based industries or human activities such as agriculture or mining sustain those living inland from Los Angeles?
10. What are the most fragile environments in or near your own community? How may they best be used or maintained?
11. What environmental factors will be significant in the future development or maintenance of Los Angeles as a large urban center?

Water supply

1. From what sources does the Los Angeles water supply come?
2. What are alternative water sources to increase the supply if the need for water increases?
3. Evaluate whether or not federal funds should be expended to increase the Los Angeles water supply.
4. Can the quality of soils and their productivity be maintained after many years of irrigation?

Transportation

1. Thinking of Los Angeles automatically brings visions of the most complex and crowded urban highway system in the world. Why is this not characteristic of large cities such as Chicago or New York?
2. Why is Los Angeles particularly susceptible to smog and air pollution?
3. What remedies may be used to relieve the severe air pollution in Los Angeles?
4. What is the possibility of a severe air pollution problem occurring in your community?
5. Why is 1975 or later to be the target date for more adequate control of the air-polluting constituents of automobile exhausts?
6. Can the vegetation already destroyed by air pollution in the Los Angeles area be restored? If so, by what means?

Culture and population

1. To what extent have the customs of Mexico influenced the culture of Los Angeles?
2. Rapid change in customs, mores, and life style seem to be more characteristic of Southern California than most of the United States. How can you account for this? Evaluate whether or not it is fair to say that Los Angeles typifies the "throw-away culture."
3. What is the relative proportion of minority and nationality groups in Los Angeles?
4. What have been the factors producing some of the racial tensions such as were evident at Watts?
5. What suggestions can be made for overcoming tensions that exist among segments of the Los Angeles population?

NEW BEDFORD, MASSACHUSETTS—NEW ENGLAND ENVIRONMENT

New Bedford is most famous as the site of one of the great whaling seaports, which reached its peak during the nineteenth century. A museum of the whaling industry interests many tourists who visit there.

With a population of more than 100,000, New Bedford is a seaport community of considerable size located on the southern shore of Massachusetts. The harbor is sheltered from high wind-driven wave action because it is located in the lee of the Elizabeth Islands and Martha's Vineyard. The severity of the typical New England winter is lessened by the moderating influence of the ocean.

Although the whaling industry has now been sharply reduced as a result of the overkill of whales, New Bedford still functions as an active fishing center. The principal fish caught are codfish, mackerel, halibut, hake, and haddock.

New Bedford represents a large seaport community in transition. Originally its environment was favored with a bounty of fish and nearby forests to supply wood for the shipbuilding of a century or more ago. The present fishing fleet is now scarcely dependent on Massachusetts-grown forest products for its raw materials. The development of the textile industry in New Bedford paralleled that of many New England communities. With the migration of many textile-manufacturing firms to the southeast, New Bedford has had an increasing activity in the production of ready-made apparel.

In this way, the original environment-based industries have given way to people-centered industries. These population-related industries, in turn, undergo modification, as labor situations or other factors affect the cost of production.

Answers to the following questions will point up New Bedford's environmental impact.

Forests

1. If there are forests in your vicinity, what was the lumber used for in the early history of your community? Are these same needs being met by forests in your area today?
2. What are some other uses for forests besides lumber production? Are any of these functions being carried out today?

Water quality

1. When a large community is situated on a narrow estuary, what particular need is there to protect such a body of water from extensive pollution?
2. What pollution of water in your area is attributed to your community? Are these conditions, if any, regulated by state or federally imposed water-quality standards? What has been done recently, if anything, to reduce the occurrence or danger of water pollution in your community?

Tourism

1. What characteristics of environmental quality attract tourists to a community?
2. Do any tourists visit your community? For what purpose?
3. Has the number of tourists increased or decreased in recent years? What improvements in environmental quality could be made in your community to increase the number of tourists?

Fishing. Many persons favor abolition of the hunting and killing of whales, as advocated by former Secretary of the Interior, Walter J. Hickel.

1. Why is it considered significant not to hunt any species to extinction? Does the danger of whale hunting typify the hostility of individuals for many parts of their environment?
2. How does a fishing industry contribute to environmental quality? What precautions must be taken and restrictions made for any fishing industry, to ensure a continuing supply of fish?

Wildlife. In the vicinity of New Bedford the seabirds, including ducks and geese, constitute an environmental treasure—so also does the wealth of crustaceans and snails found in rocky tide pools.

1. In terms of wildlife, what is the greatest treasure in your community?
2. What steps are being taken to ensure that the wildlife be protected or increased?

NEW YORK, NEW YORK—NORTHEAST MEGALOPOLITAN ENVIRONMENT

New York is so important in the American economy and society that it must be considered in this list of sample study areas. New York's problems of pollution, urban renewal, and ghettos make it a focal point for efforts to combat these urban plagues. New York's highly diversified industry (garment, printing, and publishing), its leadership in cultural and artistic fields, and its function as an entertainment and communications center—all present opportunities to explore the most complex phase of the interrelationships in the physical and human worlds. Many challenging problems can be posed to students in studying New York's metropolitan area. For example, has

New York surpassed an optimum size for cities? How would one determine such a size? Will New York be surpassed by Los Angeles or Chicago in growth and economic importance? The nature and growth of the East Coast megalopolis may be considered, in general, with a study of New York's metropolitan area.

The students may focus on New York's environment by considering the following questions.

Environment

1. What are the climatic conditions in the New York area?
2. What environmental features favored the development of New York as a city?
3. Are environmental factors still the significant influence in maintaining the size and growth of New York?
4. What is the present environmental impact of New York with respect to such factors as (a) air pollution, (b) pollution of the Hudson River and New York Bay, (c) accumulation of solid wastes, and (d) urban sprawl?
5. New York and its suburbs, especially in New Jersey and on Long Island, represent the highest population density in the world. Evaluate whether there is a limit as to how many people can have an environment of high quality in any given area. This idea of limit is called *carrying capacity.* Can it differ from one location to another? If so, what factors could influence the carrying capacity?

Urban decay. Perhaps the degradation of many parts of the central city of New York is typical of many large cities.

1. What factors have produced degradation of environments in the central city?
2. As cities face increasing costs for services to citizens, what assistance can the city expect from more distant environments (a) in the state, (b) in the country, and (c) in the rest of the world?
3. When cities develop housing for urban residents in the future, what means can be employed to ensure (a) greater successful utilization by low-income urban residents and (b) a longer useful life to the buildings or the area?
4. Evaluate the following suggestions:
   a. Urban housing and buildings should be produced for a maximum life of twenty years.
   b. Urban architecture should be placed largely underground to provide adequate and pleasant land surfaces to be used as common living space and to avoid harmful rainwater runoff now plaguing all cities.
   c. All cities should be limited in size by the carrying capacity of the immediate environment.
5. Since cities are the direct or indirect sources for most goods that are supplied to people in outlying areas, evaluate the worth of a city to a region in the following terms:
   a. Employment
   b. Source of food products
   c. Source of nonfood products
   d. Center of culture
   e. Center for education
   f. Center for human creativity
   g. Tax burden
   h. Center for organized or sporadic crime
   i. Source of environmental pollution

ATLANTIC CITY, NEW JERSEY—MID-ATLANTIC COASTAL ENVIRONMENT

Atlantic City, a resort founded in the mid-nineteenth century, is a prime example of the interaction of man and the natural environment of an offshore barrier beach. The natural beauty of this rather fragile environment has been negatively affected by population growth in terms of water pollution, particularly in the bays behind Absecon Island, on which Atlantic City is built.

The problems of a seasonal economy are related

to the social and economic problems of this area. The convention bureau, the chamber of commerce, and others have attempted to lengthen the season and thus smooth out the peaks and valleys caused by the tourist season. The convention business and the Miss America Pageant may be considered endeavors to solve the problems of the seasonal economy.

The broad question related to the interaction between people and the environment is the problem of the natural shifting of sand along the barrier beaches, the opening and closing of inlets and channels, and the continual change of the shoreline through natural means. People's vital interest in stabilizing the shoreline and in protecting their structures against the sea and winds places them in dramatic conflict with the forces of nature. Atlantic City will serve as a prime example of the deterioration of the natural environment, brought about by the sheer numbers of people who were attracted by the original beauty of that environment.

Statement of problems

1. What qualities of the physical environment support a resort here?
2. How and why did man change his evaluation of the physical environment here from nearly useless to highly valuable?
3. What are the societal functions of resorts? How are resorts related to the other cities of the megalopolis and to the industrial revolution?
4. What changes has man made in this environment?

Natural setting. The landforms of Atlantic City include offshore sandbars (barrier beaches), tidal inlets, back bays, marshes, and estuaries. Its climate involves modifications of northeastern United States climate by marine influences; contrast the climates of Philadelphia, New York City, and Atlantic City.

Natural vegetation, including occasional heavy grass, was the ground cover.

Man's changing evaluation of the natural setting

1. Why did early settlers in this region prefer the mainland, avoiding the offshore sandbars, such as the Atlantic City area, except for occasional fishing or seasonal grazing?

Future problems and prospects. Some direct experience student activities possible to simulate this environment follow:

1. Study of wave action in ponds, lakes, or seashore.
2. Monitoring daily and seasonal arrival of visitors.
3. Study of phytoplankton in ponds or streams.
4. Collecting information concerning use of pesticides–individual, community, and industrial.
5. Charting the local community's entire transportation network.
6. Quadrat and transect studies to describe one or more significant natural communities found locally.

A REPRESENTATIVE IN-DEPTH CASE STUDY

Have you ever wondered how it would be to live in a city that you share not only with 60,000 other residents, but also with more than 16 million visitors each year? During three months of the year, this city is a beehive of activity and excitement, but for the rest of the year it takes on the routine character of most other cities. This city may offer more to its visitors than to its own residents, and if you lived there, it would seem to be yours only part of the time.

Such is the character of many so-called "resort cities." For many reasons these resorts attract large numbers of visitors or temporary residents at various times of the year.

One typical resort is Atlantic City. Sometimes known as "the nation's amusement capital," Atlantic City has been a mecca for tourists, honeymooners, and vacationers for more than a century. This world-famous resort boasts the world's finest

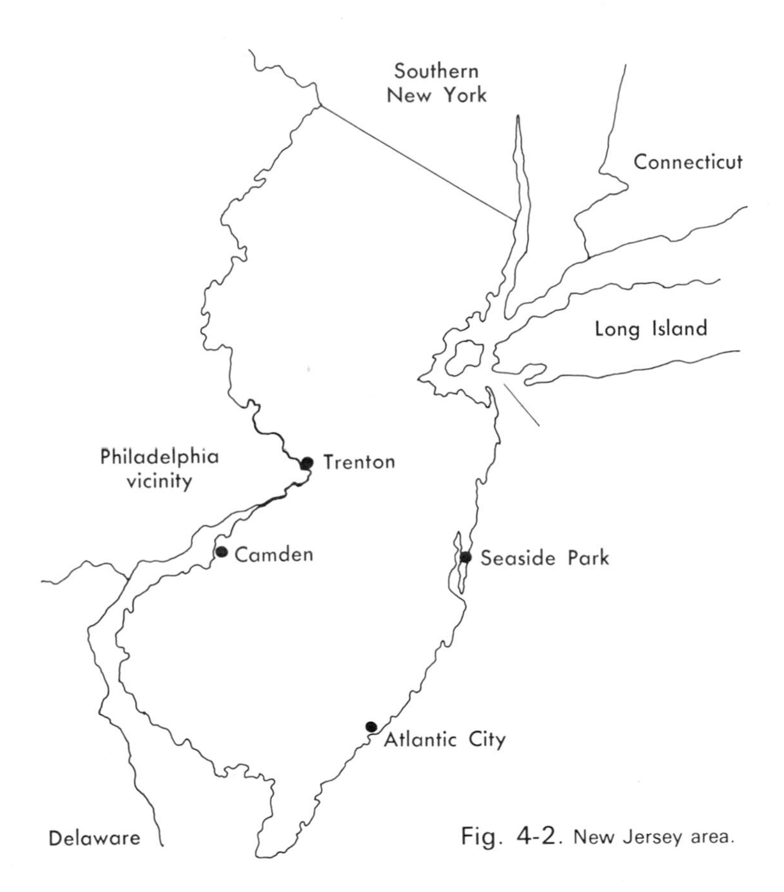

Fig. 4-2. New Jersey area.

sand beach. The natural beachfront and recreational resources of the city encouraged promotion of the area as a health and vacation resort.

Atlantic City is located on Absecon Island, some 140 miles from New York City and 60 miles from Philadelphia (Fig. 4-2). The island is more than 8 miles long, about 1 mile wide, and separated from the mainland by 5 miles of salt marsh and bay. Absecon is derived from the Indian word *Absegami,* which means "place of the swans." The shoreline of Absecon Island trends east-west, rather than north-south as you would expect. Thus it faces cool, southerly, onshore winds in summer that give Atlantic City a definite climatic advantage over rivals along the New Jersey Coast.

This city of 12 square miles served as the model for the popular game Monopoly, a long-time favorite of millions of children and adults. Names such as Boardwalk, Park Place, and Baltic Avenue, which are essential to the game, are in fact real-life street names in Atlantic City.

Atlantic City was designed in 1854 by Richard Osborne, a railroad designer, whose scheme for laying out the street pattern was unique and interesting. Streets running parallel to the beach were named for the world's oceans and seas, such as

Fig. 4-3. Part of the Atlantic City ocean front. (Courtesy Atlantic City Convention Bureau.)

Atlantic, Pacific, and Mediterranean. Streets running from the beach to the marshes are named for states and capital cities. Therefore visitors have the advantage of being familiar with the names of most Atlantic City streets.

What attracts 16 million visitors to Atlantic City each year and supports a population of 60,000?

Atlantic City has some of the most modern hotels and motels in the country. These are located primarily on the boardwalk and within one block of the beachfront. Elsewhere in the city are found apartment houses and beautiful residential areas with landscaped gardens surrounding large, imposing homes. Some streets are lined with quiet cottages and others with houses that have seen better days (Fig. 4-3).

The climate of Atlantic City has helped to make it attractive on a year-round basis. Weather records for more than fifty years show an average rainfall of 41.44 inches annually. Temperature charts indicate that Atlantic City, by comparison with nearby areas, is 10 to 15 degrees cooler in summer and 10 to 15 degrees warmer in winter. During August, hay fever victims find comfort in the "clean" air of the resort.

1. How do these figures compare to those pertaining to other large cities in the United States?
2. Complete Tables 6 and 7.

A pollen count of 7 grains per square centimeter on a slide is equivalent to 25 pollen grains per cubic yard of air. News media sometimes report the pollen count in number of ragweed pollen grains per cubic yard of air. To obtain the pollen grains per cubic yard of air, multiply the pollen count per square centimeter by the standard conversion

TABLE 6. Climate of Atlantic City and other cities in the United States

	AVERAGE ANNUAL TEMPERATURE	LOWEST RECORDED TEMPERATURE	HIGHEST RECORDED TEMPERATURE	AVERAGE ANNUAL PRECIPITATION	AVERAGE ANNUAL HUMIDITY	
					DAY (1 P.M.)	NIGHT (1 A.M.)
Atlantic City	54.2° F.	−9° F.	104° F.	40.91 in.	81%	54%
New York	52.3° F.	−14° F.	102° F.	41.63 in.		
Boston		−18° F.	104° F.	38.94 in.		
Atlanta		−8° F.	103° F.	47.58 in.		
Miami		27° F.	96° F.	59.18 in.		
Chicago		−20° F.	109° F.	31.56 in.		
Denver		−29° F.	105° F.	13.99 in.		
Tacoma		7° F.	98° F.	38.00 in.		
Phoenix		16° F.	118° F.	7.62 in.		
Houston		5° F.	108° F.	44.84 in.		
Minneapolis		−34° F.	108° F.	27.31 in.		
Los Angeles		28° F.	109° F.	14.76 in.		
San Francisco		27° F.	101° F.	20.23 in.		
Your community						

TABLE 7. Pollen count of several New Jersey cities*

CITY	NUMBER OF DAYS COLLECTED	HIGHEST POLLEN COUNT/CM²	DATE OF HIGHEST POLLEN COUNT	NUMBER OF DAYS ABOVE 7/CM² OR 25 GRAINS/YD.³ OF AIR
Wildwood, N. J.—near Atlantic City on New Jersey coast	61	11	Sept. 11	2
Newark, N. J.	45	23	Aug. 26	6
Trenton, N. J.	61	49	Sept. 2	31

*Data from Bulletin 3, Dec. 15, 1969, New Jersey Division of Environmental Health, New Jersey State Department of Health.

factor of 3.6. A ragweed pollen count of 7 per square centimeter on any one day is generally considered the pollen concentration at which persons susceptible to ragweed pollen might show symptoms of pollinosis.

Allergists have an interest in the relative levels of pollen concentration in the air from day to day, in relation to changes in the severity of hay fever symptoms in their patients. Citizens also have a general interest in pollen levels and its effect on public health.

3. Which cities have a pollen count similar to that of the New Jersey shore?
4. Which city has the highest pollen count? What possible reasons can you give to account for the variances in pollen counts?
5. Do you know how to describe the climate of your community to a visitor or a distant pen pal? How hot does it get? How much rain usually falls? Have one member of the class or a small committee write a single letter to request a yearly summary of weather data from your state weather bureau, local agricultural cooperative, newspaper, or radio station. Use each source for information only once. If there are other classes in your grade who could use this information, you may wish to share it with them.
   a. Make a bar or line graph of the average monthly temperatures.
   b. Make a bar or line graph of the rainfall for each month.
6. What other questions could you answer with this climate summary?
7. How does your climate compare with that in Atlantic City?
8. How did this resort come to gain the reputation it now has as a resort city?

Prior to 1850 a very small fishing village was located on Absecon Island, which was reached by a combination of horse and carriage and sailing ship.

Early in the 1850's Dr. Jonathan Pitney and several associates who owned ironworks or glass factories in the New Jersey Pine Barrens banded together to build a railroad from Camden, on the Delaware River, to Absecon Island. Dr. Pitney was ridiculed when he speculated that someday a resort city would develop on Absecon Island at the eastern end of the railroad. Those who saw the railroad as an aid to industry were greatly disappointed with the decline of the iron industry in New Jersey. Dr. Pitney's predictions came true, and despite the early lack of good hotel facilities. Atlantic City grew rapidly. The phenomenal growth and prosperity of Atlantic City exceeded

TABLE 8. Population statistics for Atlantic City and its suburban neighbors since 1920

	1920	1930	1940	1950	1960	1970
Atlantic City	50,707	66,198	64,094	61,657	59,544	47,859
Ventnor	2,193	6,674	7,905	8,158	8,688	10,385
Margate	249	2,913	3,266	4,715	9,474	10,576
Pleasantville	5,887	11,580	11,050	11,938	15,172	13,778
Total for Atlantic County	83,914	124,823	124,066	132,399	160,880	175,043

SUGGESTED WORK SHEET

LOCAL POPULATION STUDY

Population statistics for ______________________ (name of city).

YEAR	POPULATION	PERCENT INCREASE OR DECREASE
1920		
1930		
1940		
1950		
1960		
1970		

List what you consider to be the advantages and disadvantages of living in a large city, then of living in a small town *near* a large city.

Living in a large city
Advantages:
Disadvantages:

Living in a small town near a large city
Advantages:
Disadvantages:

On the basis of your answers, which place would you choose to live? Give reasons for your choice.

the most fanciful dreams of its early planners. By 1877 two railroads served Atlantic City, thus assuring the success of the resort.

By 1900 the year-round population of Atlantic City reached 28,000, continued to grow, and by 1930 had reached 66,000 (Table 8). Since that time the population has shown a gradual decline. Certainly the growth of nearby towns drew people away from Atlantic City.

9. What possible reasons can you give for the decline of population in many cities? What trends can you determine in the population of your community over the past fifty years? See accompanying suggested work sheet.

Atlantic City became famous throughout the world for its boardwalk, a 60-foot-wide and 7-mile-long walkway along the ocean front, made of wood, steel, and concrete. Ocean piers containing amusements and concessions of every type were extended outward from the boardwalk toward the sea.

The Miss America Beauty Pageant (Fig. 4-4), held in September of each year, became one of Atlantic City's most prominent events. Originally planned to extend the summer season beyond Labor Day, the pageant begins with the Miss America boardwalk parade, which is viewed by 150,000 persons. Beautiful girls have been coming from across the nation to Atlantic City to enter the competition since 1921. No other contest has yet matched the glamor and interest of the crowning of Miss America, which is televised for millions of viewers annually.

Another Atlantic City innovation, which now ranks second to the city's hotel-motel and restaurant business is its multimillion-dollar saltwater taffy enterprise. Visitors to Atlantic City at any

Fig. 4-4. Miss America Beauty Pageant.

time of the year would not think of leaving this resort without purchasing a box of saltwater taffy, which in fact contains no salt water. Why then the name *saltwater taffy?* Legend has it that many years ago a candy merchant stored his candy for the winter. The ocean flooded his store, soaking his candy with salt water. Afterward he liked the taste of the candy and from then on called it saltwater taffy.

10. Can you suggest any other possible reason for this name?

Mid-Atlantic coastal environment

Saltwater swimming is different. Your tongue and your eyes tell you that. Salt water has extra buoyancy, caused by the dissolved minerals, which increase the density of the water and make a swimmer's body float somewhat higher than it does in fresh water.

1. Can you explain how the minerals got into the ocean? Did you ever notice the grayish white spots left when drops of water dry up after a car is washed? Can you relate the minerals that form these spots to the process that resulted in a salty ocean?

Undertow furnishes an example of the mystery of the ocean. Most people are familiar with the word, but many have only a hazy notion of what undertow really is. If you could stand at the shore and watch the breaking waves moving toward the beach, it would be obvious that the water in each wave rolls back, making way for a new wave to throw its water on the sand. Under normal circumstances incoming water rides the surface, whereas outgoing water hugs the bottom. This returning water is properly called *undertow* and is not dangerous to a swimmer. If the swimmer stays on the surface, normal wave action prevents him from drifting out to sea.

However, when the surface water is quite warm compared to the water below, the returning water of a spent wave, especially when onshore winds are strong, does not slip readily under the shoreward-moving surface water. At this time some of the returning water finds its way back to the ocean via the surface. This means that if you were to swim parallel to the beach, you would be swept alternately seaward and landward.

When this condition exists, the seabound current is called a riptide (even though it is not related to the moon-and-sun-caused tides) (Fig. 4-5). When carried seaward by a riptide, the inexperienced swimmer is likely to panic and try to swim against it directly toward shore. The riptide has given a bad but incorrect reputation to the term *undertow.*

2. On the basis of what you have just read, what would you advise a swimmer to do if he found himself being carried seaward by a riptide?

The beach sand is a product of the waves, which are engaged ceaselessly in the beach-making process. As waves approach the shore, they are undercut by friction with the shallow bottom (the water not being deep enough for the wave to complete its vertical oscillation) and by water returning from a previous wave. The incoming waves are toppled in much the same way that a football player is when a blocker throws himself against his opponent's shins. The toppled wave crashes down onto the beach as breaking surf and creates a temporary mixture of swirling water and sand. As soon as the turbulence ends, the coarser earth particles drop out of the water. If any fine materials such as silt and clay are present, they are held in suspension by the motion of the water and by movement of molecules within the water. These fine materials are then carried seaward by the undertow and deposited as a muddy layer on the bottom a short distance from shore. If there are rocks on the shoreline, wave action tumbles them against each other and grinds them slowly into smaller pieces in the same way that stones

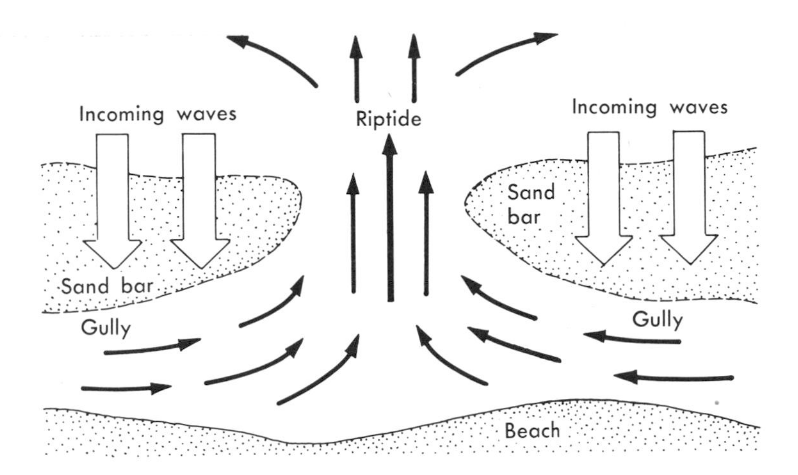

Fig. 4-5. Riptide (backwash) is really a fast-moving offshore current produced by wave action and beach topography.

and gems are ground in a hobbyist's tumbling device. (The action is quite similar to the tumbling action in a clothes dryer.)

Many descriptions of seabeaches tell of sparkling white sand. Atlantic City boasts of its white sands, but some beaches are noted for sands of striking colors such as the Playa Colorado of Venezuela.

3. You probably have a bathing beach at the edge of a lake, river, or ocean near your community. Can you find sands of other shades or colors besides white? What causes these variations? Make a chart showing location, color of sand, and possible origin of color.

At Atlantic City there are no rocks. The land is made up of soft earth materials that are a part of the Atlantic Coastal Plain extending from Cape Cod southward to Florida. These materials are layers of sediments eroded from the Appalachian Mountains at a time when the mountains were much higher than they are now and deposited along the Atlantic Coast.

As the ocean constantly "works over" the beach material, inland rivers and streams bring new deposits, which the waves eventually sort out. All running water is capable of carrying some earth materials as it flows. The faster the flow, the larger the particles that can be carried.

4. Somewhere near your school or home, you can locate a hillside or slope where no plants are growing and the earth materials are exposed. You will probably notice that some of the earth materials have been deposited at the base of the hillside. How could you locate and collect evidence there to support your answer to the following question: What do you think will happen to suspended earth materials when the speed of the water is decreased?
5. Before you visit the hillside, make a list of what you expect to look for and to find. What other questions occurred to you as you were studying the earth materials at the slope?
6. State a rule to describe how coarse and fine earth materials are sorted out.
7. Fine and coarse sand are associated with

different beach slopes. Can you suggest which one is likely to be found on the steeper slope? On the gentler slope?

The same surf action that creates the sandy beach makes other features found along the coast. Offshore breakers build raised sandy ridges, called sandbars, that run parallel to the shoreline on the ocean floor.

These sandbars are especially common at the mouth of a river or stream that carries mud, sand, and gravel as building materials which the waves sort out and pile up. The writer of the hymn with the line "Someone far from harbor you may guide across the bar" was familiar with the hazard of the sandbar that is likely to be found at the mouth of a river. Navigational charts not only show the bars but also frequently supply a written note beginning "After crossing the bar the channel is" and then go on to state how many feet deep the channel is to a specific inland location. Wherever waves of water strike the shore of a pond, lake, or ocean, the shoreline is battered and torn away to some extent. Often the shoreline appears as though there were a little step or bench between the level where the waves seldom or never touch and the water level itself.

8. Visit any lake, pond, or beach to see whether you can find this step or bench mark. Can you suggest a rule relating the size of the waves to the height of the bench mark?
9. Suppose you lived in an area where an ancient lake or sea was once located? How could you locate the boundary lines of that former body of water?

Barrier beaches such as Absecon Island, the one on which Atlantic City is situated, are built in much the same way as sandbars. Wind action is added to that of the waves so that sand dunes are formed. Coarse grass and other vegetation anchor the sand, and a relatively stable shore feature is formed. When the barrier beaches are formed parallel to and seaward from the mainland, shallow bays are established between the mainland and the beaches. These shallow bays have been given such names as back bay, sound, and lagoon. Along the eastern coast of Florida, a lengthy stretch of lagoon is called the "Indian River."

As the tides rise and fall, water surges into and retreats from the coastal lagoons through openings in the barrier beaches. In Florida and along the coast of the Gulf of Mexico, these openings are called *passes,* but along the New Jersey coast they are known as *inlets.* Thus the northern end of Absecon Island is terminated by Absecon Inlet and the southern end by Longport Inlet.

The daily inflow and outflow of water through inlets continually shifts particles of sand and silt, so that the shape of the bottom is constantly changing. Storms speed up this process, and an exceptional one can completely close an inlet or open a new one.

In recent geological times the water level has risen along the Atlantic Coast from Cape Cod to Cape Hatteras, so that the mouths of rivers and streams along the coast have been flooded. Each widened and deepened arm of a river system thus flooded is called an estuary (Fig. 4-6). These tidal estuaries have a continually changing level of water and daily changes in direction of flow, in response to lunar tides. The estuaries carry sediments from the mainland into the coastal lagoons. The sediments are distributed by tidal action in the lagoons, gradually changing these shallow basins into exceptionally flat, grass-covered marshlands.

Sometimes when you are swimming at the beach, you seem to be swept along the beach by the water. Did you happen to notice the direction of the wind when this occurred? The wind frequently strikes the coast at an angle that forces water to travel along the beach just offshore.

10. Obtain a screw-top plastic container of 1 pint or more capacity. Using a sink at home or school for a test tank, pour water into the container until it is nearly sub-

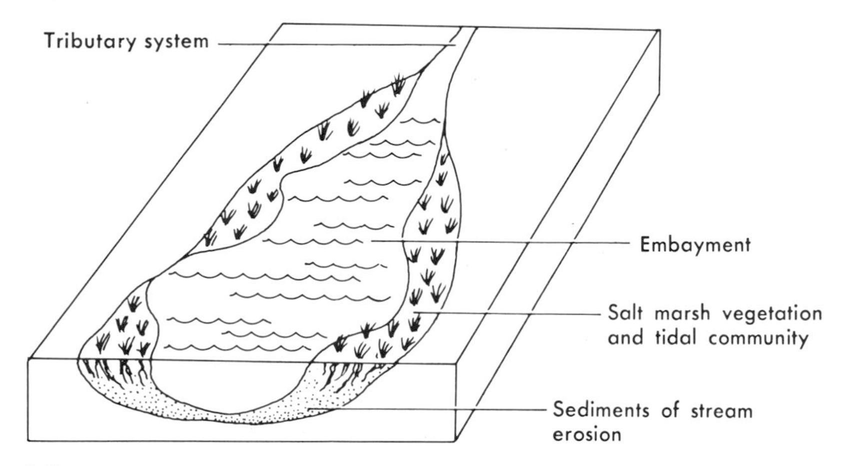

Fig. 4-6. Estuaries are formed where a river has cut a valley to the sea at a time when the ocean level was lower than at present. When the ocean level rises, the coastline is drowned, and many estuaries are formed. The eastern and southern coasts of the United States from Long Island to Galveston, Texas, are examples of a drowned coastline.

merged in the test tank. Lowering the container in the water will ensure that its movement will indicate water and not air currents. Take the water-filled container to a lake or seashore and place it in the water. It will be best to have a good length of light fishing line tied to the bottle to prevent it from moving beyond your reach.

a. Why is this precaution necessary for maintaining environmental quality?
b. How might you increase the accuracy of your observation of shore currents?

11. If you want to relate any current flow to wind direction, you will probably want to use a magnetic compass or draw a sketch map of your test site. You can get more accurate information if you bring a watch with a second hand and a 50-foot steel tape. How would they assist in obtaining more detailed and accurate information? You may want to devise a special chart on which to place your observed information before you go to the test site. How would such a chart be helpful?

This same current, which drags a swimmer along with it and makes his beach gear appear to have moved, picks up sand and carries it north or south along the Atlantic Coast. Sandy Hook was built by these *longshore* currents, as they were carried westward into Raritan Bay (Fig. 4-7). These currents are continually at work, so that Sandy Hook is being enlarged each year. In the southern part of New Jersey, southward-flowing longshore currents, joined by water flowing outward from the inlets, are adding to the width of the northern ends of the barrier beach islands, thus making the coast somewhat "stepped" in appearance.

12. Where does the sand come from for this shoreline buildup?
13. From local gas stations obtain road maps covering any shorelines, Atlantic, Gulf, or Pacific. Can you tell, using the information above, if longshore currents are there and

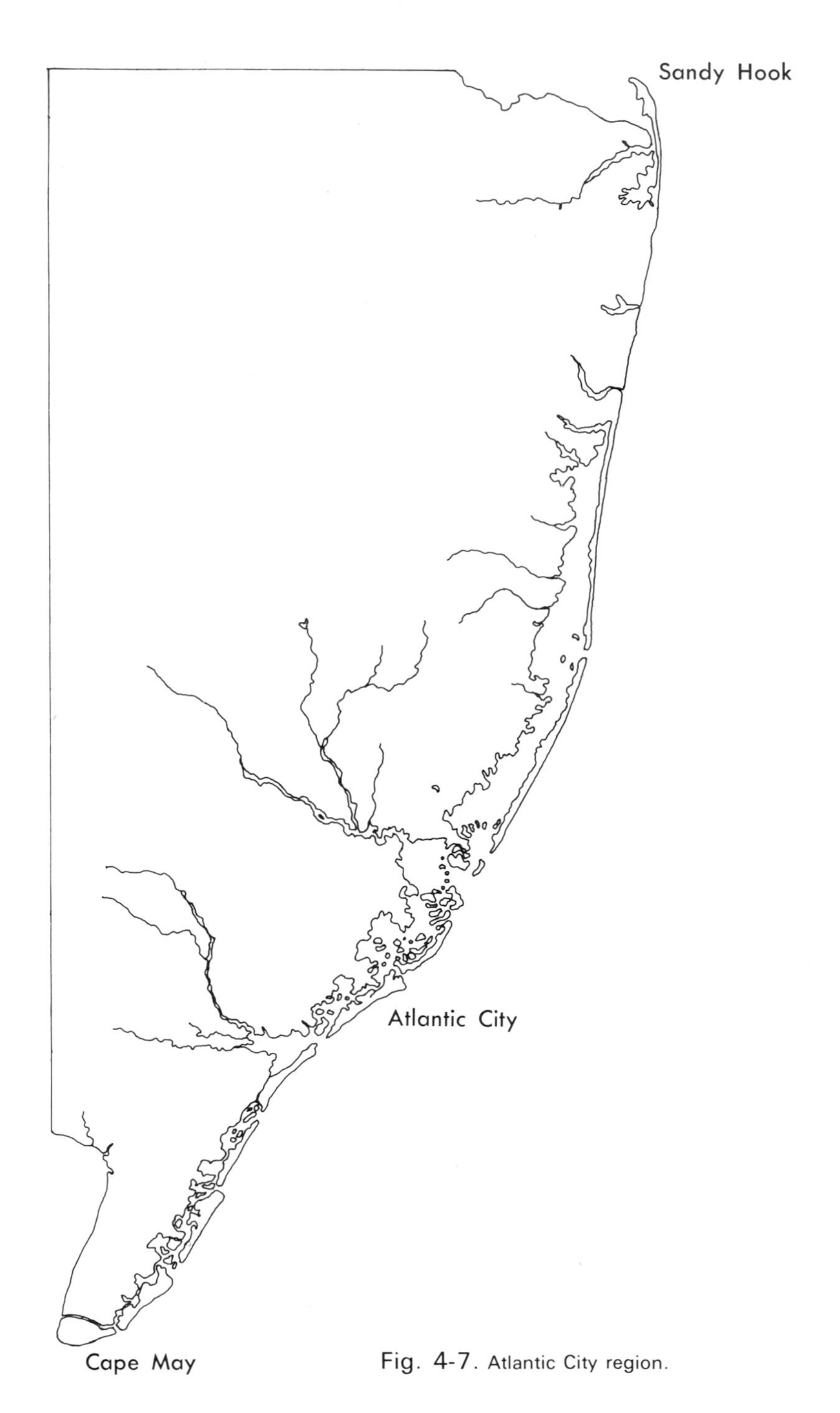

Fig. 4-7. Atlantic City region.

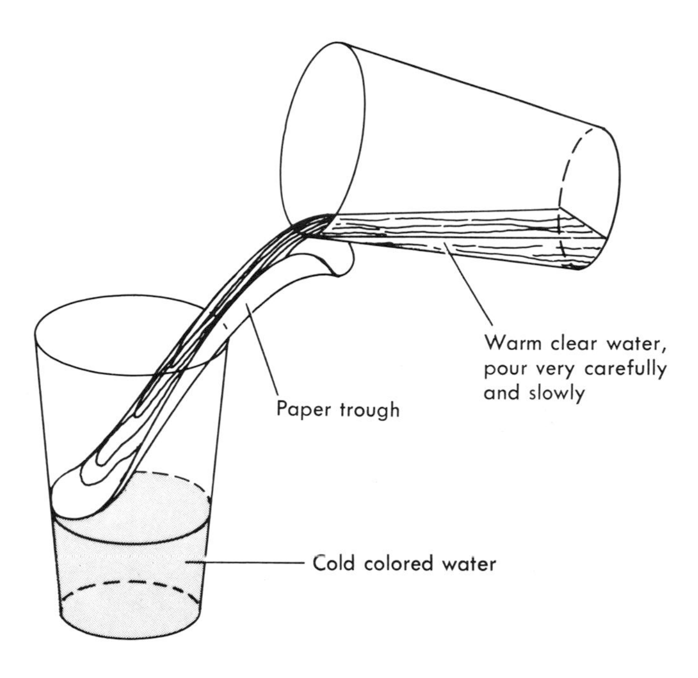

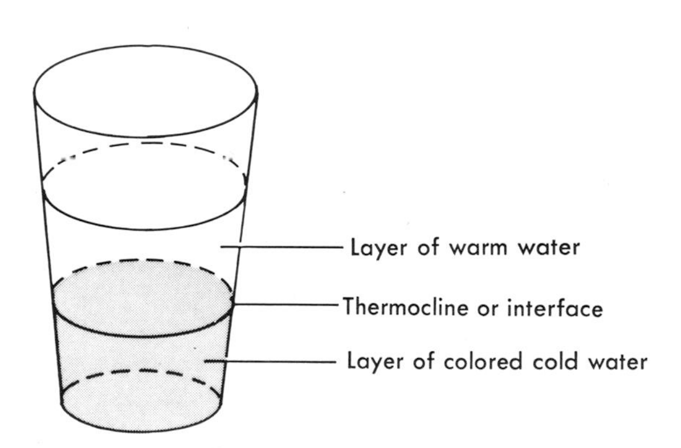

Fig. 4-8. Making a water thermocline.

in which direction they are moving? What types of evidence do you look for?

A frequent visitor to the shore often notices that a strong onshore wind (from water to land) is accompanied by above-average ocean temperatures and that an offshore wind (from land to water) is followed by below-average water temperatures. As you may have guessed, the direction of the wind brings about the change in the temperature of the water. Warm water is lighter than cold and floats on top of colder water in much the same way that oil in a salad dressing floats on top of the heavier vinegar. When the wind blows toward shore, the warm water accumulates, but when the wind blows seaward, the warm water is driven away from the coast and cold water from below rises to replace it, thus making the water at the beach cold. The sudden onset of an offshore wind can cause a dramatic drop in the ocean temperature.

14. Place some cold or ice water to the halfway mark in a glass jar or beaker and color it red or blue with vegetable or food-coloring dye. In a second jar or beaker place some warmer water (Fig. 4-8). Now place a flat piece of paper in the cold-water jar, so that it just rests on top of the water in a U shape. Pour the warm water very slowly onto the paper until the container is nearly full. Now pull and slide the piece of paper slowly from the jar, so that the edge of the paper moves gradually away from the two water layers.
    a. Do you think the water layers will remain separated? What reason or evidence do you have for your hypothesis?
    b. What other questions occur to you about this demonstration? Can you answer these new questions by your own experiments?
    c. Would it be possible to separate salt water and fresh water into layers in the same way?

If you could walk barefooted across a dry beach such as Atlantic City's on a July afternoon and then step into the ocean, you would discover that the sand feels hot and the water feels cold. However, when you retraced your steps around midnight, you would find the sand cold and the water warm. When you stop to think about the sand and water temperatures, it may occur to you that the water temperature did not change much, if any, but the sand temperature changed considerably.

15. How could you test this in your home area?

When the atmosphere at the shore is relatively calm, the alternation of hot land–cool sea and cool land–warm sea brings about a daily wind reversal that has been labelled a *land-and-sea breeze* (Fig. 4-9). Sometime around noon each day land temperatures overtake sea temperatures. When this occurs, if there are no overriding winds, the cooler, heavier air from the sea pushes toward the warmer, lighter air over the land. Depending on the atmospheric conditions at the time, the breeze from the sea may move inland from a fraction of a mile to a distance of several miles. It is this cooling breeze that attracts hundreds of thousands of visitors to the New Jersey beaches during the hot days of summer. In the early morning hours the land becomes quite cool compared to the water, which does not cool off so rapidly. When this occurs, the sea breeze ceases, and the surface air flows from the cooler land to the warmer sea, establishing a land breeze. Since ancient times coastal fishermen depending on wind to power their boats have known about and used the land breeze to propel them seaward in the early morning and the land breeze to bring them homeward in the late afternoon.

The land-and-sea breeze can be used as a model to understand the monsoons of Asia. The summer monsoon is an enormous sea breeze that blows toward the continent (land) as it heats up under the summer sun. The winter monsoon is a land breeze of continental size. As the land cools off after the departure of the summer sun, the cool, heavy air that accumulates blows away from the continent toward the ocean.

As you have already learned, the ocean modified Atlantic City's climate. Some of the oceanic influence is immediate and local, but some of it comes from a relatively great distance.

Two gigantic cells within the earth's atmosphere, each reaching from North America to Europe, are located east of Atlantic City. The

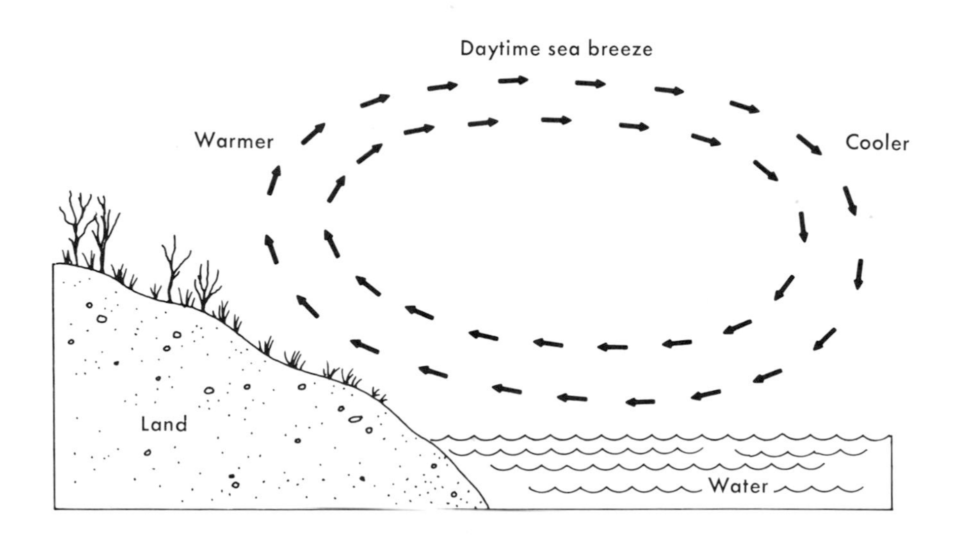

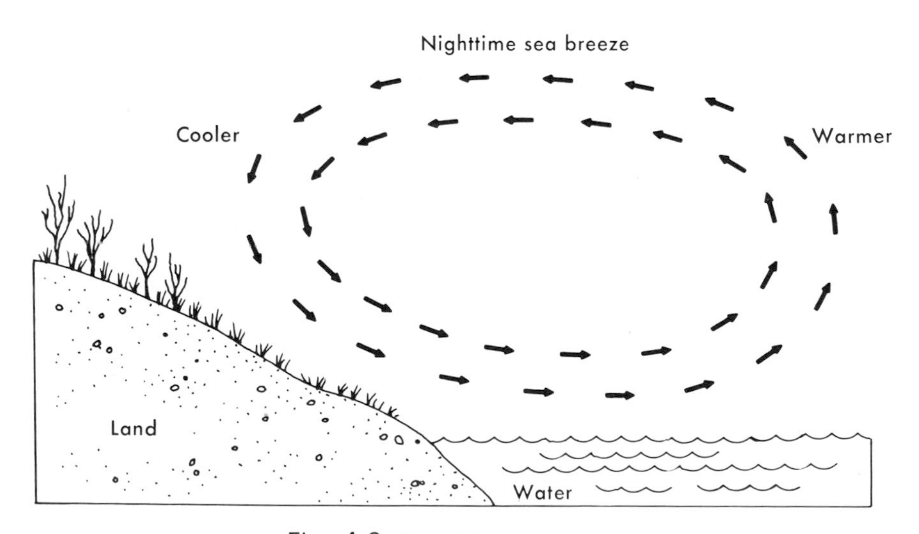

Fig. 4-9. Coastal breeze patterns.

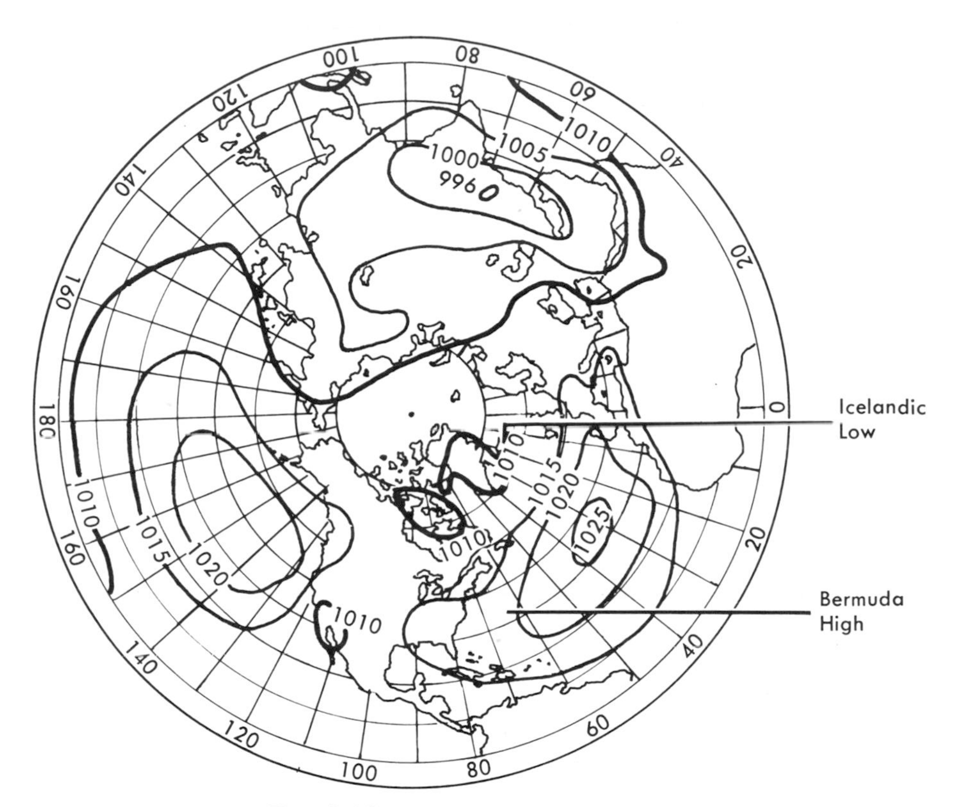

Fig. 4-10. Icelandic Low and Bermuda High.

Icelandic Low (Fig. 4-10), which circulates counterclockwise and is most active in winter, lies to the northeast. The Bermuda High with clockwise rotation and increased summer strength is found to the east and southeast. In the winter, air moving southward on the western side of the Icelandic Low frequently joins cold air that accumulates over the snow-covered surface of central Canada and reaches Atlantic City as cold, dry air, borne by north or northwest winds.

In summer the airflow in the vicinity of Atlantic City is mainly from the southwest. This air comes from the western end of the Bermuda High, which at this time of the year extends over the southeastern part of the United States. The winds coming from the Gulf of Mexico and earlier from the middle Atlantic Ocean bring the moisture that gives this part of the United States a July or August rainfall maximum. Because of the east-west direction of the coastline of Absecon Island, the summertime southwesterly airflow tends to be onshore, giving Atlantic City a predominantly sea breeze in the summer months.

Each of the two enormous cells of the atmosphere creates an ocean current on the eastern side of North America. The southward-moving air on the western side of the Icelandic Low pushes water southward as the Labrador Current.

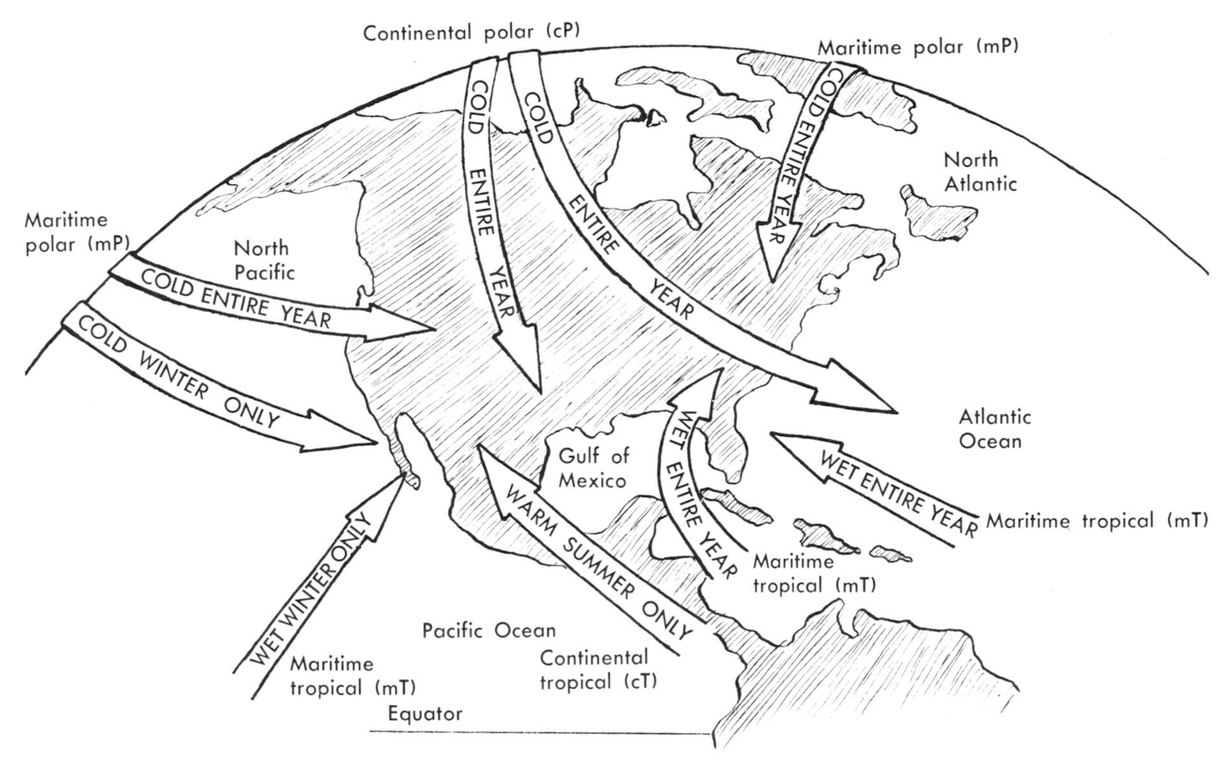

Fig. 4-11. Air masses influencing the United States. (Reprinted by permission of the publisher from Craig, Gerald S.: Science for the elementary school teacher, Ginn & Co., 1966.)

This current divides as it approaches Newfoundland. Most of the water swings toward Europe, but some of it flows south past the western side of Newfoundland and, hugging the coast, extends toward Cape Hatteras as a dead-end current called the Cold Wall. Its waters, bearing the green color characteristic of polar water, mingle with the waters that flow upward when west winds skim warm water off the top by blowing it seaward. This cold water lying close to shore is the source of the cool air that gives Atlantic City natural air conditioning, which attracts throngs of summer visitors from the large and hot northeastern cities, especially nearby Philadelphia and New York.

The north- and east-moving air of the Bermuda High drives the mighty Gulf Stream northeastward along the southeast coast of North America. Unfortunately for the people who live there the influence of the Gulf Stream on the climate of the middle Atlantic Coast is negligible. It lies outside the Cold Wall, which restricts its capacity to warm the land. Additionally, its warmth, when desired in the winter season, is carried to Europe by the eastward-trending winds of both the Icelandic Low and the Bermuda High. Fishermen who depart from Atlantic City's docks in winter may drip sweat while stripped to the waist handling fishing gear on trawlers in the Gulf Stream but find winter clothing necessary on return to port.

16. The Gulf Stream also has its identifying color. Do you know what it is? Is this color common to most tropical water? Can you find pictures of different shades of ocean water in national magazines?
17. Can you explain why polar water is green and why tropical water has its identifying color?

Earthward-moving air in the center of the Bermuda High is dry compared to the air around the edges of the high-pressure cell, so that when the center of the High moves over the coastal area, dry spells occur. Some scientists say that the Cold Wall, which induces a downward current in the atmosphere, is a factor in the recurring summer droughts that affect the Middle Atlantic States. (This process was treated in the discussion of Los Angeles, where atmospheric downfall contributes to the formation of smog.)

Although the Icelandic Low gets larger in winter, whereas the Bermuda High gets larger in summer, their day-to-day positions vary only slightly. Traveling cells, however, bring frequent weather changes to eastern North America. These are the traveling lows (cyclones) and the traveling highs (anticyclones). The highs are most likely to arrive at Atlantic City from the northwest. Normally the clockwise-rotating high accompanies our greatest import from Canada—cold air (Fig. 4-11). The passage of a high lasting about 3 days provides a recognizable sequence of weather. It begins with brisk, cold winds from the north or northwest. Because of the stirring action of the wind and because the cold air is warmed, as it moves over a warmer earth, and tends to rise, dust and smoke are distributed through a thick layer of the atmosphere, making the sky a deep blue. As the center of the high approaches, winds become light and variable, and the sky takes on a lighter blue. Temperatures inch upward. The trailing edge of the high brings light winds from the south or southwest. Slightly above-normal temperatures prevail, but the air that has been warmed by its rotational trip into southern lands is cooled again as it passes over a colder earth and tends to settle out in layers. In the absence of stirring action, dust and smoke are confined to the lower layers so that the sky becomes quite hazy. During this stage of the "high" weather cycle, temperature inversions and air-pollution alerts usually occur. If you live in the eastern half of the United States, you have seen dozens of these highs pass each year.

18. Which cities have a pollution index similar to Atlantic City? Which city in your study has the highest pollution index? What possible reasons can you give for these variances? See accompanying suggested Pollution Index Chart. You can get information for this chart from metropolitan dailies, from state departments of environmental protection, and from the federal Environmental Protection Agency (EPA).

The traveling low is a wavelike energy form that generally passes across the country from west to east, creating a complex interaction between the cold air from Canada and the warmer air to the south. It is guided from above by a high

POLLUTION INDEX CHART

CITY	MONTH	SOLIDS (SMOKE AND PARTICLES) (MCG.)	ORGANIC MATTER (MCG.)	CARBON MONOXIDE (MG.)	SULFUR DIOXIDE (MCG.)	OXIDENTS (MCG.)

altitude but shallow band of eastward-moving, high-speed air called a jet stream. The low, or cyclone, begins with a cold, northeast rain. This is followed in a day or so by clear, warm weather. Winds blow from the south or southwest. On about the third day winds swing to the northwest, and short but frequently heavy rain or snow showers signal the coming of colder weather. Described briefly, the sequence of weather in a low (cyclone) is rain and warmer, followed by rain and colder. This type of weather gives birth to the "northeaster," which drives the ocean into a frenzy of froth—so delightful to watch and in such contrast with the calm water and blue ocean found during the passage of a traveling high (anticyclone).

19. How would your perception of a northeast storm change as you moved your observation point from (a) a tenth-floor hotel window, to (b) the boardwalk, to (c) the water's edge, to (d) a fishing trawler, making port from 2 miles out?

Before permanent structures were erected on Absecon Island, it mattered little if channels shifted or shoaled, if sandbars or dunes migrated, if spring tides and high winds flooded the island, or if inlets were opened or closed. But once capital was committed to a specific location, investors acquired a strong motivation for maintaining the land-water relationships existing at the time of investment. Changes were a threat to financial solvency. *Economic man pitted himself against a restless and powerful ocean.*

The resident population of 40,000 and the up to 16 million visitors annually place exceptionally heavy demands on the 16 square mile Absecon Island. The location of a business establishment in a seashore resort is extremely sensitive to distance relationships. For example, a hotel catering to bathers must be as close to the beach as possible. If too close, high tides may be a hazard, and if not within a short walk of the ocean, it will not attract customers; thus the investors will lose money. The unavailability or high cost of water-damage insurance tends to push the site away from the ocean, but the economic facts of life thrust it oceanward. Once the site is decided on, the owners do not want the distance between the hotel and the ocean to change. The addition of sand to the beach by normal shore currents, if it increases the distance to the beach by a block or more, may mean financial disaster for the businessman. On the other hand, if currents remove the beach from the front of the hotel, the results can be equally ruinous.

Municipal, state, and federal government agencies are pressured into maintaining the shoreline's stability. They are asked to provide protection against a sea that would have been contained by sand dunes had they not been removed for private building purposes. Groins and jetties are demanded to prevent too much buildup of sand at one place or too much washing away at another. Channels that by nature are constantly shifting must be dredged. Nearby Ocean City spends hundreds of thousands of dollars annually to pump sand onto a beach that the ocean seems "determined" to wash away.

Obtaining an adequate supply of fresh water presents something of a problem on a small offshore island surrounded by salt water and as densely populated as Absecon Island is in the summer. About half of Atlantic City's fresh water is taken from wells on the mainland, the other half being supplied by a fresh-water creek on the mainland.

20. What is the daily consumption per person in your community? How does it vary seasonally? See suggested water consumption work sheet on p. 178. You may obtain information from the private company or public utility providing water for your community.

Some of the municipalities on the island have

PER CAPITA WATER CONSUMPTION FOR ____________ (NAME OF CITY)

MONTHS	JAN.	FEB.	MARCH	APRIL	MAY	JUNE	JULY	AUG.	SEPT.	OCT.	NOV.	DEC.
Gallons per month												
Monthly use per capita												
Daily use per capita												
Gallons per month ÷ population ÷ 30 = daily per capita use.												

had problems of salt water's intruding into well casings. Saltwater intrusion is a problem that has affected almost every coastal area in the United States. This problem is important because the people in the United States use more water per capita than anywhere else in the world. As the population of the United States grows and the utilization of coastal areas increases, ocean water intrusion will threaten more water wells.

One answer to the coastal freshwater problem is to take the salt from seawater–desalinization. This may be done by boiling seawater and catching the vapor, much as happens in the natural water cycle. But how can the extensive heat needed for such a process be produced? One way is to burn additional oil or coal; another way is to use the energy from atomic radiation in thermonuclear plants, which produce large quantities of hot water.

Problems such as the need for fresh water in coastal areas of the United States have no ready solution. In terms of our present knowledge and technological expertise, our society has had to accept compromise or partial solutions.

21. What disadvantages can you find with both methods? Which method is more destructive to the environment?
22. Would it be fair to limit the number of people living in coastal areas to prevent future environmental deterioration?
23. Should this nation take steps to halt population increases?
24. Who should make these difficult decisions, even though at times they may prove unsatisfactory? Should they be made by all citizens? If so, must citizens be informed about possible choices? If citizens are to be informed, whose responsibility is it?

Sewage disposal provides another headache that especially plagues seashore resorts. Sewage can be treated so that the end product–effluent–is in no way offensive. However, the cost of this kind of treatment is excessive. Can a resort city that needs only a minor part of its total sewage treatment capacity most of the year afford high-cost processing? Both municipal treasurers and voters generally say "no," so that sewage engineers are faced with difficult alternatives. One solution is to discharge less than fully treated sewage effluent into the estuaries, or inland tidal areas. People originally hoped that the scouring action of the tides would dilute and dissipate the sewage effluent and that it would cause a minimum of damage to the natural and human environment.

At the height of the summer season the sewage effluent pollutes the coastal lagoon areas to such an extent that back bay or estuary clamming is forbidden by the New Jersey Department of Environmental Protection throughout most of the

Fig. 4-12. Simplified food chain in an eastern North American (coastal) estuary.

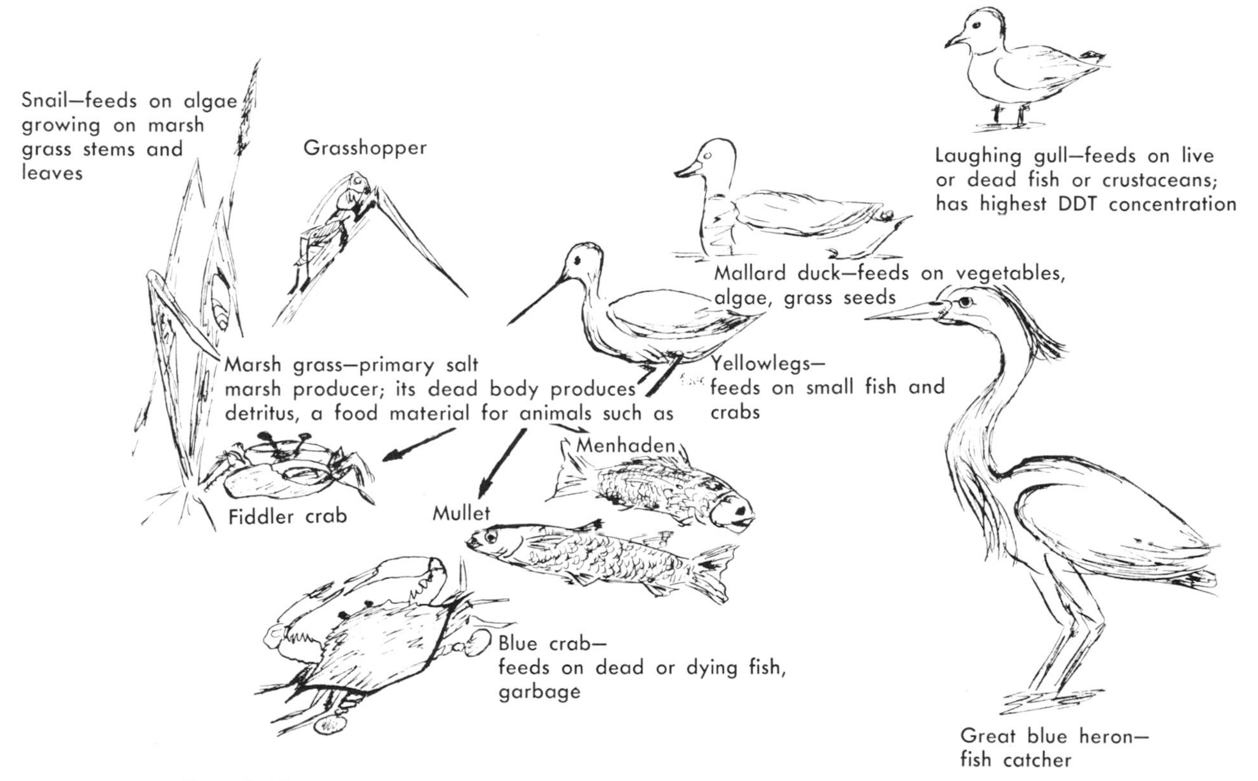

Fig. 4-13. Food web in an eastern North American (coastal) estuary. A food web is the complex of associated food chains in a particular environment.

state's coastal waters. The possibility of piping the unwanted effluent several miles out to sea has been suggested and is being studied. There is concern about how well the effluent would be dispersed. It might be carried onto the area's major resource —the beach—by unstable and unpredictable current swirls. Another serious concern is the effect of this effluent on the plant and animal life of the ocean. Much evidence has already been collected to confirm this concern.

The pollution of bays and estuaries in many coastal areas poses a very serious threat to the life in all oceans. The water in estuaries is usually shallow because earth materials brought by inflowing streams are continually being deposited there.

Warm-water estuaries are the breeding grounds for most oceangoing fish. Countless numbers of microscopic plants, called phytoplankton, float in these waters. There are also many tiny animals, zooplankton, that feed on the phytoplankton. Together they form the food of tiny fish or the developing young of larger fish.

All animals such as fish depend on plants or smaller animals for food (Figs. 4-12 and 4-13). Except for those fish that are plankton feeders, most fish eat other fish smaller than themselves. Most fish have long sharp teeth, fitted for tearing flesh. Other sea animals consume great quantities of plankton as their sole source of food. Even the baleen whale—a mammal, not a fish—lives mostly on plankton.

25. What parts of the aquatic food chain can you detect by studying the mouths of fish you have caught? See accompanying work sheet on Food Consumption of Various Fish Species.

The microscopic plants that live in freshwater ponds are not the same as those found in saltwater bays and estuaries. However, they are frequently similar in size and other characteristics. They are of comparable importance to other living things in and around the body of water in which they are found.

One of the easiest ways to collect plankton is to dip a jar into greenish colored water. If you attach the jar with wire to a long pole, you may obtain samples from a variety of depths and distances from the shore. The plankton that live on the bottom of the water (benthic organisms) are usually different from those which swim or are suspended near the surface.

You may use a convenient reference such as *The New Field Book of Freshwater Life** or *Pond Life,*† if you wish to locate the names of some of the organisms you have found.

26. Do you think the kinds and numbers of organisms in the plankton of a water body change during different seasons of the year? How could you find out? If you wish some very concentrated and active planktonic organisms, go to the operator of a sewage disposal plant and ask for a sample of zoogleal film from the aeration beds. Why

*Klots, Elsie: The new field book of freshwater life, New York, 1966, G. P. Putnam's Sons.

†Reid, George K.: Pond life, New York, 1967, Golden Press.

FOOD CONSUMPTION OF VARIOUS FISH SPECIES

SPECIES OF FISH	SKETCH OF MOUTH AND TEETH	FOOD SUPPLY

should these aeration beds be so rich in the number of life forms? Caution: Keep sewage liquids away from hands and face.

One of the most interesting studies you can do is to chart the kinds of organisms that are found where water touches land. Some scientists say that there are many zones of organisms at the water-land boundary.

One way to test this idea is to walk slowly inland from the water's edge (at the ocean, estuary, lakeside, or little pond—whichever you find convenient) and sketch the shape of the dominant living organism you see. The dominant organism is the one you see most often as you look around. If the organisms and the land change rapidly, you will want to make a sketch every 1 or 2 feet. If the changes occur more slowly, you may wish to make the sketching interval every 5 or 10 feet. Do not forget to include any dominant organisms you see in the water near the shore. Compare your sketch with the accompanying zone sketch (Fig. 4-14) of a sea-beach near Atlantic City. Does your evidence support the zone hypothesis? You may also wish to collect zonal evidence outward from the shore.

27. What did you find to be the dominant organism in your study? See accompanying suggested work sheet on types of organisms found, p. 182.
28. What variations can be found in the kinds of organisms found at different depths and distances from shore? How do you account for the differences in organisms?

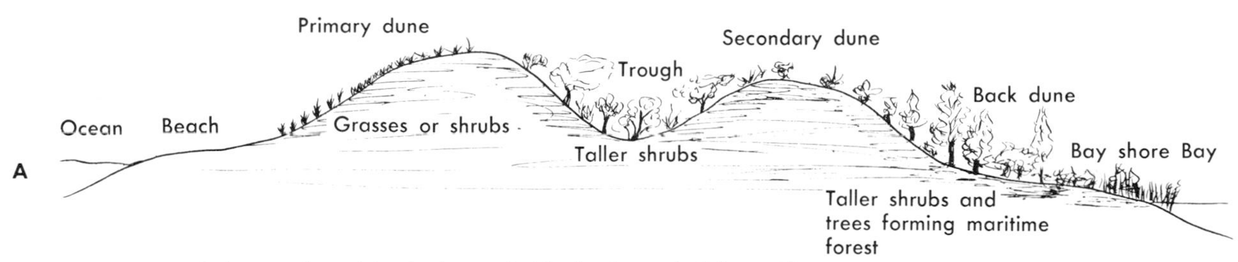

Fig. 4-14. Two zone sketches of eastern coastal United States. **A,** Undisturbed barrier beach area. **B,** Overdeveloped beach area with loss of environmental stability as regards destructive wave action and flooding.

TYPES OF ORGANISMS FOUND IN WATER OF VARYING DEPTHS

DISTANCE FROM SHORE	DEPTH	ORGANISMS

Just as changes occur from place to place in various environments, so do changes occur in one environment from time to time. Again, as human societies and technologies are changed, man's perception of the use and value of any environment are changed also.

Man's changing evaluation of the natural setting

Whenever you look at any place in the world, whether out your bedroom window, in a movie, or just walking down the street, you might wonder if it always looked like this. When you think about it, you know that the answer is no because human ideas of what to do with a particular environment keep changing. Almost any place you can name, used by man for any of his activities, looked very different in the past. We can expect that those places will look different in the future.

1. Why do people keep changing their minds about what they are going to do with part of the earth's surface? How do they go about changing it?
2. Look for old pictures of how your local neighborhood looked in past years. How have the appearances and uses of buildings changed?
3. Can you find any "old-time" residents of your community, who can tell you of the changes that have taken place in their lifetimes?
4. Can you find any old maps of your area? (Perhaps in the local historical society or in newspaper files? A local library may be able to help find these, especially an old topographical map, published by the U. S. Geological Survey.) How have road patterns, types of land use, and size of settlements changed? Can you think of reasons for these changes?

If you stepped into a time machine and went back to the southern New Jersey shore as it was in 1840, you might be surprised at what was there. Maybe you would be more surprised at what was not there! Nobody had any particular use for the offshore islands at that time. Even the Lenni-Lenape Indians had little permanent use for the site of present-day Atlantic City. We know that they visited Absecon Island to do some fishing and to dig oysters and clams. Local mainlanders in 1840 also made occasional visits to the islands to fish, dig clams, and even to bring their cattle over to graze during the summer. But except for an occasional lighthouse keeper, few people lived on the island throughout the year.

5. Try to fit yourself inside the mind of a person living in 1840 to guess why. Why did settlers avoid Absecon Island at this point in its history? What kinds of resources were settlers in this period seeking to establish permanent homes?

Like all early settlers coming to the New World, those arriving in New Jersey looked for places to establish ports. These they needed to maintain ties with their former homes and to trade with one another and with the rest of the world. The best sites for ports were the deep and protected

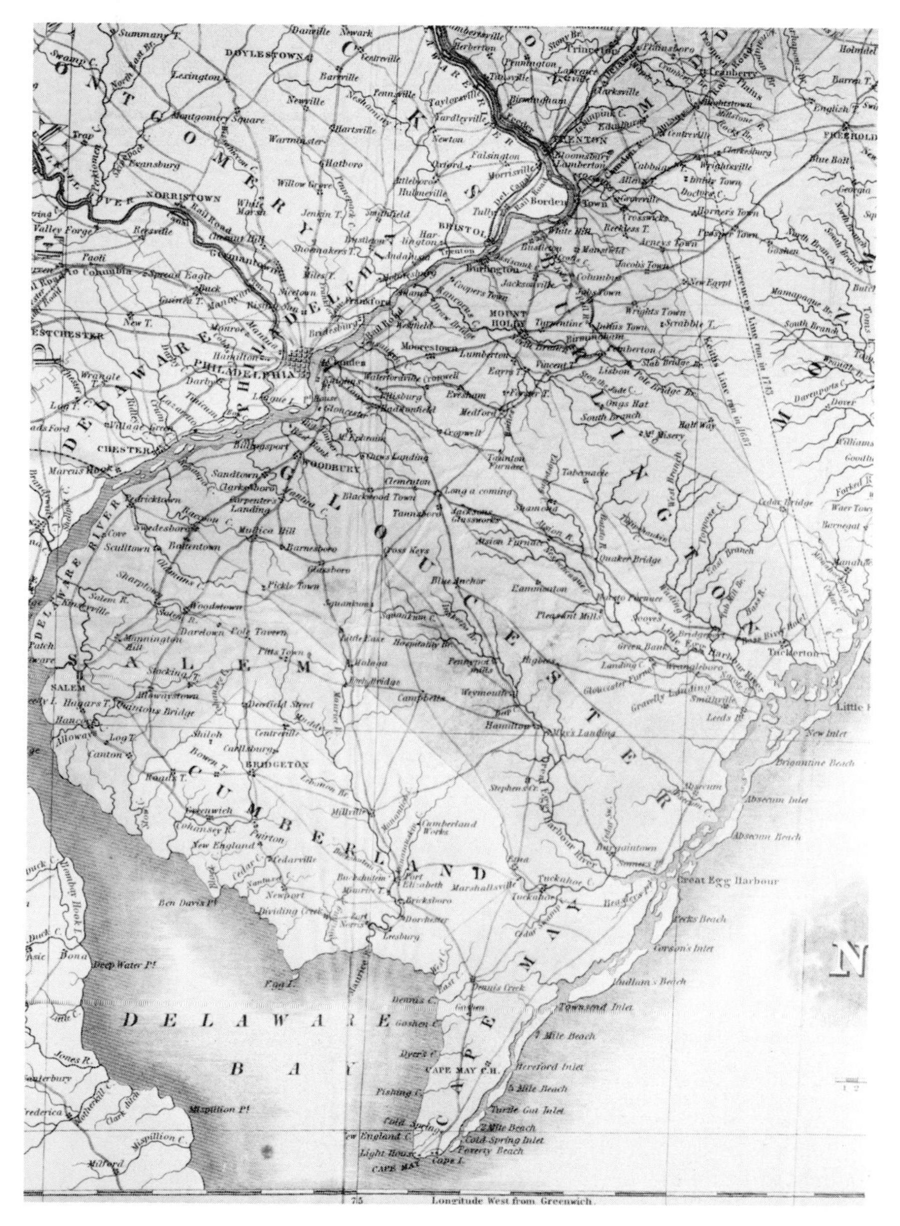

Fig. 4-15. Early settlement routes in New Jersey. (Reprinted by permission of the publisher from Boucher, Jack: Absegami yesteryear, Egg Harbor City, N. J., 1963, Atlantic County Historical Society, Laureate Press.)

waters on the western side of New Jersey, along the Delaware River, and in the northeast along the Hudson River (Fig. 4-15). Southern New Jersey's Atlantic Coast with its shallow bays, narrow inlets, and heavy surf was avoided because that kind of coast offered few opportunities for port development.

Settlement in southern New Jersey appears to have come through the "back door" from the west instead of the east. The Europeans came to New Jersey from the east, across the Atlantic Ocean, sailed up the Delaware River, and settled along the western boundary of New Jersey. Settlements spread eastward from these early sites.

As they moved eastward from the Delaware River into southern New Jersey across sandier soil, the settlers decided that the area known today as the Pine Barrens was poor for agriculture. Thus they tended to avoid that area. The Pine Barrens is a region of about 1,700 square miles, covered with pine, oak, and cedar forests. Some use was made of Pine Barrens timber for shipbuilding and as fuel for early ironworks and glassworks. There were few settlements. Roads were not extended to the islands offshore. Too few people lived on these islands to create a demand for roads.

In 1695 the islands off southern New Jersey were so isolated and of such little value that land at the site of present-day Atlantic City sold for 4 cents an acre! The present estimated value of Atlantic City real estate is more than $300 million.

A necessary ingredient in founding a successful resort was providing the link between the customers from the inland cities with the offshore island beaches. Provision of a fast and inexpensive means of getting to these offshore islands brought many visitors. Changes were taking place at that time in the nearby cities of New York, Philadelphia, and Camden. More people were living in the fast-growing cities and working in industry. These changes are sometimes grouped together and called the Industrial Revolution. The railroad reduced both time and cost of reaching the shore.

When the first railroad to the New Jersey shore was built in 1854, railroads were the fastest, cheapest, and best means of land transportation. Until highways were built to connect the mainland with Absecon Island, the railroad with its bridges and causeways was the only means of land transportation to Atlantic City.

After completion of the railroad, the new resort began to grow rapidly. Floods of visitors began to arrive from the nearby cities. Great hotels rose on the sands along with summer cottages, restaurants, amusements, and stores. Visitors to Atlantic City wasted no time in getting to the beach. The beach and the ocean, after all, were the real reasons for their coming. All the buildings were there to make the visitors more comfortable, but the original attractions were the ocean and the beach. Hotel owners found that being as close to the ocean as possible pleased most visitors. The restaurant owners and the men who opened small shops to sell souvenirs found that their customers were at the beach much of the day. The visitors wanted to enjoy the beach, and their presence there drew vendors hawking their wares. The number of people attracted to the beauty of the beach made it more crowded and less attractive than it had been. The strip of stores, restaurants, and amusements that soon developed along the beach brought about further deterioration of the esthetic and recreational quality of that environment.

6. Cite examples in which the overuse of a recreational resource has diminished the recreational quality of the environment.

Many of the visitors wanted to walk along the beach. The view was pleasant, the sound of the surf was exciting, and in the evening they could enjoy a cool sea breeze. They did have a problem, however—the sand was difficult to walk in, and it got in their shoes! But how can you walk along

Fig. 4-16. Two views of the world-renowned, **A**, Atlantic City boardwalk and, **B**, beach area. (Courtesy Atlantic City Convention Bureau.)

a beach without walking in the sand? In 1870 the problem was solved for Atlantic City by the construction of the world's first boardwalk. A wooden walkway, 4 feet wide, was laid on the sands. It has since been raised on concrete pilings, widened, lengthened, and copied in other resorts. This unique attraction afforded a view far out to sea and led to the establishment of many additional shops, restaurants, and hotels along the boardwalk (Fig. 4-16).

The phenomenal growth and prosperity of Atlantic City exceeded the most fanciful dreams of the early planners. There have always been several reasons why people would come to Atlantic City. Some like the big hotels, fancy restaurants, and fine entertainment. Others came by train on a one-day excursion to swim, walk the boardwalk, or sun themselves on the beach.

Although some persons came to spend money, others came to make it. The visitor's demand for hotel rooms, restaurant meals, and entertainment drew other people to provide those services. The permanent population of Atlantic City grew as the number of visitors increased. Many who intended to work only during the summer stayed on, hoping to live all year on their summer earnings. Perhaps the low rents available in the off-season helped them decide to stay.

Atlantic City was a prosperous offspring of the railroad era. By the time the railroad's passenger business was in decline, Atlantic City was aging. The "Queen of the Resorts" of the early 1900's has experienced changes in its population and character. Cities, like people, get older, and their ways of doing things and their likes and dislikes change. The railroad, once the king of land travel, has declined in popularity and efficiency of service. Most small towns have limited passenger service or none at all. What has replaced passenger trains? Cars, buses, and planes. The widespread ownership of automobiles combined with good highways has induced many people to drive their own cars on vacations and even on one-day trips. This preference for cars means, of course, that Atlantic City must tackle the problems of highways and parking.

7. Where do you think the busloads of visitors to Atlantic City are coming from? A map of the United States may help to answer that question.
8. Would you be willing to ride on a bus for more than a few hours to get to the beach, especially if you were only going for one day? If the buses travel over major highways at an average speed of 60 miles per hour, approximately how many people live within 3 hours of Atlantic City by bus? Have you heard people measure distance by time rather than space, such as "I live about 20 minutes from here"? Why is time more important than space when people talk about distance?

Atlantic City had the first municipal airport in the United States, Bader Field. A larger airport has been built near Atlantic City on the mainland. But Atlantic City has never had a major airport, in terms of commercial plane traffic, like New York, Chicago, or Miami.

9. Why have not the crowds of visitors coming to Atlantic City, estimated at 16 million annually, created a demand for air service there?

The larger mainland airport offers some intercity service. However, most air passengers are shuttled between smaller but closer Bader Field and Philadelphia International Airport. People in Atlantic City refer to Philadelphia International Airport as the "Gateway to Atlantic City" because Philadelphia, unlike Atlantic City, is connected by regular flights to all the nation's cities and many world capitals.

Many important changes in how people organize their vacation time are affecting Atlantic City as well as other United States resorts. Americans tend to spend more of their vacation time on the move, rather than in one hotel at one resort. They want to see more places and do different things, and their cars make this easy.

10. Many people come to your community in their own automobiles. By what other means of transportation do they arrive?
11. The class may form a group of committees to visit local transportation centers such as bus terminals, railroad stations, airports, car rental agencies, and others to determine how people travel to your community. You may also wish to consult the Highway Safety Council and the traffic division of the police department.
    a. Can you determine the percentage or proportion of people using each transportation method?
    b. How can you guard against overlapping information?

We would think of the old-fashioned resort hotel as a kind of "vacation factory." Everything that visitors needed and wanted was right there or, at least, around the corner. But many people now cover hundreds of miles during their vacations, staying at one place only a few days before moving on. As airplane fares become cheaper, many will go to foreign cities and resorts. It might not really be more expensive to vacation overseas than in Atlantic City or a similar United States resort. The wages paid to workers in the resorts of other nations may be much lower, thus reducing hotel and other costs.

12. Do you think that Americans tend to like the new, exciting, and glamorous, rather than the old and familiar? Has the image of Atlantic City as the "Playground of the World" faded? Have other resorts such as Las Vegas and Miami Beach replaced Atlantic City as leading centers of top-name entertainment?

Part of Atlantic City's glamour remains in the famed Miss America Beauty Pageant. The seasonal nature of the tourist economy is a serious problem for Atlantic City. During the winter the enormous hotels and numerous restaurants, souvenir stands, and amusements are lightly patronized; some even close for the season. One response to the winter business doldrums by Atlantic City's businessmen has been the encouragement of conventions during the off months.

Although the quality of the natural environment has been deteriorating under the pressures of numbers, Atlantic City's hotels and related facilities have taken on additional appeal. The ocean and beach are physically less attractive now than in the beginning of Atlantic City's career. The buildings and services for summer visitors now provide reasons for coming to Atlantic City in other seasons. This change of emphasis is related to the growing importance of conventions.

13. Probably someone you know attends or works at conventions. Can you identify some cities that host conventions? Look for and clip articles in your newspaper datelined Atlantic City. Collect the information that identifies convention dates, numbers attending, and significant news.

With a growing population and an expanding economy, conventions, which may be held for two days to a week or more, are larger in attendance than ever before. It is not unusual for a convention to draw 20,000 persons. The convention of the New Jersey Education Association, held annually in Atlantic City, has an attendance of up to 55,000. The 1964 Democratic National Convention brought 40,000 persons to Atlantic City. Only very large cities can absorb the sudden increase in visitors that a major convention produces.

Conventioneers must have hotel or motel rooms as close to central meeting points as possible. Convention goers spend money in restaurants, souvenir and gift shops, and other stores. Convention cities usually schedule one convention right after another and provide special meeting halls. Because of scheduling, convention visitors must be moved in and out again within a day or two of one another. Atlantic City, with a tourist season concentrated in the summer, has many hotel rooms and restaurants that are available for convention use. Without convention business these facilities would go unused during most of the year.

Conventions can use the capacity of Atlantic City to serve these large numbers of people, and Atlantic City's businessmen can use the off-season money! Almost half a million conventioneers come to Atlantic City every year and bring over $60 million. The convention goers are not particularly interested in the ocean and the beach. They are more interested in meeting one another, attending meetings, and finding out about the latest ideas in their field. The major convention seasons are spring and fall.

Why are conventions so popular and why are they becoming more important each year? We often hear that, with modern long-distance communications, we humans need not actually be in personal face-to-face contact with one another, but these half million conventioneers who travel every year to Atlantic City must think otherwise.

14. Atlantic City exists to entertain visitors from all over the world. They come for seaside recreation, conventions, and sports events. What brings people to your community? You and your classmates may find answers to this question by sending a representative to your local chamber of commerce or office of the mayor. You may wish to collect some firsthand information for yourselves by organizing the class to watch all the roads leading into the city on a weekday and a weekend day and to get some variations by season if any. See the sample work sheet below.
15. One of the most important decisions the class will need to make is how to tell visitors from persons who live or work in your community. Does your community have more visitors on weekdays or weekends?

SUGGESTED WORK SHEET

COMMUNITY TRANSPORTATION

Types of transportation used by visitors to ______________ (name of city).

Sources of information ______________ Month ______________

____

____

FORM OF TRANSPORTATION	NUMBER OF VISITORS	PERCENT OF TOTAL VISITORS
Airplane Bus Horse and buggy		

Is there a seasonal change in the number of people who come to visit your community?

Atlantic City is plagued by problems common to all cities. Its role as a resort community is one of the underlying causes for some of its special problems. The seasonal nature of the Atlantic City resort industry creates high unemployment during the winter months, although manufacturing and other year-round jobs have increased in the area. Primarily geared to vacation and convention business, employment rises and falls with activity in the trades and services.

The city's basic economy is in motels, hotels, restaurants, retail trade, and resort-oriented enterprises. Most job opportunities call for workers having skills in occupations related to those industries. This situation has provided little encouragement for manufacturing industries to locate in Atlantic City. However, some industry has come into the area recently, creating jobs for semiskilled workers in enterprises such as clothing manufacturing. Many of these industries are located on the cheaper mainland. During the tourist season, when jobs are available, a substantial influx of outsiders competes with permanent residents for jobs. Young local people must match their often limited qualifications against visiting college students for jobs in hotels and restaurants.

Summer is a happy time in Atlantic City. But for almost nine months of the year, when the unemployment rate swings from 4% to 15%, living conditions are harsh.

16. What is the unemployment rate in your area? Does it change seasonally? How does it compare to the national average? See the work sheet below.

The length of ocean shoreline in the United States is limited, but the number of Americans seeking recreation by the sea continues to increase.

17. What will competition for land near the seashore do to the price of land there? Who do you think could pay more for oceanfront land—a man planning to build a large new hotel or one planning to build a new clothing factory? Which man would have to

SUGGESTED WORK SHEET

COMMUNITY EMPLOYMENT

City ____________________ Year ____________________

MONTH	JAN.	FEB.	MARCH	APRIL	MAY	JUNE	JULY	AUG.	SEPT.	OCT.	NOV.	DEC.
Total number in labor force												
Number employed												
Number unemployed												
Percent unemployed												

choose a site near the beach and which could move nearer the bay or even the mainland?

A brief tour through Atlantic City would document its housing problems, poverty, and socioeconomic complexities. About 30% of the population is nonwhite. An examination of the census tracts shows that each tract is almost entirely all white or all black. About 90% of the nonwhite population lives in nine census tracts, making Atlantic City a highly segregated city with distinct boundary lines.

According to 1960 census figures, the following factors are related to the housing picture in Atlantic City:

33.5% of the families earn less than $3,000 a year.
51% of the population over 25 years of age have eight years or less of formal education.
25% of the persons in the city are over 60 years of age.
Approximately 91% of the housing units in Atlantic City were built prior to 1939.

18. How do each of these factors relate to housing in Atlantic City?
19. In what part of Atlantic City would persons who earn less than $3,000 per year be likely to live?
20. What limitations does the lack of education place on an individual? What effect does a large number of persons with limited education have on a community?
21. What problems are faced by old people in locating and maintaining housing in Atlantic City?
22. Why do you think little new housing has been built in Atlantic City since 1939?

What is it like to live in Atlantic City? The answer depends on who you are and what you are seeking. If you are a retired pensioner, this resort city provides excellent places to spend the twilight of your years. If you are among the many unemployed adults, you look forward to the beginning of a new summer season to make ends meet. As an owner of a small hotel, motel, or other seasonal business, you also look forward to the summer season to produce your yearly income. Or perhaps you look at Atlantic City as a place to share with millions of visitors in summer and with your friends and neighbors in winter.

Many large cities have photo folders of the most outstanding scenes and interesting buildings that a visitor might wish to see. These folders usually do not describe what the people in that community do or see in their daily lives.

23. You and your class might wish to produce a photo series that shows important locations or scenes in the lives of one or more local residents. Some may wish to depict the life of an adult, whereas others may wish to follow the scenes of a child's everyday life. What kinds of residents would you choose to be the subjects of a photo log?
24. How would you tell someone what it is like to live in your town or city?
25. Have you ever made a list of everything you do from the moment you wake up until you go to sleep at night? Would your day differ in winter, spring, summer, and fall? If there are any important seasonal differences in your life, is there anything special about your community to account for these differences?
26. If you decide to test this idea, in what form would you suggest that the "day-in-my-life" story be organized?
27. How would you describe the environment about you? Do you suppose that the physical environment of Atlantic City is one reason that so many people make the city their year-round home?

No matter what permanent residents do in Atlantic City, they are always aware that they live on a coastal island. The ocean dominates their environment.

5 EVALUATION

Evaluation for any educational endeavor is more than an attempt to test whether or not students have acquired certain knowledge or skills. Contrary to many established practices, evaluation begins with the development of the curriculum.

For environmental education any curriculum should be created to satisfy the needs that engender a study of environments. President Nixon in his introduction to the First Annual Report of the Council on Environmental Quality, August, 1970, called for the development of "environmental literacy for our society, a new understanding and new awareness of man's relation to his environment." The President wrote further, "This will require the development and teaching of environmental concepts at every point in the educational process."

NEEDS OF ENVIRONMENTAL EDUCATION

A definition of environmental education, given in the Senate Report for the Environmental Education Act of 1970 (P.L. 91-516), provides a detailed statement of scope and purpose.

> Environmental education is an integrated process which deals with man's interrelationship with his natural man-made surroundings, including the relation of population growth, pollution, resource allocation and depletion, conservation, technology, and urban and rural planning to the total human environment. Environmental education is a study of the factors influencing ecosystems, mental and physical growth, living and working conditions, decaying cities, and population pressures. Environmental education is intended to promote among citizens the awareness and understanding of the environment, our relationship to it, and the concern and responsible action necessary to assure our survival and to improve the quality of life.
>
> Environmental Education is a life-long process. It is a way of looking at life, fostering awareness of other life and of inter-relationships, learning to recognize the effects (good and bad) we have on physical surroundings, and the responsibilities we must accept for the mere fact of our presence and of our activities in our environment. It should enable us to make sound ecological decisions and foresee their consequences; to make value judgments, and act accordingly. It is acceptance of life values and ways of living which minimize destruction and maximize those relationships that enchance life. It is learning how to contribute to the quality of life, and the constructive use, rather than exploitation, of the environment.
>
> It is important to understand that EE is much more than a schoolhouse approach to ending the degradation of man-made surroundings and the pollution and destruction of the natural world. Environmental education will not simply provide an understanding of pollution problems and provide the nation with skills to meet or solve those problems. It is not merely a course in school or a curriculum combining elements of the natural and physical sciences into a new department or specialty. Nor is it just another name for outdoor education, resource management or conservation education.
>
> Environmental Education provides alternate ways of thinking—a synthesis—which colors and affects the humanities, languages, social sciences, history, economics, and religion as dramatically as it does the natural sciences. It will give an ecological perspective to every aspect of learning.

ENVIRONMENTAL EDUCATION IS A UNIQUE VENTURE

This mandate for what environmental education should do is unique. It is intended to affect society for the immediate present and for the foreseeable future. If the utmost significance of the intended effects of environmental education cannot be truly evaluated until youngsters have left school and have become decision makers, it seems inescapable that the schools must reach out to participate in present-day society's environmental decisions.

This implies the following:

- Children will frequently leave the classroom to study various environments firsthand.
- The school and the community will learn to communicate with each other about environmental problems and decisions.
- The school and the community will interact by planning for the improvement of environmental quality.
- They will execute some of those plans *together.*

In view of these expectations, an environmental education curriculum will not concentrate on knowledge alone, indispensable as knowledge is. Furthermore, that knowledge must come from many branches of learning; environmental education is broadly interdisciplinary.

The curriculum in environmental education will be equally concerned with the development of an environmental ethic and with societal action that emanates from the ethic.

ASSUMPTIONS BASIC TO A CURRICULUM IN ENVIRONMENTAL EDUCATION

Assumptions are basic to all human endeavors. They represent whatever the persons involved believe to be true, even if the truth of the statements cannot be demonstrated. The environmental education described in this book is based on the following statements, *assumed to be* true and acceptable.

1. Environmental education is needed in all schools.
2. EE in the schools will be significant in the present and future improvement of environmental quality.
3. A curriculum in environmental education should be included in each grade, K-12.
4. Such curriculum should require the firsthand study of many environments in the community.
5. A curriculum such as this should encourage and support student investigations of the quantitative and qualitative aspects of many environments, particularly local ones.
6. Such curriculum in environmental education should provide opportunities for students to "work within the framework of local democratic government, which has as its tenet the freedom of individual choice and respect for the individual person."*
7. Efforts in environmental education should not be dogmatic with respect to existing social or religious values or coerce ethics or behavior but should offer alternatives. These must be developed in a context of balance and perspective that will assist individuals and groups with decision making, particularly in relation to environmental questions and problems.*

A BROAD VIEW OF EVALUATION

Evaluative practices in education have traditionally been limited to some type of procedure to test for selected outcomes of instruction.

But outcomes, whether immediate or long-range in scope, should not be the only goal of any educational enterprise. Full evaluation really means that the school should scrutinize its entire operation carefully at frequent intervals to determine

*From EE—the education that cannot wait, U.S.O.E., 1971, p. 13.

whether or not the best strategies and procedures are being employed to achieve the stated goals.

REAPPRAISING NEEDS AND GOALS

Since the broad goals of instruction are developed from recognized needs within a society, it is reasonable to assume that needs and therefore broad goals may both be modified by time and a complex of societal factors outside the school.

For example, in the years previous to Earth Day in 1970, it seemed that most people were not aware that environmental deterioration was a serious problem and that many projected developments which would modify the environment were being planned without consideration of ecological knowledge. For this reason the term *environmental awareness* was coined to communicate both a *need* and a *goal.* Today most middle-grade youngsters, older students, and adults who are exposed to the mass media in school or out seem to have this awareness to some degree. Now, the need for environmental knowledge, the need to look at the historical development of land use, and the need to make decisions on the basis of knowledge of the complex interrelationships present in most environments all seem to be more significant than the need for awareness alone. Perhaps environmental awareness can be profitably retained as an instructional goal for primary-level children in particular.

Needs and broad goals in environmental education probably require reappraisal at least every three years, to take advantage of the progress of science and society toward the appropriate goals.

EVALUATING RESOURCES AND PROCEDURES

An educational enterprise must also evaluate itself by assessing how well its resources are able to bring about the achievement of both broad goals and specific objectives. Resource evaluation begins with an assessment of personnel and their capacity to achieve stated goals in terms of both capability and time. For environmental education other resources include areas available for environmental study, school plants and their equipment, and the entire system's ability to institute or adapt to change.

For example, many larger school districts are so complex in their present organization that change can only be effected slowly, if at all. Teachers are often poorly prepared to guide students in studies of local environments, since environmental studies are just now becoming part of teacher-training programs. If environmental education is to become a significant and permanent part of the school curriculum, then the personnel resources must be readied to achieve such modified tasks. In addition, the following deficiencies exist:

1. Teachers have not been encouraged to induce students to delve deeply into local problems and their previous or projected solutions.
2. Teachers have not been prepared or encouraged to study environments firsthand away from the classroom:
3. Schools in general have not heretofore been encouraged to gather information for or to become influential in environmental decision making.

Educational or instructional procedures are the game plans, or strategies, suggested and used to achieve stated objectives. Certainly notable effort has been made before today to arouse people to the environmental crisis, but the fact that the crisis became acute so quickly is ample evidence that procedures in conservation and environmental education have not been sufficiently effective hitherto.

ORGANIZING RESOURCES AND PROCEDURES AROUND A MODEL OF NEEDS AND GOALS

Discussions in Chapters 1 and 5 of this book and in other sources have defined the needs and goals of environmental education. A simple model for organization may be constructed from key terms found in those statements.

A curriculum in environmental education might well develop the following capabilities or attributes for each child:

1. *Environmental awareness.* Each child should be aware of his absolute dependence on natural environments and should experience environments in various stages of degradation. The development of environmental awareness is probably a major concern for primary grades.
2. *Environmental knowledge.* Each student should have abundant experiences inside and outside the classroom on which to build the broad concepts of interrelatedness and interdependency within or among environments.

The conceptual schemes listed in Chapter 1 (pp. 17 and 18) form the framework around which environmental knowledge may be built. For each conceptual scheme a number of lesser generalizations and facts will be needed for suitable illustration and study. A group of lesser generalizations is listed with one conceptual scheme on pp. 17 and 18.

In Chapter 2 several units of study are reproduced. Each one has its own set of generalizations to specify the environmental knowledge to be derived therefrom. The acquisition of this environmental knowledge is probably best projected from kindergarten to the twelfth grade and beyond.

ENVIRONMENTAL ETHICS

An environmental ethic is a series of beliefs about people and their relationships with and values concerning the environment, which beliefs, in turn, motivate them to their present practices of utilization of land, air, space, and all other resources.

A statement and rationale for environmental ethics appears in Chapter 1. In Chapter 2 several statements of environmental ethics have been included as generalizations in the sample study units. The discussion of ethics and values, along with their environmental consequences, are a significant part of the model and can be a continuing aspect of instruction from kindergarten on.

MAKING ENVIRONMENTAL DECISIONS

An effort should be made to train students to make or suggest environmental decisions on the basis of the most *precise* and *complete* information available. Decisions presumably should be made on the basis of knowledge, ethics, and wisdom. Environmental wisdom comes from knowledge of the results of previous environmental experiences, tempered with an understanding of the generally inevitable complexities of modifying intricately balanced ecosystems, both natural and man-made. In such situations compromises or trade-offs are often required. The training and practice of decision making can begin in the middle grades and continue through higher or adult education or both.

COMMITMENT TO ECOACTION

A democratic society draws its strength from the participation of as many as possible of its members. The achievement of environmental quality in particular requires the influence of a large number of informed citizens. However, a great percentage of citizens seems unwilling to commit themselves to societal action. To overcome this attitude, students in the middle grades, secondary schools, and colleges should be encouraged to take positive action to reflect their own environmental decisions—decisions made hopefully with the benefit of ecological knowledge and wisdom.

EVALUATING THE ACHIEVEMENT OF SPECIFIC OBJECTIVES

The most common practices for detecting advancement toward specific objectives include written tests to determine how many facts or generalizations can be recalled by students. In many disciplines, notably mathematics, science, social studies, and literature, problem-solving situations have been used with increasing frequency as part of a testing, or evaluative, procedure. Other specific objectives may be measured by "practicals," or performance tests, often employed in science laboratories, industrial education, physical education, and home economics education.

Many educational experiences are characterized by direct contact with some aspect of the environment that evokes student responses far more readily than some of the more abstract and formalized classroom procedures. For this reason oral and written reports, skits, dramatic presentations, or art projects employing a broad spectrum of materials and techniques can provide accurate indices of students' feelings and beliefs. Because these techniques do not belong to the so-called objective variety of testing is no reason to disregard them as valid tools for evaluation.

One of the hallmarks of environmental education activities is the utilization of small work groups. The work groups seem to operate most successfully when they have a chance to work together on a relatively long-term basis—several weeks or more.

Changes in students' perceptions of their peers may be measured through the use of sociometric techniques, such as the sociogram. Sociograms made before and after a number of environmental education experiences usually show a change in the peer status of many students within the groups. This seems especially evident when a class or two share a resident experience of several days duration.

AN "OBJECTIVE TEST"

Following is a copy of generalizations used in a secondary unit of study to consider the effects of pertinent legislation on the environment. Following this is a multiple-choice response test designed to examine many of the issues and problems encountered during the course of the unit. It would be unfortunate if this were the sole means for evaluating the immediate and long-term objectives of this unit of study, but it may prove useful to many readers.

ENVIRONMENT AND THE LAW

SOME GENERALIZATIONS PERTINENT TO THIS STUDY

1. Strict laws with high local and national standards would provide for the improvement of environmental quality; however, such laws are relatively useless unless compliance and enforcement can be secured.
2. Because of the difficulty of enforcing laws that regulate environmental use and quality, voluntary compliance with all environmental laws should be an educational and societal goal of the highest priority.
3. Master planning in accordance with ecological principles and considerations can be proved to be scientifically sound.
4. The adage "Law is rule without reason" has often caused confusion and resistance, since it has led people to believe that the law subverts or threatens justice; therefore knowledge of the rationale for laws is valid in environmental education studies.
5. Compliance with laws and standards regulating environmental quality will be weakened by three significant factors:
   a. The increasing volume and diversity of pollutants, which will require escalating costs
   b. The difficulty in detecting violations
   c. The slowness of the judiciary process
6. The development of any parcel of land large or small has important and far-reaching effects on the continuing ability of surrounding land to support life.
7. Public awareness of and participation in the development of regulations that govern environmental protection are essential for the maintenance or improvement of environmental quality in a democratic society.
8. It is ecologically desirable to limit the number of persons using any public resource at one time; however, restrictions that directly or indirectly discriminate against any segment of society are inimical to the quality of the social environment.

MULTIPLE-CHOICE TEST DESIGNED FOR EVALUATION OF A UNIT DESIGNATED *ENVIRONMENT AND THE LAW*

1	2	3	4
Agree	Don't know	Disagree	Don't understand

1. The local government utilized sound ecological principles when they planned our community. 1 2 3 4
2. Only government has the right to legislate land use. 1 2 3 4
3. The best communities have no slums. 1 2 3 4
4. Today's suburbs may be tomorrow's slums. 1 2 3 4
5. Ecologically planned communities discriminate against industrial development. 1 2 3 4
6. Strict laws with high local and national standards would provide for the improvement of environmental quality; however, such laws are relatively useless unless compliance and enforcement can be secured. 1 2 3 4
7. The law discriminates against land owners. 1 2 3 4
8. People have the right to do anything they want with their land. 1 2 3 4
9. Certain selected individuals should be allowed to regulate land use in the community. 1 2 3 4
10. Zoning ordinances are designed to aid the orderly development of communities. 1 2 3 4
11. A master plan for community development is not necessary, since it is not protected by law. 1 2 3 4
12. Because of the difficulty of enforcing laws that regulate environmental use and quality, voluntary compliances with all environmental laws should be an educational and societal goal of the highest priority. 1 2 3 4
13. The value of master planning is its ability to restrict low income housing. 1 2 3 4
14. Master planning in accordance with ecological principles and considerations can be proved to be scientifically sound. 1 2 3 4
15. Public officials are often poorly prepared to make zoning decisions. 1 2 3 4
16. People should not be allowed to own land. 1 2 3 4
17. State and federal government, rather than local government, should regulate all land use. 1 2 3 4
18. The adage "Law is rule without reason" has often caused confusion and resistance, since it has led people to believe that the law subverts or threatens justice; therefore knowledge of the rationale for laws is valid in environmental education studies. 1 2 3 4
19. Large shopping centers have been a great help to small businessmen. 1 2 3 4
20. The local government should be responsible for the recycling of reusable resources in its community, i.e., water, air, bottles, cans, soil, or other resources. 1 2 3 4
21. Laws regulating industrial development are too strict and not in the interests of the public. 1 2 3 4
22. Communities have known about good and poor land use for over a century. 1 2 3 4
23. Citizen advisory groups, such as Environmental Commissions, should be instituted to advise local planners, zoning boards, and the municipal governing body. 1 2 3 4
24. Compliance with laws and standards regulating environmental quality will be weakened by three significant factors:
    a. The increasing volume and diversity of pollutants, which will require escalating costs.
    b. The difficulty in detecting violations
    c. The slowness of the judiciary process 1 2 3 4
25. If there were no builders on planning boards, there would be better planning. 1 2 3 4
26. The wetlands, those lands affected by tide waters, should be filled in to increase the amount of usable real estate near the shore. 1 2 3 4
27. Most sea life avoids the shallow water areas of creeks and estuaries. 1 2 3 4
28. There are not enough public lands or recreation areas in your state. 1 2 3 4
29. Fees for parks and other public lands should be paid by the people who use them. 1 2 3 4
30. The development of any parcel of land, large or small, has important and far-

reaching effects on the continuing ability of surrounding land to support life. 1 2 3 4

31. Industries that do not pollute waterways or other resources should be given incentives such as tax relief. 1 2 3 4
32. Laws should be definite and unalterable; too often large, influential industries are allowed to bend laws to fit their own advantage. 1 2 3 4
33. Universal, far-seeing environmental goals are more important to society than personal, economic gains. 1 2 3 4
34. Future population growth will make it necessary to develop public lands in order to house our people adequately. 1 2 3 4
35. Public awareness of and participation in the development of regulations that govern environmental protection are essential for the maintenance or improvement of environmental quality in a democratic society. 1 2 3 4
36. It is ecologically desirable to limit the number of persons using any public resource at one time; however, restrictions that directly or indirectly discriminate against any segment of society are inimical to the quality of the social environment. 1 2 3 4

BEHAVIORALLY STATED OBJECTIVES

The use of objectives in behavioral terms can make the task of evaluation more precise. Chapter 1 describes some of the advantages of behavioral objectives, whereas the study units in Chapter 2 provide numerous examples of these objectives and means of reaching them.

If the generalizations and the facts supporting them are the cognitive, or knowledge goals of instruction, then each generalization should be represented by one or more behaviorally stated objectives (if behavioral objectives are judged to be useful).

Similarly, if environmental ethics, stated as generalizations, are accorded a high priority in environmental education, then a series of index behaviors that indicate an action-producing attitude can be designed to evaluate whether a student holds or acquires a particular environmental ethic, or value. Most of the units in Chapter 2 include a series of index behaviors intended to be used for evaluative purposes. Of course, for each statement of an environmental ethic, literally hundreds of index behaviors can probably be developed.

ULTIMATE GOAL

The ultimate goal of environmental education is to create a citizenry that is environmentally literate. Lay persons must be able to marshall facts to support decisions about projected environmental changes and developments and also must have the commitment to engage in appropriate societal action to implement the desired changes. To achieve the long-term goal, an environmental education program should provide each of these kinds of experiences during school years. *The content of the curriculum as it pertains to environmental education is not so significant as the concern it engenders for whatever environment is being considered.*

Although evaluation in formal education has been taking place for a long time, only recently has serious attention been paid to the selection and evaluation of the achievement of educational objectives. These beginning stages in the attempt to evaluate experiences and activities in environmental education in general reflect the uncertainty that attends evaluation of all educational activities. If any broader horizons have been glimpsed through the foregoing discussions relating to environmental education or its evaluation, it is hoped that they will lead to an increasing concern for improving the learning environments in which our students are nurtured.

INDEX

A

B

C

D

E

P

Q

R

S

T

U

V

W

Z